PORTRAIT OF YOUTH MINISTRY

Maria Harris

For Martha, sister and friend—
Maria
June 1995

PAULIST PRESS
New York/Ramsey

for Mary Tunny Harris
with all my love

Library of Congress
Catalog Card Number: 80–84512

ISBN: 0–8091–2354–1

Published by Paulist Press
545 Island Road, Ramsey, N.J. 07446

Printed and bound in the
United States of America

CONTENTS

CONTENTS

iv

CONTENTS

ACKNOWLEDGMENTS

In writing this book, I have been graced by the support and the work of many people. Youth Ministers, DRE's, and teachers throughout the country, Catholic and Protestant, have shared experiences with me. However, no group has been more insightful than my own students, and to them I owe my deepest thanks. Nancy Elder, Steve Wayles, and Gene Langevin have been especially helpful. In addition, I am happy to acknowledge the following: Sue Olmstead, Walter Pitman, Diane Root, Brian Benoit, Meg Curran, Donna Cieply, Karen King, Marc Nagel, Barbara Gianino, Chuck Ericson, Eric Bascom, Nancy Adams, Karen Moeschberger, Stephen Fisher, Frank Armstrong, Patrick Ryan, Charles G. Campbell, Bruce Sandy, Anne Squire-Buresh, Timothy Morrison, Susan Wilson, Mary Byrider, Lyle Jenks and Barbara Sinclair.

The book began as a response to classes and conversation at Andover Newton in 1976, and a program designed at the request of Joseph Moore in Attleboro, Massachusetts the summer of 1978. It was completed in an environment of Rhode Island hospitality provided by Delia Lynch and Marge Tuthill. The friendship and critique of Joanmarie Smith has been, as always, invaluable, and the always original and creative thought of Gabriel Moran continues to be fundamental to my own.

Whatever is wanting is due to my own limitations, but all that is good and true, I dedicate to the always young Mary Tunny Harris, a woman beyond compare.

The following additional acknowledgments are probably in order. In Chapter 4, "Leiturgia: The Ministry of Prayer," the material appeared in different form in "Prayer and Vision," P.A.C.E. 10 (Winona, Minn.: St. Mary's Press), and in the November-December, 1979 issue of *Religious Education.* Some of the material on Catechesis appeared, again in different form, in the September, 1978 issue of *The Catechist Magazine,* in the article entitled "Catechesis as a Form of Sacrament."

INTRODUCTION

For several years, I have been working with church educators throughout the United States; this book is a result of that work. In it I address a number of issues receiving increased attention among those educators, the most prominent of which is ministry. Today, the word ministry is enjoying unprecedented use by people in the church. Not by all people, by any means, but by people who are and have been at the heart of church life for decades: parish coordinators, directors of Christian or religious education, catechists, Sunday School and CCD principals, parochial school teachers, church-school superintendents, and judicatory and diocesan staff members.

Among Catholics, "apostolate" as the word describing what church educators do when they work *as* church has been replaced by ministry. No longer is ministry a word referring exclusively to the ordained. Usage is similar among Protestants, although here attention focuses on the *title* minister as in the phrase "Minister of Education." This shift from the previous title *Director* of Christian Education signifies far more than a change of name. It goes to the very nature of *what* it means to minister in today's church and *how* the educator engages in ministry. Given these circumstances, my intention in this book is to explore what ministry means in our day, and to try to describe what that ministry might look like in the local parish or local church. This is the reason for the title *Portrait of Youth Ministry*. I intend to paint a portrait with my words.

In order to sharpen the picture, I concentrate attention on youth. More and more, church educators are speaking of their work with adolescents and young people as youth ministry. It seems to me this emphasis is educating our understanding of ministry as a whole, and my point of departure in this book will therefore be ministry as it is engaged in for, and with, and by young people. However, I hope the resulting understanding of ministry is not limited

1

by this factor, because my intention is a broad and possibly pretentious one: to offer a description that can serve as a model for ministry among all in the church, whatever their age. I base the model on two convictions: (1) Youth is not only a time of life with special characteristics and issues, but also a quality of life. "Youth" and "youthful" are descriptions of ways of being in the world. Furthermore, as adults, although it is as useful for us to be in touch with the young as it is for the young to be in touch with us, we need to remember that residing *within* us is the young person we once were, who has influenced us, and who in some sense we continue to be.[1] (2) More importantly, if we call an activity *ministry,* that term ought to have a constant meaning. Thus, youth ministry, hospital ministry, campus ministry and even ordained ministry differ not because of the second word in each phrase but because of the first. To be genuine, ministry is always ministry no matter with whom it is carried on, or it is never ministry at all.

I also wish to stress the importance of intelligence, thought, critical judgment and the questioning of assumptions to our understanding and practice of ministry. I admit to experiencing dismay after many recent conversations concerning ministry because its meaning as reflected in such conversations seemed based on private opinion, present feeling, particular circumstance, or unexamined presuppositions. If, as an entire body of church people, we are ever to achieve a learned ministry (a learned clergy has been an ideal for centuries) we will have to attend seriously to the best exercise of our mental powers. Intelligence must be brought to bear, for example, on such questions as whether everything the church person does can be called ministry. The impression is abroad that such is indeed the case, and I suspect most people know of what I write. It was brought home to me last year when a speaker was identified as engaged in the "ministry of hanging around." The laudable intention embodied in that and similar phrases can lead to a trivializing of ministry by extending its meaning to so many activities it eventually covers none. I am not convinced that everything and anything we do can be baptized as ministry by preceding the action by the phrase "ministry of." In contrast, I submit that if we in the church consider ourselves involved in ministry, we need to know

---

1. Edward Robinson (ed.) in *Living the Questions* (Manchester College, Oxford: Religious Experience Research Unit, 1978), p. 24, writes of childhood in this way, as "an integral and continuing element in each individual." I think it is true to say of youth, too, that it is an integral and continuing element in each person.

what that means, and the knowledge needs to be informed by study, thought and awareness of tradition. If we then wish to change or enlarge the meaning, we will be able to do so free of the charge that such change or enlargement is arbitrary or whimsical.

A final set of questions I want to raise is related to those called Youth Ministers. Who are they, what are they expected to do, what are their qualifications, their desires, their gifts? As a role, is the Youth Minister a fad soon to be replaced or joined by the family minister, the young adult minister, the mid-life crisis minister, the senior citizen minister? Do we need ministers for particular age groups? Perhaps more important—certainly this is true for most of the church personnel whom I meet—how is the Youth Minister related to others in the parochial setting? Basic to all of these questions, of course, is the one that underlies and is the canvas for the portrait of ministry: What is the church? For ministry is, at root, an ecclesial question, and it will be addressed as the primary question it is only as people come to understand themselves as a communion of human beings who form one body.

THE DESIGN OF THIS BOOK

· The book has three sections. In *Section One*, I address the nature of ministry first, drawing on scriptural and theological sources. I then devote the second chapter to youth, writing about young people from the perspective of what they are *not*. I hope my viewpoint in that chapter makes sense: anyone who has read about youth knows the literature on this stage of life is voluminous, and it is not necessary to repeat it. Nonetheless, I think it important to highlight a few areas that may be in danger of too much shadow.

Section Two is the main section of the book and has five chapters. I devote one chapter to each of the five traditionally ecclesial areas of ministry, explaining its meaning in contemporary terms and suggesting agenda items critical for ministry with youth in each area. I conclude each chapter with suggested activities and exercises Youth Ministers have found helpful in their work and consented to share with me for inclusion in this book. I hope it becomes clear as these chapters progress how each is related to the other and how all are interrelated.

Section Three is a one-chapter section concerned with Youth Ministers. In that chapter, I share some responses received from young people and from Youth Ministers on the most important qualities desired from the latter, and some institutional suggestions directed to building a grace-filled ministry. I conclude with comments under the general heading, "Where Do We Go From Here?"

WHY THIS PARTICULAR BOOK?

Why another book on ministry? Allow me to name those reasons that influence me in the conscious writing of this one.

Item #1: The Necessity of a Common Language. At a recent symposium of religious educators, Dwayne Huebner noted,

Theologians, academics, religious educators, and laity share responsibility for the way they give voice to our educational experiences as religious people and as Christians. Could some of the difficulties and problematics of the practice of Christian religious education be associated with our collective failure to share responsibility for this collective voice, this needed public language?[2]

My own answer to his question is yes, and the work I have done with Youth Ministers and ministers of education over the past few years convinces me Huebner is naming a critical problem. Our work suffers badly from lack of a common language. Talk about educational ministry in church circles is hampered because we have no agreed-upon usage in conversation as the ground for common, public discourse. Thus, if ministers of church education, DRE's, Youth Ministers and others are to engage in any kind of profitable exchange with one another, it is to our advantage to use the same words, giving to those words an agreed upon, albeit general meaning.

The point is illuminated for me further by a comment of Erik Erikson. He writes, "It would be fatal to underestimate the degree to which the future always belongs to those who combine a universal enough new meaning with the mastery of a new technology."[3] I believe we are rich in the technology of ministry; procedures, plans, models, and patterns of activity are constantly being developed. What is needed, however, is a "universal enough meaning" for what we are doing. My hope is that by focusing on *didache, leiturgia, koinonia, kerygma* and *diakonia* I can offer such a meaning

---

2. See "The Language of Religious Education," in *Tradition and Transformation in Religious Education,* edited by Padraic O'Hare, (Birmingham: Religious Education Press, 1979), p. 109.

3. Erik Erikson, *Young Man Luther* (New York: Norton, 1958), p. 225.

by pointing to a language in our history that lies at the heart of ministry.

Item #2: The Necessity of Theory. Religious educators in the church are not well known for an insistence on theory; indeed, we still suffer from traces of anti-intellectualism. I hope the reader will not be disappointed to learn that, as well as the practical, this book has much theory to it. Indeed, I hope readers will join me in the adventure of spinning out the theory undergirding the practice of ministry. I am using the term theory as Abraham Kaplan does in *The Conduct of Inquiry,* where he speaks of it as a "device for interpreting, criticizing and unifying established laws, modifying them to fit data unanticipated in their formulation, and guiding the enterprise of discovering new and more powerful generalizations."[4] At the same time, I hope to highlight the more ancient meaning of *theoria* from the Greek for "contemplation," and *theastai* "to observe," recalling Whitehead's dictum that there is absolutely no inevitability as long as there is a willingness to *contemplate* what is happening. We need to know why we do what we do; we need to question assumptions; we need to observe; we need to trace the history of our institutions. All these help create a learned ministry, and in each of them, theory can help.

Item #3: The Necessity of Paths to One Another. Books are another way of creating the bondings we often experience at workshops, at conferences, or at the four- or six-week summer schools so many of us attend across the nation. Much of this book is the fruit of work with ministers of education and Youth Ministers, affirmed by them, and it is thus an opportunity to share with others some of what we have done together, creating bondings and alliances in the process. At this point, however, I am not looking for consensus so much as searching to name a field and its issues. Cooperation can always be elicited by not reaching the real issues that divide people from one another, or by diverting attention from fundamental where-are-we-going-anyway questions. "Many errors of judgment can be traced to too much consensus too early in the game."[5] At this point, therefore, I want to turn to the fundamental issues of ministry, of youth, and of the priestly and prophetic elements that underlie them. Eventually, I do hope that a community of ministers will be created in the churches, a community that shares a common

---

4. (San Francisco: Chandler Publishing Co., 1964), p. 297.

5. Harlan Cleveland, *The Future Executive* (New York: Harper and Row, 1972), p. 87.

vision, and a common hope for the world. For the present, it may be wise to dwell in patience within the questions which ministry itself poses, content that some day answers will become clear.

Be patient towards all that is unsolved in your heart and try to love the questions themselves like locked rooms ... Do not now seek the answers; that cannot be given you because you would not be able to live them. And the point is, to live everything. Live the questions now. Perhaps you will then gradually, without noticing it, live along some distant day into the answer.[6]

6. Rainer Maria Rilke, *Letters to a Young Poet* (New York: W.W. Norton, 1934), p. 33.

SECTION ONE

Chapter One
MINISTRY: PRIESTLY AND PROPHETIC

"When I use a word," Humpty-Dumpty said in a rather scornful tone, "it means just what I choose it to mean—neither more nor less."

"The question is," said Alice, "whether you can *make* words mean so many different things."

"The question is," said Humpty-Dumpty, "which is to be the master—that's all."[1]

The word under consideration in this chapter is *ministry*. The reality of words and the meaning given them is a function of power. If ministry is to be reclaimed by all in the church and if that ministry is to be empowered, we need to engage in study of the word and the meanings given to it, not only in our own time, but throughout history. Such is my intention in this chapter. I will begin by examining some meanings given to ministry in the recent past. Then I will move back to the scriptural roots of the word, trying to discern what biblical tradition can tell us. I will then describe what a contemporary rendering of that tradition might look like, and conclude with a number of features to be borne in mind not only by Youth Ministers but by all engaged in the ecclesial journey.

---

1. Lewis Carroll, *Through the Looking Glass* (New York: New American Library, 1960. First published 1871), p. 186.

THE RECENT PAST

The way that rediscovery of ministry as an ecclesial activity, proper not only to the ordained but also to the whole body of the church, has occurred is a good example of theory brought to bear on present life. I mean here theory in both senses. Ministry has come to the fore first, because people contemplated what was happening in their midst (*theoria*) and began naming it; and because, at the same time, scholars were supporting this naming with intelligent study, expressed in a way that interpreted, unified and criticized experience. The contemplatives at the grass roots were largely religious-education personnel. Dennis Geaney does not hesitate to state that "The most revolutionary breakthrough in the emerging concept of nonordained ministry" was the "parish religious education coordinator."[2] This is the same conclusion I reached at the end of *The D.R.E. Book*[3] where I wrote of the coordinator creating a new understanding of religious ministry. On the next to last page of the book, I found a profound and disturbing consciousness dawning: ministry was indeed the engagement in priestly activity. If that was true, however, then the use of the term was "of enormous significance . . . if one looks closely this raises the issue that a priest is not something one *becomes,* but that priestliness is an activity that is called for by a community."[4] My conclusion, which by this time has become a conviction, was reached largely on experiential grounds, because the DRE's with whom I was working were speaking of what they did as ministry, and often as "doing what priests do." Margot Hover engaged in an enterprise similar to mine. She asked people in families she taught to describe their understanding of ministry and discovered that most of the definitions spoke of caring, reaching out, being of service to others, although she was also told it was "Anyone involved in religion—priests, etc."[5] Often, descriptions of ministry were beautifully poetic, as in Hugh Kennedy's speaking of it as "Sacramentalizing God's presence among people,"[6] and often, in the early seventies, one could

---

2. In *Emerging Lay Ministries* (Kansas City: Andrews and McMeel, Inc., 1979), p. 51.

3. (New York: Paulist, 1976), pp. 186–190.

4. *Ibid.,* p. 188.

5. "Ministering to Families, A Research Report," in *The Living Light,* 15, 4 (Winter, 1978), pp. 501–502.

6. "Ministry," unpublished manuscript (Santa Fe: Center for Christian Renewal), p.13.

trace the meaning to the influence of Henri Nouwen, who in *Creative Ministry* named what many felt but as yet had not articulated:

Ministry means the ongoing attempt to put one's own search for God, with all the moments of pain and joy, despair and hope, at the disposal of those who want to join this search but do not know how.[7]

At the same time, on more official levels, churches were changing ministry. In Catholicism, the seventies saw the abolition of minor orders, the restoration of the diaconate, the reinstitution of acolyte and lector as ministries, and the emergence of rites for catechists.[8] These occurrences were not uniformly received as great positive strides, of course, and disparate groups have responded to them quite differently. Among these are the persons who believe that all ecclesial ministry derives from and is controlled by the office of ordained priesthood,[9] others who question whether the structures of ordained ministry may be dysfunctional for the church in a global setting,[10] and church groups who feel ministry is regressing since it is seen "as the laity's participation in work traditionally assigned to priests or sisters."[11] Despite such reactions, the more general meaning of ministry as the work of all the people appears to be here to stay.

While the language has been changing, scholarship has been increasingly directed to study of ministry, especially to reclaiming its biblical roots. Bernard Cooke's monumental ten-year study, for example, has given strong undergirding to the notion of ministry for all. In that work he writes,

Though intrinsically it was the entire community that was body and sacrament, the bulk of Christians (the laity) was early reduced to passivity within the life of the church. This passivity found ex-

---

7. (New York: Doubleday, 1971), p. 116. It is this passage that is quoted in the United States Catholic Conference statement, "A Vision of Youth Ministry" (Washington: USCC, 1976), p. 3.

8. Matthias Neuman, "A Shared Responsibility for the Parochial Teaching Ministry," in *The Living Light*, 14, 2 (Summer, 1977), p. 187.

9. *Ibid.*, p. 191.

10. In a talk delivered at Episcopal Divinity School, Cambridge, Massachusetts, April 24, 1979, Nadine Foley asked this question.

11. "Lay role regressing, 47 Catholics charge," in *National Catholic Reporter* (December 23, 1977), p. 16.

pression in the laity's role (or lack of role) in liturgy, in the retreat of laity from active evangelical witness, and most basically in the laity's Christian self-image. Fortunately, in more recent times there has been some recovery of the understanding that the entire Christian community is the body of Christ, sharing in Christ's prophetic-priestly role, "ordained" in baptism to evangelical witness, to concerned service in the world and to Eucharistic worship of the Father in union with Christ.[12]

Although Cooke's work is probably the most authoritative with reference to the beginnings of church ministry, other scholars continue to flesh out the picture. Elizabeth Schüssler Fiorenza, for example, is helping women to understand their original place in the early Christian missionary endeavor as equal to that of men like Barnabas, Apollos or Paul,[13] and Harvard's Stillman Professor George MacRae ties the present, rediscovery, and the need to elaborate a new meaning together, writing, "Any period of theological creativity ... is also a period of rediscovery. As we strive to elaborate a theology of ministry for our own situation, we must rediscover the meaning of Christian ministry at its roots."[14] It is to those roots that I now turn.

NEW TESTAMENT BEGINNINGS

A number of passages in the Christian scriptures have become classic examples of the meaning of ministry. Ephesians 4:11–14 names the fivefold ministries of apostle, prophet, evangelist, pastor and teacher; Galatians 3:28 affirms that in the Body of the Christ there is neither slave nor free, male nor female, Jew nor Greek; 2 Corinthians 6:4–10 describes the circumstances in which God's ministers are called to act, and the qualities they are asked to exhibit; and 1 Corinthians 12 acknowledges the diversity of roles, gifts and charisms. However, the clearest description of ministry as the church's work is found not in Paul but in the second chapter of Acts. It is there that *the kerygma* is first announced: *"This Jesus God has raised up and we are all witnesses"* (Acts 2:32), and it is

---

12. *Ministry to Word and Sacrament* (Philadelphia: Fortress, 1976), p. 195.

13. See "Women in the Early Christian Movement," in *Womanspirit Rising,* edited by Carol Christ and Judith Plaskow (San Francisco: Harper and Row, 1979), p. 91.

14. "Ministry and Ministries in the New Testament," in *The Living Light,* 14, 2 (Summer, 1977), p. 168.

there that we have the most detailed description of what the first Christian community did, as a community.

And they continued steadfastly in the teaching *of the apostles and in the* communion *of* the breaking of bread *and in the* prayers ... *And all who believed were together and* held all things in common, *and* would sell their possessions and goods and distribute them among all according as anyone had need. *And continuing daily with one accord in the temple, and* breaking bread *in their houses, they took their food with gladness and simplicity of heart,* praising God *and being in favor with all the people (Acts 2:42; 44–47).*

These few verses, found in Acts, are the first portrait of ecclesial ministry we have, but it is not only first in time, it is pristine. In the description, Luke gives us the central elements in ministry: continuing in the teaching, the *didache;* praying, breaking bread and praising God, or *leiturgia;* being in communion and holding all things in common, or *koinonia;* speaking the word of the Christ, of Resurrection, and witness—"this Jesus God has raised up"—or *kerygma;* and moving outward to those in need, or *diakonia.* It is this apostolic ministry in which the Christian ministry receives its decisive formulation.[15] It is not a repetition of the ministry of Jesus, just as ministry today cannot be simply a repetition. "The apostles in the book of Acts do not repeat Jesus' sermons; their gospel is the same gospel that he preached but, in the new situation created by his death and resurrection, they take the responsibility of finding new ways of expression for the gospel."[16]

Those engaged in ministry today must engage in a similar work, finding expression for the gospel just as the first followers of Jesus did. Nevertheless, it seems to me both possible, and to our advantage, to articulate a meaning for ministry that is intimately related to the ministry described in the New Testament, and going back even further to the Hebrew scriptures. For this reason, I suggest that the best way to define ministry is this: MINISTRY IS THE PRIESTLY AND PROPHETIC WORK OF THE CHURCH. Traditionally, it is the priestly role to preserve the past. Priestly responsibility is threefold: to preserve tradition, celebrate in ritual prayer, and gather community. We find each of these in Acts: *didache,*

---

15. James D. Smart, *The Rebirth of Ministry* (Philadelphia: Westminster, 1960), p. 37.

16. *Ibid.*

koinonia, leiturgia—or teaching, community, and prayer. But we discover a prophetic role in Acts as well: the speaking of a word that transforms, that challenges, that calls to account—the *kerygma,* and the journey outward to those in need, even to the selling of wordly possessions—*diakonia.* It is evident that the impetus for the priestly-prophetic role is Jesus' ministry. But it is also evident, in the early church, that the source of the ministry and the agent of the ministry is the entire body of the church. "On any analysis, ministry gets its meaning from an understanding of the church, since the mission of Jesus is felt in the New Testament to be entrusted to the church, not to ministers, at least not as individuals."[17] It is the entire people who are called to be priestly: Let *us* be accounted as servants of the Christ and stewards of the mysteries of God (1 Cor. 4). But the entire people are called to be prophetic as well, an element in ministry that has received less attention than the priestly,[18] at least in the thinking of many in our local churches. The prophetic is the work of the church in pushing back boundaries, in speaking the word nobody wants to hear, and in challenging institutions by action in the world guaranteed to be disquieting. Classically, historically, and theologically, the prophetic is that aspect of ministry where the community emphasizes its responsibility beyond itself, where it dares to call both itself and others to judgment before God, and where it insists that personal and structured evil must be confronted and condemned. It is noteworthy from an educational perspective that the inner life of prophecy is described in Isaias 50:4 as having "the tongue of a learner" and an ear that is wakened "to hear as a learner." "An ear open continually toward God to hear what God has to say to weary, broken, stumbling humanity, and a tongue ready and disciplined to speak the cauterizing and healing words—that is the true portrait of the prophet."[19]

If ministry is to be genuine, both the priestly and the prophetic must be present. No one work will be exclusively priestly or exclusively prophetic; instead these will tend to overlap and even merge. Nevertheless, as we engage in the work of ministry, church educators and youth ministers will probably be seen emphasizing now

---

17. MacRae, *loc. cit.,* p. 173.

18. The work of liberation theologians is changing this; see also Matthew Fox, *On Becoming a Musical Mystical Bear* (New York: Paulist, 1974) and *Compassion* (Minneapolis: Winston, 1979), for examples of conscious inclusion of the prophetic element.

19. Smart, *op. cit.,* p. 55.

this aspect, now that. Such emphasis is not destructive as long as both are present. The danger occurs if either is completely lost. But danger also lies in failure to recognize that the priestly and prophetic work of the church is lifelong and cannot be rushed. Ministry is a continuing task that can engage one for a lifetime, ultimately received from the saints gone before us as the *traditio,* and ultimately handed on to our children and our children's children.

INDIVIDUAL ELEMENTS

The priestly and the prophetic are the two overarching components of genuine ministry. Within them, however, as I have indicated, are more specific activities, to each of which I will devote a chapter (3 through 7 below). I have already named them, but I want at this point to make a few comments about each one generally, saving more concrete and specific applications and references to youth for the five chapters in Section Two.

In their pastoral letter, *To Teach As Jesus Did,* the United States Catholic Bishops wrote, "The educational mission of the church is an integrated ministry embracing three interlocking dimensions: the message revealed by God (*didache*) which the church proclaims; fellowship in the life of the Holy Spirit (*koinonia*) and service to the Christian community and entire human community (*diakonia*)."[20] The passage and the pastoral letter have been widely used and widely accepted as a way of understanding education in the Catholic Church, and their use points to an essential validity for this particular interpretation. In speaking of *didache, koinonia,* and *diakonia* in what follows, then, I do not intend to denigrate that document. However, I do wish to offer another interpretation of those three central activities, adding to them a particular rendering of *kerygma* and *leiturgia* as well. I offer the interpretation on the grounds that (1) "message," "community," and "service" are insufficient translations of *didache, koinonia* and *diakonia* in our day; (2) *kerygma* and *leiturgia,* often translated as word and sacrament, are essential ministries for all in the church and not separable from the first three; and (3) it is more accurate to speak of each aspect of ministry within the church as having an educational dimension to it, rather than to speak of the church's educational min-

---

20. National Conference of Catholic Bishops, *To Teach As Jesus Did* (Washington: USCC, 1973), n.14.

istry, as if that could be contained in only *some* of the church's work. I would argue that no matter what aspect of ministry we are considering, we are educated by it and to it. We are educated by *didache* and to *didache,* by and to *leiturgia,* by and to *koinonia,* by and to *kerygma,* and by and to *diakonia.* None of them is exempt.

Didache. The first point to make about *didache* is that it does not mean "message"; it means *teaching.* Originally, *The Didache* was an anonymous church treatise of the second century, possibly the first, known as "The Teaching of the Twelve Apostles." The word comes from the Greek *didakhe,* "a teaching," and is related to *didaktikos,* "skillful in teaching" and *didaskein,* "to teach." Actually, *didache* is the art and science of teaching, or what Paulo Freire calls *pedagogy,* an activity whose personal, social and redemptive power he has demonstrated brilliantly.[21] If our ministry is to have the same kind of power, we need to return to teaching as a central activity of ministry.

Teaching within the church begins with catechesis. All of the church's teaching is not catechetical; actually and historically the term catechesis was not even used in the New Testament.[22] Eventually, when it did come into use it referred to the instruction of the catechumen prior to the reception of the sacraments. It is tied to and continues to be related to the processes of initiation and education into sacramental life: this is its essential focus.[23] It refers not only to the ritual acts of sacramentality, however, but to initiation and education into the complete living of sacramentality throughout life; to experiencing sacramentality as a necessary religious component of life from birth to death.[24]

Following catechesis, however, there is another kind of instruc-

---

21. See *Pedagogy of the Oppressed* (New York: Herder and Herder, 1970); see also *Education for Critical Consciousness* (New York: Seabury, 1973).

22. Jacques Audinet, "Catechesis," in *Sacramentum Mundi,* edited by Karl Rahner *et al.,* Vol. I, p. 263 (New York: Herder and Herder, 1968).

23. *The New Catholic World,* 222, 1329 (July-August, 1979) devotes an entire issue to reflections on the value of such catechesis, which is precatechetical and postcatechetical, or mystagogical, as well. The focus is the Rite of Christian Education for Adults. I prefer to distinguish between catechesis and *didache* as the two elements in the church's ministry of teaching.

24. Here I would also point out that a most interesting *nonuse* of catechesis occurs in Catholic seminaries. Although it is often episcopal documents that equate religious education and catechesis, I know of no seminary professor who speaks of his or her work as catechetical even though the work is directed to preparing for the sacrament of orders. It would be interesting to pursue the question of why this is so.

tion necessary, traditionally referred to as didactics, where a person is educated toward an understanding of the tradition. Here I am referring to what at another time was known as the learning of Christian doctrine (the CCD, or Confraternity of Christian Doctrine got its name from this work). Although didactic teaching includes that, it is not limited to it. Instead, this stage in the ministry of teaching is the time and the opportunity to learn one's own story and the story of one's people from the inside, from within the community itself.

In the last few decades we have been falling short in this area as a church. We need to restate George Albert Coe's question, "Shall the primary purpose of Christian education be to hand on a religion or to create a new world?"[25] so that it reads, "How can a community engage in teaching so that it not only hands on its *traditio,* its religious perspective, but also instructs in the possibilities of recreating the world?" A people can best create a new society as they understand what has brought them to where they are, and as they come to know the people who have made them who they are. Chesterton once wrote that tradition is the extension of the franchise to that most obscure of all classes, our ancestors. "It is the democracy of the dead. Tradition refuses to submit to the small and arrogant oligarchy of those who merely happen to be walking about."[26]

Didache, then, includes catechesis and engagement with the tradition. Two other points are essential. The first is a realization on the church's part that the ministry of *didache* does not belong to an individual but to the corporate body as agent. *Didache* is "the whole church teaching the whole church." The doer of the teaching and the receiver of the teaching are the same: the Christian community.[27] The second is that genuine teaching is often provocative, discomforting, and frightening, and can lead to unexpected conclusions. A fundamental question for us who engage in the ministry of teaching, therefore, is just how completely and seriously we will undertake an enterprise which at its best includes a radical refusal to limit perspectives, to limit questioning, and to limit creativity, even if that means a decision on the part of the learners to challenge, confront, and perhaps let go.

---

25. In *What Is Christian Education?* (New York: Scribner's, 1929), p. 29.

26. *Orthodoxy* (Garden City: Image, 1959), p. 48.

27. Gabriel Moran, *Religious Body* (New York: Seabury, 1974) devotes an entire chapter to this and related points. See Chapter 5, "Education as Religious," pp.145–186.

Leiturgia. "The religious life and experience of a people is the background and context of their liturgical prayer; their liturgical prayer expresses and deepens the people's religious experience."[28] This comment of John Gallen in the introduction to *Eucharistic Liturgies* helps focus on the twin concerns of that aspect of ministry called *leiturgia.* One is the public, communal, sacramental prayer of the people gathered together to worship God as a priestly people. The other is the religious experience of individual persons, and their lives of prayer and contemplation. Worship and contemplation are interwoven; nevertheless, each can be considered distinctly though they cannot be completely separated.

The first aspect of the priestly ministry of *leiturgia* is worship. As with the other aspects of ministry, it belongs to the entire people, not to the sacramental celebrant, or to the ordained. From an educational perspective, attention to worship is many-fold, and we need to address it from at least three perspectives: (1) The environment for liturgy, the physical setting, must be taken into account. This includes special attention to the cultural and subcultural differences within individual situations.[29] (2) The content of the public service must be attended to with reference to the words, symbols, gestures and images used, especially to whether these are both appropriate for the God addressed (or more accurately, not inappropriate), but also capable of being appropriated by all present. This comment applies especially to the exclusive use of gender-specific words for the Holy (He, Him, His) but is also directed to awareness of the kind of God (militaristic, magisterial, hidden, transcendent, tender) assumed by our prayers, our hymns, our rituals. (3) The purpose of liturgical prayer must be the worship of God—not a well-prepared liturgy, a well-rehearsed liturgy, a well-designed liturgy— but the worship of God. Preparation for liturgy is important, certainly, but the essential purpose is not ultimately a well-planned service. The purpose of liturgical prayer is the worship of God, "God, that inexpressibly good power which spirals through the universe, creating and recreating our being, our imagination, our faith."[30]

I suspect that one of the reasons we forget that God is the center of liturgy is the inattention we have given to the contemplative

---

28. (New York: Newman, 1969), p. 1.

29. Tissa Balasuriya, *The Eucharist and Human Liberation* (Maryknoll: Orbis, 1979), elaborates on this point, pp. 146–148.

30. Carter Heywood, *A Priest Forever* (New York: Harper, 1976), p. 8.

aspect of prayer. The time has come to return to conscious and careful instruction and practice in contemplation and in those activities
that express and value solitude, emptiness, no-thing-ness, not-do-
ing, and use-less-ness. Such instruction is based on the realization
that contemplation is also a work of liturgy, and is related to remembering the mystics and mysticism of our own Western tradition. The educational dimension of the ministry of *leiturgia,*
therefore, concentrates on the realization that we need to learn,
once more and again, to pray. We need to learn how to teach each
other to pray, we need to be with each other as we pray, and we
need to leave one another alone to pray. "When Rabbi Mendel was
in Kotzk, the rabbi of that town asked him 'Where did you learn
the art of silence?' He was on the verge of answering the question,
but then changed his mind and practiced his art."[31] As a people,
both corporately and as individuals, we need to practice the art of
leiturgia.

Koinonia. Koinonia is the priestly element in ministry that,
while celebrating and gathering in toward community, strives to go
always beyond it. The ministry of *koinonia* is toward healing and
wholeness. Linguistic detective work results in the discovery that
health, healing, hallowing and holy all stem from the same Indo-
European root, *kailo.* In the appendix of any good dictionary, one
finds that *kailo* means "whole, uninjured, a sign of the good." This
leads to a way of answering the questions: how can the life of the
community be whole? Holy? How can we surmise that we personally, as well as the people of the community and church in which
we live, are tending toward the divine, that is, toward the Holy? Let
me make four suggestions. The first ones reflect the interpersonal,
religious, psychological nature of *koinonia;* the others reflect its so-
ciological and societal dimension.

(1) *Koinonia* is directed to a healing of divisions within and
among humans; those in our midst, yes, but those outside us as well.
It is also directed to the nonhumans. Where "community" conveys
the sense of a union of human beings, of men, women and children,
"communion" reminds us of our responsibility to the nonhumans as
well: the trees, and the animals and the earth. I believe that one
of the reasons young people are so drawn by ecological and environ-
mental issues is their natural sense of the need to be in communion
with all the earth, and I would suggest that "Communion" is actu-

---

31. Sally Palmer, "Meditation and Silence," *The NICM Journal,* 2, 2 (Spring,
1977), p. 10.

ally a more comprehensive and richer rendering of *koinonia* than is community. Not only does communion include community, it goes beyond it as well.

(2) Communion and cooperation with other religious traditions—Christian, Jewish, Muslim, Native American—is not a luxury or an afterthought in a pluralistic world.[32] I am often surprised that the churches in a community do not, at least occasionally, cooperate with one another on identical tasks (food, clothing drives) and I suspect it is precisely *noncommunal* factors that hold us back. One of these factors is a latent elitism or lingering suspicion of those who are not like us—the "non-us-es" in Marie Augusta Neal's phrase; the other is the still prevalent misconception that community is by its nature a bland, sugary, friendly, polite reality where no one ever disagrees, argues, or takes an opposing stand. Although wholeness is the eventual ideal, the way to it, like any exciting path, necessarily includes obstacles, pitfalls and difficulty.

(3) Those concerned with the educational dimension of *koinonia* need to demonstrate awareness of the diversity of communal forms in which people live.[33] Most church materials addressing community are still geared to father-mother-child units, and this seems to me to illustrate a refusal to admit that the majority of people do not live in such units: 16 percent of U.S. adults head single-parent families; 21 percent are single, widowed, separated or divorced; 23 percent live in childless or post-child-rearing marriages.[34] Many people, hearing these statistics, say "I know, I know," but as far as I can judge, in this area not much has changed.

(4) Finally, even if it wishes to, a church cannot assume that it will always be possible for it to provide community. In Edward Wynne's superb study, *Growing Up Suburban,* for example, he points out that more affluent and better-educated persons, although they may go to church or be affiliated with a church, "focus on the rational, cognitive and social service elements of religious activities, as opposed to the affective, ceremonial and expressive."[35] He concludes that this focus may therefore lessen the appeal of

32. See George Rupp, *Beyond Existentialism and Zen. Religion in a Pluralistic World* (New York: Oxford, 1979).

33. Gabriel Moran, "The Way We Are: Communal Forms and Church Response," in Maria Harris (ed.) *Parish Religious Education* (New York: Paulist, 1978), pp. 25–40.

34. News Release, U.S. Bureau of Labor Statistics, March 8, 1977.

35. (Austin: University of Texas, 1977), p. 54.

churches to the young especially as community-building forces, "since community building requires intensity, expressive elements, and powerful symbols: as it were a certain degree of parochialism."[36] Wynne's work is sobering, but necessary. We cannot assume that if only we work hard and diligently, our churches will provide an experience of communion for their members. Other factors come into play and may be far more powerful than the best good will in the world. What we might do in such instances, however, is provide opportunities for alternative experiences (art and theater come most quickly to mind) in order to offer the intensity, expressiveness and symbolic richness essential to *koinonia*.

I wish to turn now to the more prophetic elements in ministry. I reiterate that no aspect of ministry is solely priestly nor solely prophetic. Nonetheless, the three elements just considered seem to me more obviously related to the inner life of the church and less obviously reflective of its engagement with and involvement in the wider society. In turning to *kerygma* and to *diakonia,* however, this emphasis is reversed. The focus now becomes the world beyond the church's own experienced life. Ministry now becomes prophetic in the sense of taking seriously injustices within political, social and economic reality as a primary emphasis, speaking directly to those injustices, and attempting to do something about them.

Kerygma. I have already indicated my understanding that *kerygma* means word, and takes its essential meaning from the original and primary *kerygma,* "This Jesus God has raised up, and we are all witnesses of it." Jesus the Christ, resurrection, witness: this is the first *kerygma,* or message, from which all kerygmatic activity proceeds. For some, it is best translated and understood as the activity of preaching. However, what I want to suggest here is a meaning of *kerygma* that sees it as a message fleshed out in human activity (as was the Word Incarnate). It is a message best understood as the witness of human beings living their words by their lives.

The Good News is addressed to the person in all aspects of his or her being. This means that the reality of one's life needs to be taken into account if the Good News is to have meaning for the one hearing it ... If it is a message that is meant to touch the whole of life, then the message will lack meaning *unless it recognizes the right to a*

---

36. *Ibid.*

human existence and unless those who announce it are willing to become engaged in bringing it about and in completing it.[37]

The contemporary rendering I suggest for *kerygma* is *advocacy*. Advocacy as prophetic activity is fundamentally a way of speaking; it *is* embodied speech. An advocate is one who argues for a cause, a supporter or defender of a position. An advocate is one who pleads on another's behalf, an intercessor. An advocate is one called to give evidence, a defender. Notice in each definition the emphasis on speech—advocacy is speech directed to speaking up, out, and forth for the sake of another. It is not an accident that the Holy Spirit is given the title Advocate by Jesus. My own argument is that the meaning of the message (*kerygma*) of Christians is best interpreted in our day as advocacy in this particular and precise sense of *speaking the word for others*.

When John's disciples came to Jesus and asked whether his message and person were valid, Jesus replied, "Go and relate what you have seen: the blind see, the lame walk, the lepers are cleansed, the deaf hear, the dead rise, the poor have the gospel preached to them" (Luke 7:22). So too with those engaged in ministry. The validity of our prophetic ministry is demonstrated by our speaking forth in the role of advocate. The areas claiming attention are numerous, but in Chapter 7 I will stress three that are of particular concern to contemporary youth: sex, power, and resources. Attention to sex as a focus for advocacy is threefold: Jesus' own emphasis on bodiliness (Matthew Fox has suggested that one of the original phrases in Luke 7:22, later deleted, was "the impotent are making love"), the need for religious affirmation of sexuality, and the urgent necessity to overcome the oppression of the female sex throughout the world. Attention to power is important, too, and nowhere so much as in education about legal issues and the understanding of civil, political and religious rights, especially for the young. A less obvious but equally essential aspect of power is empowering the powerless to become doers as well as receivers.[38] Attention to resources is recognition of the area of advocacy that takes seriously more equitable distribution not only of money but of the food, clothing, shelter and necessities intimately connected with socio-economic realities.

---

37. John P. McManus, "An Approach to Evangelization," in *Proceedings: CARA Education Workshop* (Washington: CARA, 1978), pp. 70–71.

38. Freire, *op.cit.*

Diakonia. The final element in ministry, a prophetic ministry in itself, is variously known as outreach, service or mission. As with advocacy, it is often accompanied by and demands a good deal of risk on the part of the minister. Its scriptural and traditional understandings have been enumerated in the spiritual and corporal works of mercy, from feeding the hungry and visiting the sick, to counseling the doubtful and burying the dead. For our day, I want to refer to it as the ministry of *troublemaking.*

As a noun, trouble is a state of distress, affliction, danger or need; something that contributes to such a state: exertion, effort and pains. As a verb, it means to agitate, to stir up, to afflict with discomfort. It can also mean to cause confusion, to inconvenience and to bother. I would submit that the church, as an institution, can best clothe the naked, feed the hungry, and free the oppressed by troubling, challenging, afflicting and stirring up institutions, itself included, to address head on issues of peace and justice. The specific and peculiar element in *diakonia* as troublemaking is its ministry to *institutions.* Other ministries concern themselves with institutions, it is true, but more often their focus is persons. The church is, however, besides being a pilgrim people, a very strong and very powerful institution, to be reckoned with by other strong and powerful institutions from governments to industry, as the Communist government of Poland and the Nestlé Company have recently rediscovered.

Since troublemaking can be a politically prophetic act in many circumstances, it necessarily requires both knowledge of and sophistication in the ways of engaging institutions, as well as deciding which ones to choose.

It requires much effort to learn which questions should not be asked and which claims must not be entertained. What impairs our sight are habits of seeing as well as the mental concomitants of seeing. Our sight is suffused with knowing, instead of feeling painfully the lack of knowing what we see. The principle to be kept in mind is to know what we see rather than to see what we know.[39]

Such seeing will assist ministers to name the illusions concerning institutions that spread curious ideas about bigness and complexity. Some of these illusions are that things are run by a small number of conspiratorial but shadowy "bosses"; that the management of in-

---

39. Abraham Heschel, *The Prophets* (New York: Harper, 1962), p. xv.

stitutions is so out of control that no ways exist for making change; and that one cannot achieve freedom inside institutions, but only outside them.[40] Such seeing will also help those in ministry to discriminate *which* institutions they will choose to agitate, and toward which they will decide to take pains. No dearth of candidates exists, but certainly with reference to the young, churches need to be concerned with the world of work, of school, and of the military, as well as with the youth industry, that complex of institutions whose clients and consumers are young people. Such ministry will involve, as educational dimensions, assisting the young to find viable alternatives rather than to adjust; to understand rather than to immediately accept; and to learn how and in what ways their own freedom is hindered by institutional forms, in order that they might eventually make intelligent decisions as they engage in the journey toward adulthood.[41]

In writing about these issues, I have tried to emphasize their New Testament roots. Teaching is *didache,* prayer is a filling out of *leiturgia,* communion is *koinonia,* advocacy is the enfleshed, bodily *kerygma,* and troublemaking is a contemporary rendering of *diakonia.* If we engage in these areas and our engagement bears fruit, we may draw the reaction similar to that received so often by Jesus of Nazareth. People will say to us, "I'm not sure what you mean by that, but I'm certain I don't like it." Nonetheless, it is important to try, with conviction, with lightness of touch, and with a resolution to stay at such ministry in season and out. The task is enormous, but engaging in it is symbolic testimony that we take seriously the responsibility to move in the direction of a new creation.

In the next chapter, I will turn to youth, the focus of the ministry about which I have just written. However, to conclude this chapter, I want to highlight three features of the portrait painted thus far that will assist in illuminating what is to follow.

The first is that we need to keep in mind that ministry as I have been describing it is a gift God gives the church, not a gift to any one individual. (In fact it is probably a gift God gives beyond the church as well.) Parish ministers would do well to avoid the bias or appearance that ministry is the gift of some and not all, since it refers to a work that is the vocation and the responsibility of all

---

40. Cleveland, *op. cit.,* pp. 136 ff.

41. Jeffery Schrank, *Teaching Human Beings: 101 Subversive Activities for the Classroom* (Boston: Beacon, 1972) consistently demonstrates such attitudes toward young people.

who would consider themselves baptized Christians. The bias toward ministry as "mine" and not "ours" shows up in language; one hears of ministers *of* a congregation, shepherds *to* a flock, priest *and* people. This creates a tension with the vision of ministry being etched and painted today, the vision of the church as a community where all enable one another, where sometimes one leads, sometimes one follows, and where the entire community educates the entire community.

If this is kept in view, then the image and metaphor of rhythm can be aptly drawn, and drawn upon. I have said that some elements of ministry are more priestly than prophetic, and others are the reverse, although none is exclusively one or the other. Forgetting this can lead to the teacher worrying that teaching is getting in the way of contemplation, and the advocate worrying that community is being left out, worries that mushroom when one feels, and is made to feel, responsible for everything. The distinction between background and foreground is illuminating here.

Certainly both sets of strengths or virtues may be present. But insofar as ... intentional activity is in the foreground, receptivity is in the background. Effective work or successful communication may well require a constant movement between the two terms of the polarity. That rhythm is not, however, the same as simultaneity. Instead, a valuing of both ... requires a rhythm from one polar term to the other.[42]

When rhythm is understood, stress on one aspect of ministry—teaching, communion, advocacy—can be encouraged without causing the distracting concern that one should really be doing something else. This is because at root one is part of a body of people where all of ministry is being addressed somewhere in the life of that body.

I think that the attitude best calculated to serve this view is an attitude of humor. In ministry, we may be tempted to work *hard;* humor reminds us to work *soft,* since what is needed for this most serious endeavor is the lightest of touches. Many of us are in danger of thinking that we and our particular work are the center of ministry, at best an exaggerated claim. Humor is the inner gift reminding us that we are only one in a very large community weathered

---

42. See George Rupp, *op.cit.,* pp. 83–84.

by centuries of similar striving. Yes, we are important, but probably not essential. Our striving can be peaceful if we pray with lightness and humor,

> Creator Spirit, please let your
> soft lamp the soul of our poor
> land illumine and its
> amber comfort us. I am
>
> familiar with your grace when you
> call me to look out the window
> and quiet with its stars is heaven,
> and people doing what they can.[43]

---

43. Paul Goodman, *Little Prayers and Finite Experience* (New York: Harper, 1972), p. 52.

Chapter One
STUDY AND PRACTICE

ACTIVITY 1
The Meaning of Ministry

The following questions are for small group discussion, and are intended to create further understanding of the central ideas in this chapter.

1. What new meaning of ministry has had the strongest effect on you?

2. What are the implications of saying that "ministry is no longer only for the ordained"?

3. What is the difference between ministry *to* and ministry *with?*

4. How might the word "ministry" be applicable to persons who are not church members?

5. Is everyone in your church a minister? Give reasons for your answer.

6. Complete the following: If I could change one thing about ministry as it exists in the present, I would _____.

ACTIVITY 2
The New Testament and Ministry

1. Divide participants into small groups of three to five people. Ideally, each person should have a copy of the New Testament.

2. Assign or have each group select one of the following texts:
   Ephesians 4:11–14   1 Corinthians 12
   Galatians 3:26–28   2 Corinthians 3:12–17
   Colossians 3:12–17

3. After reading and reflecting on the text, each person should individually complete the following three topics: (a) What ministry *is* in the text. (b) What ministry *is not* in the text. (c) How this would affect our church, if we used it as a theme.

4. Compare responses within the group. Each group should come to a consensus concerning the one response they wish to share with the large group.

Allow about forty to sixty minutes for this project.

ACTIVITY 3
Dreams for Practice in Ministry

The purpose of this activity is to discover as many possibilities of meaning and practice for each element in ministry as participants can dream.

PROCEDURE:

1. Individually or as a whole group brainstorm by writing or calling out an activity that could be part of the suggested ministry.

2. Choose those responses that are the top priorities.
   In each case, two activities are suggested to get the group started.

TEACHING: Hold a recruitment fair; design an intergenerational lesson plan.

PRAYER: Conduct a retreat; spend a day in complete silence.

COMMUNION: Visit a local dog kennel; cook dinner for a new family in town.

ADVOCACY: Invite a local lawyer to speak on the rights of children; observe one session of the local government.

TROUBLEMAKING: Plan a way of changing one aspect of local TV programming; interview one local business that employs no young people.

STUDY AND PRACTICE

ACTIVITY 4
Central Elements in Ministry

The following role play is designed to (a) emphasize the five central elements in ministry; (b) investigate whether it is possible to interrelate all of them. Participants should be given their parts beforehand. Twenty to thirty minutes should be devoted to the role play. A debriefing session should follow that allows participants and observers time for comment.

1. After three years in Youth Ministry in one state, you have moved to another section of the country. You are being interviewed for the position of Youth Minister in a church where you will be the first to take on this role. You believe strongly that *all* elements of ministry are important, although your talents lie in teaching, and you are uncomfortable with prayer and with troublemaking.

2. You are the chairperson of the group interviewing the candidate. Your main objectives are to make sure everyone is heard, that whoever has questions gets to ask them, and that unless a grave problem appears, you are able to hire the candidate for the position. For you, personally, the most important part of ministry is someone who will make the young people do what they are "supposed to," although you are open to other people's positions.

3. You are the representative of the young people, a high-school junior. Your major and overwhelming desire is to have someone in the Youth Minister's role who will be an advocate for the young people with the rest of the church. You are not especially interested in teaching or prayer—you just want your rights.

4. You have taught in the parish for years and are convinced that young people know less and less of their faith. You are ready to leave aside every aspect of ministry except teaching and do not believe prophetic ministry is appropriate in your church.

5. Your background in the Peace Corps and in Civil Rights has convinced you that a ministry to institutions is of the utmost importance, and that the next generation must engage in political action toward churches, business corporations, the military, and

schools so that young people are not exploited by these institutions. Presently, you are convinced that in general, the young are hurt by most institutions. In your view, the driving force to change this is the gospel, and you do not hesitate in pushing your position.

6. You believe that unless the young are seen as part of the community the church is failing in its purpose. However, you believe the young people themselves must also work at community. You are very strong about offering your own help if it is needed, and in insisting that ministry is not *to*, but *with* the young.

7. You do not believe a genuine ministry is possible without prayer, both public and private. You would like to know about the candidate's personal prayer life, plans for instruction in prayer, attitudes toward worship and hope for including the young in worship, but you are also uncomfortable raising these issues.

ACTIVITY 5
Study Projects on Youth Ministry

This activity is designed for a group who will be studying Youth Ministry over a period of several days or several weeks. After reading and reflecting upon this chapter, divide the group into five sections, and determine mutually agreeable times and dates for each section to work with the whole.

PARTICIPANTS IN SECTION ONE: Your task is to design a program for the whole group where the focus is the ministry of teaching. Decide on your goal, objectives, the tasks and processes you will engage in prior to the program, the resources needed, and the ways in which you can involve everyone from all sections in the finished program.

PARTICIPANTS IN SECTION TWO: Your task is to design a program for the whole group where the focus is the ministry of prayer. Decide on your goal, objectives, the tasks and processes you will engage in prior to the program, the resources needed, and the ways in which you can involve everyone from all sections in the finished program.

STUDY AND PRACTICE

PARTICIPANTS IN SECTION THREE: Your task is to design a program for the whole group where the focus is the ministry of communion. Decide on your goal, objectives, the tasks and processes you will engage in prior to the program, the resources needed, and the ways in which you can involve everyone from all sections in the finished program.

PARTICIPANTS IN SECTION FOUR: Your task is to design a program for the whole group where the focus is the ministry of advocacy. Decide on your goal, objectives, the tasks and processes you will engage in prior to the program, the resources needed, and the ways in which you can involve everyone from all sections in the finished program.

PARTICIPANTS IN SECTION FIVE: Your task is to design a program for the whole group where the focus is the ministry of troublemaking. Decide on your goal, objectives, the tasks and processes you will engage in prior to the program, the resources needed, and the ways in which you can involve everyone from all sections in the finished program.

NOTE THAT: "the whole group" in these directions may refer to the group studying together, but it may also refer to a youth group with whom you are working or to the entire congregation.

Chapter Two
YOUNG PEOPLE IN
U.S. CULTURE

At the beginning of his extraordinary study of adolescence, *Rites of Passage,* Joseph Kett points out that United States society between 1790 and 1840 was composed of children and young people. The median age of our population was sixteen in 1800; 150 years later, in 1950, it had risen to 30.8. The corollary to these statistics is that in the early nineteenth century, there were relatively few middle-aged people in the country. Those aged forty-five to sixty-four comprised only 9 percent of the population.[1] In contrast, that portion of our population had almost tripled by the mid-seventies, so that by 1976, the ten to nineteen age group and the forty-five to sixty-four age groups were almost even in numbers, each accounting for roughly 22 percent of our people. (As of 1976, the last year for which statistics are available, the first group numbered 41 million, and the latter 43 million. Persons over sixty-five now make up 30 percent of our population.)[2]

I cite these statistics because our social institutions have had to adjust to these changing patterns, and in adjusting have changed the life-styles of youth and to some extent its nature. Just as ministry is very recent as a focus for the entire church, so too the picture of youth as we see it today is quite new in our history. In the late eighteenth and early nineteenth century United States, for example, children were *emotionally* and *economically* independent at

---

1. *Rites of Passage. Adolescence in America 1790 to the Present* (New York: Basic Books, 1977), p. 38.

2. Demographic, Social and Economic Profile of States, (Washington: Bureau of Census, Department of Commerce, Spring, 1976).

an early age, but remained *morally* and *intellectually* dependent on parents well into their maturity. Today the reverse is far more likely to be true.[3] In addition, dependence has shifted to peers in a way less obvious formerly. "There is one generalization one can make about adolescence. It is the age when one greatly needs one's contemporaries; when one must interact closely with them to try out one's capacity to think, feel and make decisions; the time when one becomes truly part of one's own generation."[4]

The social institution that has at present the greatest impact on youth is the school. We have reached a time when school has come to be the place for the young to be, by law; the place that more than any other shapes their image of themselves as success or failure.[5] Stress on the cognitive skills of the young has been so successful that we have reached the highest literacy rate in the world, compulsory schooling has been a most effective element in destroying the abuses of child labor, and the young are now going on to college and professional schools in unprecedented numbers. On the other hand, concern is continually voiced with reference to our schools, particularly as we note those experiences the schools do not, and cannot, provide. At present, most of the young are not given (a) experience with persons differing in social class, subculture and age; (b) experience of having others dependent on their actions; and (c) experience of interdependent activities directed toward collective goals.[6] A striking characteristic of the school (more true of junior high and high school than of elementary school or college) is that it brings together persons who are almost identical in age. At no other time in life does one spend such an extraordinary amount of time, for so long a period each day, with persons within two or three years of one's own age. The circumstance has many effects: some of the deepest friendships of one's lifetime tend to be made during these years; a multi-million person professional class of youth workers has emerged; communities come to be centered not only around the school but around its extracurricular activities. More germane to my consideration of youth here, however, is that

---

3. Kett, *op. cit.*

4. Gisela Konopka, *Young Girls: A Portrait of Adolescence* (New Jersey: Prentice-Hall, 1976), p. 84.

5. Maxine Greene of Teachers College, Columbia University, in an unpublished lecture, "We grade and degrade."

6. See James S. Coleman (ed.) *Youth: Transition to Adulthood.* (Chicago: University of Chicago Press, 1974).

the need has grown up for information about this time of life so that those working with the young can do so with intelligence and understanding. Hence we have turned to developmental studies, as youth workers, youth teachers, and youth ministers, in the apparent hope such studies will answer most of our questions.

In this chapter I want to look at these developments. My focus will be twofold: First, I want to challenge the unspoken assumption that all young people are the same. The assumption is usually unexamined and is obviously untrue; we know in our hearts that human beings of whatever age are infinitely varied. "The school apparently gives great weight to individualism. It talks about individualized programming, uses tests and counselors to identify individual skills, and individually evaluates the work of each student. But much of this 'individualism' is rather specious. That is, when two to three thousand comparatively young persons are put in one building at the same time, it is essential that many common conventions be articulated and followed."[7] This lumping together, herding together, and bringing together of age cohorts during the teen-age years can create circumstances where willy-nilly, adults are pushed into treating youth as if they *were* all the same, and into the even more damaging circumstances of considering as deviant those who do not "fit." "Our society provides a ladder of age-graded experiences for young people—sports, clubs, schools—which in theory conforms to their needs but which in practice often does not. At least part of the trouble now arises because a young person's status as an adolescent is *too* well defined."[8] This sharp, clear definition does not apply to all young people, however, and then the society, as well as the young person, loses. "We found that if a child is not white, or is white and is not middle class, does not speak English, is poor, needs special help with seeing, hearing, walking, reading, learning, adjusting, growing up, is pregnant or married at age fifteen, is not smart enough, or is too smart, then in many places school officials decide that school is not the place for that child."[9]

Given such factors, it seems to me that we need to at least go easy on developmental study and use what has been learned from Piaget, Kohlberg, Erikson, Goldman, Fowler and others only in the wider social, political and economic contexts where young people

---

7. Wynne, *op, cit.*, pp. 16–17.

8. Kett, *op. cit.*, p. 81.

9. From a report by the Children's Defense Fund (New York Times Service, Washington, D.C., 11/22/74), quoted in Konopka, *op. cit.*, pp. 124–125.

live. For this reason, a secondary emphasis in this chapter will be brief comment on developmental research.

It is to these two issues that I now wish to turn. I will devote most of what follows to consideration of what young people are not, and then move to some remarks on developmental study.

WHAT YOUNG PEOPLE ARE NOT

1. *Young people are not children; they are not adults.* Ministry with young people could be made much simpler if we could assign precise ages to the group about whom we were speaking. Ideally, we should be able to say, "By age 15, all young people should be able to —" or "Once a boy or girl is 16, he or she will know —" Ideally, we would have precise definition and be able to say, "Youth are all those between the ages of 10 and 19," something in the manner of the United States Bureau of the Census. Unfortunately for us, it is not that easy; and social developments have added to the difficulty. Adolescence as a stage of life emerged only in this century, beginning in 1904 with the publication of G. Stanley Hall's *Adolescence: Its Psychology and Its Relations to Physiology, Anthropology, Sociology, Sex, Crime, Religion and Education.*[10] Prior to that time, most young people went from puberty to some kind of job or apprenticeship, and were not thought of as a separate time of life. Obviously, Hall did not discover adolescence, but he did perform the service of naming a stage of life that was clearly identifiable. More recently, Kenneth Keniston, who has been studying young people for many years, suggested that our own times were witnessing the emergence of yet another stage of life, one he called "Youth."[11] In doing so, he was acknowledging a group of people, post-high school, who were being called "late adolescents" or "young adults," phrases whose very "mouth-filling awkwardness" testified to their inadequacy. In the same area, the church's ambivalence is demonstrated by the use of such phrases as "youth minister" and "young adult minister." Librarians are among others acutely aware of the problem, forced daily to decide what does or does not go on the "Young Adult" shelves.

Throughout this book, I wish to focus on those young people who are roughly of high-school age, but I do so asking the reader

---

10. (New York: D. Appleton and Company, 1904.)

11. See the essay, "Youth as a Stage of Life," in his *Youth and Dissent* (New York: Harcourt Brace Jovanovich, Inc., 1971), pp. 3-21.

to keep in mind that such a limitation is very hesitantly made. Youth Ministers who speak of the young as "students" will, I am sure, identify with the problem. Because it is so difficult to give exact description of this age group, a first definition, possibly as helpful as adolescent or youth is this: young people are not children; they are not adults.

Another way of stating this is that from a religious perspective, youth is a totally new experience of death and a totally new experience of life. The death is the death of childhood: of the dependent, un-self-conscious, and often responsibility-free time of life, and a movement through the stages of dying. We see the young deny the change, and this is manifested by their acting one day like grown-ups, the next like small children. We see it in their anger, often irrational although genuine, at circumstances that would not have touched them earlier; by the depression and gloom that can envelop them for apparently no reason; by the almost continual bargaining for greater freedom to experiment, and finally by the first stages in accepting their new identity. I do not use death here as a metaphor; I use it as a realistic description. Youth is a primary experience of death—the death of childhood.[12]

Youth is also, however, a totally new experience of life. The beginning of puberty in its physical manifestations symbolizes a newness of life of more profundity and depth than the physical alone. The possibility of generating life, of actually giving physical birth is related to the possibilities now glimpsed for the first time in relationships toward other people and the first "fallings" in love; poetry, often beautiful poetry, is written with passion; birth of a new life toward the social world is manifested in a new taking of responsibility. Adelson gives one example of the latter in his study of the development of political consciousness. Asking what is the purpose of law to twelve- and thirteen-year-olds, he was told, "So that people don't get hurt. If we had no laws, people could go around killing people."[13] By fifteen and sixteen they had come to realize that the

---

12. The sequence here is drawn from Elisabeth Kübler-Ross's *On Death and Dying* (New York: Macmillan, 1969). Hers is the best-known analysis of stages, and needs the caveat that not everyone passes through all of them nor should they be expected to.

13. Joseph Adelson, "The Political Imagination of the Young Adolescent," in *Twelve to Sixteen: Early Adolescence,* edited by Jerome Kagan and Robert Coles (New York: Norton, 1972), p. 108. The viewpoint, however, must be qualified, and Adelson also found significant differences among U.S., British and German young people. See pp. 131 ff.

purpose of law was to ensure safety and enforce government. Eventually, the vision of a new life in community is born, as the sociocentric emphasis of genuine adulthood comes into play.

This not-child, not-adult status is characterized by an easily understood wavering that can be prolonged when the young person is isolated from diversity. One manifestation of such isolation is the state of transportation, especially if the persons live in suburbs. "Until the children are old enough to drive a car, their out of school life is limited to the experiences that (1) are within walking distance, (2) they are 'ferried' to; or (3) may be available via bicycle in some seasons and for some age groups."[14] Here not-child, not-adult time comes between puberty and driver's license, a time that can be extended and exacerbated by lethal and nonresponsible driving practices on the part of the young. A more subtle but no less real prolongation of the period is accomplished unwittingly by many adults in contact with the young. Such adults romanticize and extol adolescence, glamorizing and idealizing it beyond recognition, while setting up and demanding unrealistic standards of perfection and innocence. The reasons are many, beginning with a desire to relive one's own youth. Whatever the reason, however, one result is to magnify for the young a confusion about themselves already felt all too strongly by many during this period. I submit that what is needed, instead, is not more reinforcement of their own ambivalence about themselves, but an experience of definiteness, strength, and mooring that it is in the capacity of adults, especially Youth Ministers, to provide. In the view of James DiGiacomo, such people can structure situations in such a way that truth is discovered rather than imposed. He gives as an illustration a situation where a teacher has engaged young people in a discussion that has run its course, but has not arrived at even tentative consensus. At such times, he writes, it is most appropriate to say something like this:

Well, we have had a very interesting discussion about stealing (or cheating, or abortion, or premarital sex, etc.), and we haven't arrived at a consensus. I'm glad that you feel free in this class to express your honest feelings and opinions, to disagree with one another, and to disagree with me. So what I'm going to say now is not meant as a put-down. I think you're wrong. As a Christian and as a human being, I reject not you but your opinion. I believe that the conclusions you have reached are dangerous and potentially destructive. Act on

---

14. Wynne, *op. cit.*, p. 12.

them, and you may hurt yourself and others. I know you don't see it this way, and I don't question your sincerity. I don't want you to say things you don't believe, or stop thinking for yourself. I don't even deny that possibly—just possibly—you may some day be proven right, and I may be proven wrong. But meanwhile I have a responsibility to myself and to you to stand up for what I believe and to caution you against behavior that I consider irresponsible. I have to do this, because I love you, I care about you, and I take you seriously.[15]

Such caring, such love, and such being taken seriously is eventually the strongest catalyst for the young as they seek to walk through this precarious in-between stage of their life.

2. *They are not invested.* In *The Uncommitted,* Kenneth Keniston wrote of a somewhat older group of young people whom he described as alienated.[16] I acknowledge that there are young in our society who are indeed deeply troubled, deeply alienated. In Gisela Konopka's study of young girls, for example, 57 out of the 940 interviewed had *attempted* suicide—a very high and significant number.[17] Others are characterized in Erikson's words by showing "a sharp and intolerant readiness to discard and disavow people (including, at times, themselves)"; a repudiation which is "often snobbish, fitful, perverted, or simply thoughtless."[18] Nonetheless, in speaking here of the young as not invested it is a more generalized and less stark set of issues to which I refer.[19]

Four of the more obvious elements in this noninvestment are: (1) in the economic area, the young are not yet at the stage of paying for student loans; working for food, board or housing money; tying themselves to mortgages; and putting down the kind of roots that marry them to credit and finance. (2) In the area of life choices they are still exploring options, particularly with reference to parenthood, marriage, work/vocation, and religious commitment. (3) Not only do they, at least theoretically, have multiple options, but they have multiple *power* to pursue these options, a thesis Joan-

---

15. "Follow Your Conscience," in *The Living Light,* 15, 3 (Fall, 1978), p. 396.

16. (New York: Harcourt, Brace and World, Inc., 1965).

17. Konopka, *op. cit.,* p. 95.

18. Erik Erikson, *Young Man Luther* (New York: Norton, 1958), p. 42.

19. The idea of not invested has some relationship to Erikson's idea of a "psychosocial moratorium." See Erik Erikson, *Identity Youth and Crisis* (New York: Norton, 1968), pp. 156–158. Feminist concerns would undoubtedly have some impact on the idea as it is discussed in relationship to women. See pp. 282–283.

marie Smith has articulately explored in discussing recent findings on adolescent superiority, not only in the physical realm, but in the moral realm as well.[20] (4) As they come into contact with many adults, they see that adulthood for these persons is, today, very fuzzy as a concept in the sense that men are becoming more hesitant to hold up a super-rational, "macho" and work-oriented ethic, and women are more hesitant to hold up the "marry and live happily-ever-after" ethos.[21] This shores up any latent desire or inclination not to rush toward adulthood, since for many who have *apparently* reached that stage, what they have rushed toward is ambiguous at best, and fallen-apart at worst.

Such a time of not-yet-being-invested suggests to me that those in Youth Ministry might focus on their own work with young people in a manner that complements this characteristic, a manner that I would name "exploratory." I mean by this a concentration on what they do as an exploration rather than as an arrival, and I would center this exploration in the areas of life-choices, of social structures, and of religious ideals.

With reference to life-choices, there almost certainly must be a wiser and more open exploration of sexuality and parenting. In her interviews Konopka asked almost a thousand girls what they thought a young girl should do if she were pregnant and unmarried. Her comment after extensive reflection was, "It is significant that this is a subject they thought about a great deal just as they thought about premarital sex. It is definitely not a 'hidden' or unimportant subject."[22] Then she concluded with this judgment: "*It is distressing that adult society gives girls so little opportunity to discuss it, except when they become pregnant.*"[23] Girls, and boys too, need opportunities to explore the particularities and ramifications of this life-investment.

Youth Ministers would also do well to explore the values the young put on the institutions with which they are involved, rather than assume they are the same as the adult value of the institution, or the values articulated when the structure was first set up. Mer-

---

20. "The Next Generation: The Heroic Age," in Harris, *Parish Religious Education*, pp. 74–83.

21. See Moran, *Education Toward Adulthood, loc. cit.,* esp. Ch. 2, "Meanings of Adulthood," pp. 17–36, for a development of the meaning of adulthood I am working from in these comments. He is especially sensitive to feminist concerns and to the destructive nature of some historical ideals of adulthood for both men and women.

22. Konopka, *op. cit.,* 36.

23. *Ibid.*

ton Strommen's work in this area is known to many;[24] the issue is reflected in the Konopka interviews with reference to the school in her finding that the most significant aspect of school from the young person's point of view was not its educative value, but that "it was a place *to meet and be with friends.*"[25] And, while in no way suggesting that schools lower their academic standards, she does comment that "Schools seem to underrate this part of their function. They often consider it only a by-product. But this function is the most significant one to the young people themselves and has a deep impact on their whole attitude *toward people* and *learning.*"[26] Given such a strong formative influence, the school needs to be examined and explored in this area, an exploration toward which Youth Ministers might naturally gravitate. And, although the school is the most obvious institution to explore, church, work, family and government must undergo similar scrutiny. In Chapters 5 and 7, I will provide some of this examination.

With reference to religious ideals, the exploration must take into account the experience of sin, of responsibility and of hope. The exploration of sin I am suggesting is not toward immorality; rather it is a move toward understanding the true nature of religion. "The utmost security of letting oneself go, of letting oneself sin, which we call by the ancient name of religion, is at the same time the greatest step forward. Because of the inner experience of the grounding of our identity, a return journey is necessary."[27] Adults are often so protective of the young that they will not allow them to fall, and when they do evidence failure or sin, will either ignore it, excuse it, or tolerate it. My argument here is that the journey in the direction of investment of oneself almost necessarily involves sin, and the Youth Minister can be a support when this occurs, if in no other way than by naming it accurately for what it is, acknowledging it as part and parcel of the human condition, and pointing the way to forgiveness.

Responsibility is the second religious theme to be cultivated in this not-yet-invested time—certainly, a statement which is not new. The angle of vision I would offer, however, is that we are already

---

24. See his *Five Cries of Youth* (New York: Harper and Row, 1974).

25. Konopka, *op. cit.,* p. 114.

26. *Ibid.*

27. See Dorothee Soelle, *Death by Bread Alone* (Philadelphia: Fortress, 1978), p. 126, for a development of the religious significance of the point I am trying to underline here.

long on preaching responsibility to the young and what is first needed is a grasp of the idea of human response. The young are not yet invested, that is, responsible toward, because as yet there has been so little exploration of the *what* toward which their responsibility is to be directed. "There can only be authentic responsibility where there is a genuine response. But response to what? Every given hour with its contents of world and destiny is a personal message to whoever is attentive; being attentive is all that is required to start reading the signs one receives."[28] Cultivation of response is intimately related to attitudes of stillness and contemplation, a theme to which I will return in Chapter 4. Here I will simply note the Youth Minister's responsibility to design zones of quiet, of silence, and of prayer in order to enhance the possibility of being attentive.

Finally, a religious ideal that must be held out, one becoming increasingly difficult in a world of nuclear buildup, global hunger, boat people, political assassination, terrorism, and war, is the possibility of hope. I suspect that a very strong argument for refusing to invest one's life is the absence of evidence for reasons to do so. Undoubtedly the assertion of hope not only has the appearance of foolishness, it *is* foolishness, and may possibly be offered only in the context of a religion that affirms death and resurrection. Nevertheless, it is a gift that must be given to the young, and is most clearly seen if embodied in other human beings. What is hope? "Hope consists in asserting that there is at the heart of being, beyond all data, beyond all inventories and all calculations, a mysterious principle which is in connivance with me, which cannot but will that which I will, if what I will deserves to be willed and is, in fact, willed by the whole of my being."[29]

3. *Young people are not welcome in the world of work.* When one reads the most recent Census Bureau figures, which indicate that in 1976, 65 percent of all persons sixteen to twenty-four were in the labor force, and that in the 1980's, when this figure declines by 2 million it will be mainly because of the sharp drop in the 1960's birth rate,[30] the impression may be given that the young *are* welcome in the world of work. My argument is the opposite: the

---

28. Gabriel Marcel, *Searchings* (New York: Newman Press, 1967), p. 85

29. Gabriel Marcel, *The Philosophy of Existence* (New York: Philosophical Library, 1949). p. 16.

30. "Characteristics of American Children and Youth: 1976," (Washington: Bureau of the Census, Department of Commerce), p. 40.

young have been systematically excluded from the world of work, and although this is true across the board it is even more pertinent to females and to nonwhite males in our population.[31]

My concern here, however, is not basically a statistical one. Rather it is an informational and philosophical one. I want to point out that a very powerful socialization process excludes young people who are the concern of Youth Ministers from a work-world that is almost certainly to be theirs throughout their lives, and which ought to be part of their present experience. To back up this thesis, I offer the following reflections.

At some point in the nineteenth century, urban life began to force discontinuities between age groups and to deprive teen-agers of social roles and economic functions.[32] By the turn of the century, adolescence had been invented, largely in response to the social changes that accompanied U.S. economic development. David Bakan has argued, brilliantly in my judgment, that the years of childhood were thus prolonged into the teen-age years largely because social, economic and political forces became linked with the major humanitarian agencies concerned about the exploitation of the young. And, without faulting the work of the reformers who were desperately concerned with the plight and abuse of children and teen-agers, he does illustrate the ways in which compulsory schooling, child-labor laws, and the establishment of criminal procedures for juveniles effectively removed the young from the labor force, creating a situation with us to this day.[33]

I cannot do justice to Bakan's essay in these few paragraphs and I urge the reader to study the original. What I can do, however, is to name some of the provocative issues that a critique such as his raises. One is that young people have little access to jobs and are carefully proscribed by law from taking on innumerable kinds of jobs, without very detailed certification procedures (e.g., working papers). They are also carefully prescribed by law to go to and stay in school, even if it is obviously not the right place for them to be. An accompanying element is that they also have very little experience of seeing people at work, or actually engaged *in* a job, except

---

31. *Ibid.* "Black high school graduates with no college were twice as likely to be unemployed as their white counterparts. Among those with some college education, Black youths were three times as likely to be unemployed as White youths."

32. Kett, *op. cit.,* p. 86.

33. See David Bakan, "Adolescence in America: From Idea to Social Fact," in Kagan and Coles (eds.) *op. cit.,* pp. 73–89.

for school personnel. Especially when a parent works at a distance from the home, such geographically remote work "makes it hard for young people to see work as either comprehensible or interesting. Nor do they find simple images of tangible work activities in the complex modern institutions that provide efficient services to many . . . supermarkets, teams of doctors and aides, branches of quick-service food chains."[34]

Another issue raised by this nonrelationship is that little if any distinction is made between job, work, and vocation. Where Thomas Green could write that "work is that activity by which men (and women) refuse to acknowledge that life is vain,[35] job is a modern concept that refers to something partial and something for which you usually get paid."[36] In distinction, *vocation* is the calling of a lifetime and takes decades of growing-into before it is eventually ours.[37] Contrast the usual understanding of these terms in most literature relating work and the young. As only one example, Wilson and Scharf write that "Work-Experience/Study Programs have been historically associated with the ritual of 'training' lower-class students in public high schools to perform the more menial tasks of an industrial society."[38]

In many ways, girls and women are especially harmed by such issues. The image of their mothers who may be involved in child care and care of the home as *nonworking* and *therefore unproductive* is one with which many boys and girls grow up, whether that mother is on welfare or not. Daniel Moynihan has pointed out that when everyone is taking care of one's own children, none of that activity is counted in the GNP. When one takes care of another's children, that is counted. "If American society recognized homemaking and child rearing as productive *work* [italics mine] to be included in the national economic accounts (as is the case in at least one other nation) the receipt of welfare might not imply dependency. But

---

34. Wynne, *op. cit.*, p. 13.

35. In *Work, Leisure and American Schools* (New York: Random House, 1968), p. 16.

36. Gabriel Moran, "Work, Leisure, and Religious Education," in *Religious Education*, 74, 2 (March-April 1979), p. 162.

37. I am assuming that in Catholic circles, "vocation" is no longer limited to choices of single life, marriage, or membership in a religious order.

38. Peter Scharf and Thomas C. Wilson, "Work Experience: A Redefinition," in Ralph Mosher (ed.) *Adolescents' Development and Education* (Berkeley: McCutchan, 1979), p. 433.

we don't."[39] Only recently have basic elementary-school textbooks in reading, social studies, and literature begun to change the image of women working outside the home, and thus counteract the resentment children may feel about their mother's working, since the prevailing image has been "that her (or his) mother's work is less important than her (his) father's or that the mother works only because there is no father in the family, and the child is therefore doubly deprived."[40] The growing girl, however, is triply deprived: (1) considered unproductive if she wishes to work at home; (2) considered of secondary importance if she wishes to work outside the home; (3) without positive role-models whatever her choice, since the choices themselves are not legitimated.

In the light of such considerations, what might the Youth Minister offer? A first possibility is simply giving attention to work, job, and vocation, not as that for which the young are being prepared, but as essential human realities to be studied in themselves. What is human work? Where might we go to observe and participate in it? Is it an evil? Is it a joy? More to the point for their lives at present, however, the Youth Minister might help the young examine their own personal relationships to work. The hidden curriculum in much of their lives is the teaching: Don't live in the present—your existence right now is a preparation for life. But youth need to explore those experiences in their lives that presently *are* work, those that they consider *jobs*, and that which they suspect might be their eventual and fundamental *vocation*.

A more radical idea might be to investigate with the young the laws of compulsory schooling, so that they could understand how their present almost-universal social designation as "student" or "pupil" came about, and even, as some have suggested, work toward a revision of such laws.[41] Such investigation might lead to young people learning that law affects their own lives, and is not—as is so often implied—a reality that has to do essentially and uniquely with crime and criminals. Certainly, the Youth Minister could consider with the young whether the present distinction between "academic" and "vocational" schools is one that is helpful,

---

39. *The Politics of a Guaranteed Income* (New York: Vintage, 1972), p. 17.

40. Jamie Kelem Frisof, "Textbooks and Channeling," in Diane Gersoni-Stavn (ed.) *Sexism and Youth* (New York: Bowker, 1974), p. 307.

41. See Dwayne Huebner, "Poetry and Power: The Politics of Curricular Development," in William Pinar (ed.) *Curriculum Theorizing* (Berkeley: McCutchan, 1975), p. 274.

or is actually doing violence to their understanding of work and vocation as components of all life.

Such ideas are based on the religious view that the young person has been gifted with freedom, and that it is within his or her right as a free human person to pose the possibility of challenging societal form—certainly of examining it. In no area is this so obvious or so urgent, since the finding of one's vocation in life is each human being's inalienable birthright. Although he uses the term "occupation," it was this view of vocation about which John Dewey wrote in 1916:

A right occupation means simply that the aptitudes in a person are in adequate play, working with the minimum of friction and the maximum of satisfaction. With reference to the other members of a community, this adequacy of action signifies, of course, that they are getting the best service the person can render.[42]

The presentation of such possibility to the young with whom they work is part of the "vocation" of the Minister to Youth. The confirmation of its value may be that in offering it the Youth Minister begins to engage the young in understanding their own present and eventual roles in ministry as well.

DEVELOPMENTAL STUDIES

The last comment on what young people are not is also the second issue I wish to address in this chapter. I save it for last not because it is the most, or least, important, but because at this time developmental issues are receiving so much prominence they cannot be avoided. In view of such attention, it is important to assert: (4) *Young persons are not the equivalent of developmental stages.* To the reader whose first reaction may quite honestly be, "But nobody says they are," I direct you to such phrases as, "She's a stage two; He's a stage four; Has a six been interviewed yet?" which have become part of the language about young people and others in church, educational, and religious circles. My concern is to counteract such speech and the unexamined assumptions it can lead to. I have no intention of dismissing the work of the theorists of this century who have helped so much in assisting all of us to understand ourselves

---

42. *Democracy and Education* (New York: Macmillan, 1916), p. 308.

and one another. Instead, I would advocate understanding the meaning of developmental theory; affirming what has been helpful; naming those whose work is central, and offering complementary viewpoints.

In simple and uncomplicated language, Norman Sprinthall explains the idea of developmental stages, recalling that it was John Dewey who originally formed the idea that children and teen-agers move through stages of development.

A child is not, in this view, a midget-sized adult who simply grows from small to large in a quantitative sense. Instead children and teenagers grow and develop in a series of qualitatively distinct stages. Each stage is unique, a special way of organizing the thought process as to how a person makes meaning and understands the world. Qualitative growth can be compared to the transformations of the egg to caterpillar to butterfly sequence. Each stage of development is unique and separate yet the succeeding stage builds upon and is dependent upon the prior stage.[43]

The idea of stages of growth and development have been an enormous boon to human understanding. They have assisted educators in the development of curriculum and eliminated demands that cannot be met, simply because a person has as yet not "developed" the capacity for fulfilling them. It has influenced the design of many kinds of environments, from classrooms, to churches, to theaters, to museums, so that the subject matter being designed is offered according to the mode and the capabilities of the receiver. It has undoubtedly removed the label of "stupid" from many who are now recognized as simply not yet ready (or as it is sometimes—and far less felicitously—stated "developmentally disabled").

Certain great names are associated with different aspects of human development. Jean Piaget, the Swiss epistemologist, is the foremost theorist of cognitive development, and his work has had the greatest impact in explaining how structures of knowledge develop. Erik Erikson is the best known of those describing psychological development, although the more accurate term is psycho-social development, since Erikson links human stages of growth with so-

---

43. "Moral and Psychological Development: A Curriculum for Secondary Schools," in Thomas Hennessy (ed.) *Values and Moral Development* (New York: Paulist, 1976), p. 42.

cial structures. Lawrence Kohlberg is by far the leading name when one comes to speak of "moral development," although that is an inaccurate and incorrect label, since Kohlberg himself speaks of stages of moral *reasoning*. Recently James Fowler's name has been added to these because of his work on faith development, although Ronald Goldman in the 1960's used the work of Piaget to describe the way "religious thinking" develops from childhood to adolescence.[44] Many other theorists might be noted; I will limit my comments to Piaget, Erikson and Kohlberg here, and address Fowler's work in Chapter 4.

The name of Jean Piaget is almost synonymous with the study of cognitive development. One of the few authentic geniuses of this century, Piaget has spent more than half a century describing how the structures of the mind grow. "Piaget's discoveries of children's implicit philosophies or systems of belief, the construction of reality by the infant, and the stages of mental development have altered our ways of thinking about human intelligence."[45] Not all of his writing has been translated into English, and until his recent death he worked vigorously. His conclusions about thought have by now influenced anyone who works with the young, whether that person is aware of it or not.

Because Piaget's central focus has been the growth of thought, especially the description of how a person achieves the ability to think about thought, construct ideals, and reason realistically about the future, the impression can develop that thought and rationality are our *only* ways of knowing. This is the danger to which I wish to alert Youth Ministers and youth workers. Because they are persons who work with others in the realm of the religious, I would urge upon them an openness not only to understanding the development of reasoning, but toward understanding modes of knowing more accurately named intuitive, artistic, and mystical.[46] This is not because the work of Piaget is unimportant; on the contrary it is invaluable. Nevertheless, it still seems necessary, in my

---

44. See Ronald Goldman, *Religious Thinking from Childhood to Adolescence* (New York: Seabury, 1964); see also his *Readiness for Religion* (New York: Seabury, 1965). The work of John H. Peatling has extended the research of Goldman through the seventies. (Schenectady: Union College Character Research Project.)

45. David Elkind, *Children and Adolescents: Interpretive Essays on Jean Piaget* (New York: Oxford, 1970), p. 8.

46. A most helpful collection has recently been published. See Gloria Durka and Joanmarie Smith (eds.) *Aesthetic Dimensions of Religious Education* (New York: Paulist, 1979).

judgment, to right the imbalance in our culture that gives precedence and prestige to the linear, the logical and the abstract, and by extension to people whose gifts lie in these areas. Thus it is a religious issue, since the lure of the divine is often along nonlinear paths;[47] it is a political issue, since the use of power is often narrowly defined as the power to plan rational procedures; and it is a human issue since the dancer, the poet, the mystic and the dreamer have yet to be fully recognized and affirmed, not only in the young, but in all of us.

Like Piaget, Erikson is one of the century's great geniuses. His *Identity, Youth and Crisis*[48] continues to be a major resource for all Youth Ministers, and his descriptions of the stages of human life from trust through integrity have influenced our understanding of the human psyche. They are of particular value because Erikson relates them to the growth of the institutions of religion, law, economy, technology and ideology/aristocracy, thus achieving a social as well as a psychological focus.[49] While affirming his work, I would note several issues that ought to be addressed for a rounding out of Erikson's thought.

The first is his notion of the psychosocial moratorium. He suggests that both males and females be granted a period of delay prior to adult life, describing it as "a period that is characterized by a selective permissiveness on the part of society and of provocative playfulness on the part of youth which leads to deep, if often transitory, commitment on the part of youth, and ends in a more or less ceremonial confirmation of commitment on the part of society."[50] The issue is whether this vision is idyllic and thus open to being viewed cynically by those millions of young people without the societal and economic support that would allow for such a moratorium.[51]

Another important issue is the examination of life crises from a feminist viewpoint. While noting that *Childhood and Society* is "one of the finest books on adolescents" known, Gisela Konopka writes that like most books on adolescence, it too "consider(s) girls

47. William James, *Varieties of Religious Experience* (New York: Modern Library ed., 1902); see also the more recent work of Edward Robinson, *The Original Vision* (Oxford: Religious Experience Research Unit, 1977) and *Living the Questions* (Oxford: RERU, 1978).

48. *Op. cit.*

49. *Childhood and Society* (New York: Norton, 1950), pp. 258ff.

50. *Identity* . . . p. 157.

51. Bakan, *op. cit.*, p. 85.

not at all or only as an afterthought."[52] Works such as Penelope Washbourn's *Becoming Woman,*[53] which builds upon Erikson's understanding of life crises by focusing on such events as menstruation and childbirth, can be important resources in opening the psychological focus on man's search for meaning to women's search for meaning too. In this way, Erikson's work can be affirmed for the contribution it is, while it is critiqued in those places that must be revised or enlarged.[54]

In addition, such comments as Konopka's should give us pause whenever we base our understanding of the young on psychology, and should warn us never to interpret them solely in psychological categories. Obviously, none of us is reducible to any one perspective. But more to the point here, all youth workers should be aware that, as Joseph Adelson wrote in 1979, "Adolescent psychology as we now know it is essentially the psychology of adolescent boys, and our view of the period will be entirely transformed once we are able to achieve a more evenhanded view of gender."[55] This is not, in my judgment, a side issue to guide us occasionally; it is a fundamental issue that must rigorously inform everything we do with boys and with girls.

I find it more difficult to be as essentially positive in addressing Lawrence Kohlberg's work as I have been in speaking of Piaget and of Erikson. It may be the work itself; it may be the conclusions that disciples and devotees have drawn. At any rate, I urge consideration of a number of significant points to anyone relying on the Kohlberg schema as the basis of understanding moral development.[56] The reasons for my caveats are many, but I will limit myself to four: (1) The main basis for Kohlberg's stages is his original interviewing of fifty Chicago-area males, middle and working class, ages ten to sixteen.[57] These subjects have been interviewed every three years since 1958, and most of them are now in their thirties. (Hundreds of other persons have been interviewed since as well.) My reservation is with the limitation of this sampling—all males,

---

52. *Op. cit.,* p. 3.

53. (New York: Harper and Row, 1977).

54. This is especially true with reference to Erikson's chapter "Womanhood and the Inner Space," in *Identity, Youth and Crisis.* See pp. 261–294.

55. "Adolescence and the Generalization Gap," in *Psychology Today,* 12, 9 (February, 1979), p. 37.

56. One of the most recent and complete studies of Kohlberg is in Peter Scharf (ed.) *Readings in Moral Education* (Minneapolis: Winston, 1978).

57. Sprinthall, *op. cit.,* p. 2.

all urban, all under forty—as the basic and essential starting point. All subsequent work has been asked, to some degree, to "fit" this original formulation. (2) The highest stage in the series is one where justice is the epitome. My reservation is with the position that justice, as distinct from, say, care or mercy or love, is assigned the highest position.[58] (3) Underlying the theory is the presupposition that one progresses through these stages in a straight line, invariant, sequential, hierarchical manner. My reservation is with *any* description of human development whose underlying metaphor is so unambiguously linear. (4) Devotees of Kohlberg insist on calling his theory one of moral *development*.[59] His own designation, stages of moral *reasoning*, is far more apt, but even here, in my view, too broad. It might be better described as a schema describing a sequence of responses to hypothetical dilemmas of conflicting rights.[60]

Among the most telling critiques of Kohlberg's work is that of his colleague, Carol Gilligan.[61] Something of the flavor of her approach can be discerned in some of her interviews, which were not with young men about hypothetical dilemmas, but with women all of whom were pregnant, and all of whom were considering whether to continue or to terminate the pregnancy. Anyone seriously studying Kohlberg should study Gilligan as well; the cogency of her critique is illustrated by the following response he made to it:

Carol Gilligan would also make the claim that there's male bias built into our scale by the kind of moral dilemmas we choose to look at, which emphasize justice, property and conflicts in rights. She would argue that some other kind of dilemmas, which involve issues of caring and responsibility toward the community—for example, how much you should sacrifice for the community—might show more women at the upper end of the scale. I would agree.[62]

---

58. See Carol Gilligan, "In a Different Voice," in *Harvard Educational Review*, 47, 4 (November, 1977), pp. 481–517 for further development of these ideas.

59. Note, for example, the title: Ronald Duska and Mariellen Whelan, *Moral Development: A Guide to Piaget and Kohlberg* (New York: Paulist, 1975), one of the most successful interpretations.

60. See Gilligan, *op. cit.,* p. 515.

61. *Ibid.*

62. Howard Muson, "Moral Thinking: Can it be Taught?" in *Psychology Today*, 12, 9 (February, 1979), p. 57.

To the Youth Minister interested in this area, the options are neither as limited nor as narrow as the Kohlberg schema indicates. Perhaps moral development can be enhanced further not only by posing dilemmas and searching for discursive conclusions, but by returning to the great novels, plays and stories of Western culture and rediscovering the power of art to educate moral sensitivity.[63]

In concluding this chapter, I think it important to summarize by underscoring two main issues. The first is to name the starting point for Youth Ministers. Let me contend that it must be the environment of youth, with its political, social and cultural dynamic. We shall never understand young people apart from their own time and place. Each of them possesses not only a personal location, but a social location as well, and the latter is at least as influential and often more so than the former. The second is awareness that always—always—human beings know far more than they are able to say. The immediacy of the experiences of awe, of religious exultation, of sexual ecstasy, and of death are only some of the occurrences in life that shatter the boundaries between speech and silence; and often, the most profound of life's happenings cannot be stated. Thus to base understanding of humans too completely on what can be summed up in language, even the precise and informed language resulting from extensive interviews and observation, is to do all of us a disservice. As Youth Ministers, we can rely on a developmental schema only to a point. The rest, as Shakespeare knew, is silence.

---

63. See Maria Harris, "From Myth to Parable: Language and Religious Education," in *Religious Education*, 73, 4 (July–August, 1978), pp. 393–395.

Chapter Two
STUDY AND PRACTICE

ACTIVITY 6
The Journey from Child to Adulthood

This exercise is designed to help Youth Ministers in remembering their own time as not-child, not-yet-adult.

PROCEDURE:

1. Have participants draw a 7- to 8-inch time line similar to the one below. Then direct them to do the following:
   A. At the left of the time line, write the year of your birth.
   B. At the right of the time line, write your age now.
   C. Divide the time line into five-year segments. Put a (c) under those years when you consider yourself as a child. Put an (a) under those years when you view yourself as an adult. Put an (ns) under those years about which you are not sure.

2. After each participant has completed the time line, discuss the following:
   A. What are three life experiences which taught you that you were not a child?
   B. What are three life experiences where you found it hard to be sure whether you were a child or an adult?
   C. What are three life experiences that symbolize your participation in adult life?
   D. What are other comments you wish to make?

EXAMPLE:

1955 _____ /_____ /_____ /_____ /_____ /_____ today
       c   c   ns   ns   a   a

STUDY AND PRACTICE

ACTIVITY 7
The Dying of Childhood

This is an exercise for teen-agers and is for private use. It is not to be shared, except at the request of the teen-ager.

1. Is there anything about yourself as a child you would like to forget, or are tempted to deny? Is this still a part of you? Can you draw a symbol for it?

2. Do you ever find yourself feeling very angry? Can you name those occurrences which make you feel this way? Are they connected to being "treated like a child"? If so, why do you feel angry when they happen?

3. About what experiences in your life now would you like to do some bargaining? With your friends? With your parents? With your teachers? With . . . ?

4. Do you find yourself feeling depressed about things that did not bother you as a child? Do you expect the same things will bother you as an adult?

5. What do you accept about yourself today that you would not have admitted two years ago? Five years ago? Last year?

ACTIVITY 8
Work, Job, and Vocation

This is an exercise for young people and Youth Ministers. For the purposes of this exercise, some terms are defined below.

JOB: A modern concept that refers to something partial and something for which you usually get paid.

WORK: That activity by which men and women refuse to acknowledge that life is vain.

VOCATION: The calling of a lifetime.

53

After looking over the above definitions, discuss the following:

1. As you examine your life right now, what jobs do you have?

2. What is your main work in life right now?

3. What sense do you presently have about your life vocation?

4. If you could choose the job of your dreams, what would it be?

5. If you could choose the work of your dreams, what would it be?

6. If you could choose the vocation of your dreams, what would it be?

7. To what, if anything, do you feel called by God?

8. How can you get there?

ACTIVITY 9
"What Does Your Mother Do?"

This activity explores ideas about women and work.

1. Choose at random any of the textbooks you are now using in school. Examine the pictures in these books for what they tell you of the work of women. What are your conclusions?

2. Choose at random one-half hour to watch television for images of women and work. Count the situations where women are working. What kind of work, if any, are they doing? What are your conclusions?

3. Choose at random one Sunday service at a local church. Examine the service from the point of view of the work of women in the worship or liturgy. What are your conclusions?

4. Is housework work, a job, a vocation, or other? Should/do men and women share it equally? What are your conclusions?

STUDY AND PRACTICE

ACTIVITY 10
Designing Zones of Quiet

This activity is designed to help young people and Youth Ministers in the areas of response and attentiveness. The activity can be used in several ways: (a) as a follow-up to a discussion on prayer or quiet; (b) as a starting point for prayer, where people can collect their thoughts in quiet; in the midst of a worship service as a period of silence.

PROCEDURE:

1. Make sure each person has a circle approximately 5 inches in diameter, like the one below, and a pencil.

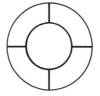

2. Have participants sit comfortably and quietly.

3. In the center circle write or draw a symbol for the place which is your favorite quiet spot.

4. In one-quarter of the circle, write the name of someone with whom you find it easy to be quiet.

5. In one-quarter of the circle, name or draw something you like with you when you are quiet.

6. In one quarter of the circle, write one word you like to repeat when you are quiet.

7. In one-quarter of the circle, name or draw one sound you notice when you are quiet.

8. Conclude with each person sharing *one* of the responses. After each response the entire group should repeat the phrase, "Be still and know that I am God." (Based on a suggestion by Patty Forbes, *Encountering Prayer and Meditation,* Atlanta: PCUS, 1979, p. 8.)

SECTION TWO

Chapter Three
DIDACHE: THE MINISTRY OF TEACHING

Apollinaire said:
"Come to the edge."
"We might fall."

"Come to the edge."
"It's too high."

"COME TO THE EDGE!"

And they came,
And he pushed them.

And they flew.
—Christopher Logue.

The first of the ministries described in Acts is teaching: "And they devoted themselves to the instruction of the Apostles" (Acts 2:42). To speak of teaching in the context of the church, it is necessary to make a number of distinctions at the outset. To begin with, teaching is not equal to religious education, just as education is not equal to schooling.[1] As a ministry, it is accompanied by, and companion to, prayer, communion, advocacy and troublemaking (*diakonia*), each of which has an educational dimension. Of these,

---

1. Religious Education, for example, might mean education in the area of religion, the intersection of the religious and the educational; the study of religion, etc. Since "church" and "religious" are not synonymous, it is obviously not limited to education carried on by the church.

teaching is the human activity most associated with others learning something, pushing them to the edge of knowledge so they might fly and perhaps even soar. When we teach, we intend that the other or others will know more than they did when we started. Nevertheless, it is not the only and often not the most significant catalyst for education and learning, to be blamed for all ills or congratulated for all good. It is one limited but essential activity. Done poorly, it can stultify and deaden; done well, it can change lives forever. It is this limited but important ministry that is the subject of the present chapter.

One of the most saddening discoveries I have made in the past few years, traveling through the country, is the bad name much church teaching receives, and in some cases the disrepute with which some hold it. For many it has become synonymous with imparting information, and that in a dry-as-dust manner. The main adjective that persons who shy away from such teaching will use is not "terrible" or "disastrous," but one far more deadly: "boring." For others, it is looked on as guiding, facilitating, drawing out, and counseling, putting the "teacher" into the role of a therapist. These activities often draw the charge of manipulation, coercion, or psychologism. I wish to challenge such understandings and attitudes in these pages. I will begin with a definition and description of teaching, name its central components when viewed as ecclesial ministry, and move to concrete suggestions for this ministry in the context of work with youth.

TEACHING

There is no one best way to teach. Learners have different styles as do teachers; particular subject matters must be dealt with in ways integral to them; and environments, both physical and mental, can alter methods of approach. Despite these obvious differences, 90 percent of teaching, once the learner is of high-school age, tends to be the so-called lecture. (I say "so-called" because a lecture in actuality is straight *reading,* and very few teachers are either so good they can carry that off, or so bad they will resort to it.) Because this form of presenting material is *modeled* most, it continues to be *used* most. Nevertheless, " ... the best general advice to the teacher who would lecture well is still, 'Don't lecture.' That is, for most of teaching, think in terms of discourse—talk, conversation—rather than lecture. Second, respect silence, both the teacher's and the student's. Third, shift from a total dependency on verbalizing to other means of animating, illustrating, and reinforcing talk."[2]

In working with hundreds of teachers, both beginners and advanced, I have discovered that most *are* willing to try other procedures besides the lecture or direct presentation of material. The resources that can assist teachers in doing this are enormous[3] but often the strongest influence is the teacher's own awareness of the need for a repertoire of teaching "models" or procedures, based on the conviction that learning occurs within a perspective characterized by rhythm. The rhythm can be named several ways. One is Whitehead's influential analysis where he describes the move from romance to precision to synthesis.[4] The teacher takes this into account whenever she or he takes time for the playing around—fooling around—getting to know the material via less-structured processes that might be called "romance," before moving to the more careful verbal activity of precision.[5] Another is the rhythm of developmental growth, especially the work of Piaget and Erikson already mentioned, which allows the teacher to work differently with child, adolescent, youth and adult, in the realization that not all of the entire body of Christian doctrine must be mastered in the eleventh grade. And finally there is a realization that all minds move through a natural rhythm that begins in an *uncritical* stage where all is light, progresses to a *critical* stage where the main activity is cursing the darkness, and emerges into a *post-critical* phase that might well be named "informed tolerance." What must be underlined about such rhythms as they apply to the act of teaching is that they are not one-time occurrences. Perhaps it is especially true of youth that a cyclical rhythm is characteristic, even with reference to the same material. Of this repetitive rhythm, Thomas Merton wrote:

Keeping a journal has taught me that there is not so much new in your life as you sometimes think. When you reread your journal, you find out that your latest discovery is something you already found

---

2. Kenneth Eble, *The Craft of Teaching* (San Francisco: Jossey-Bass, 1976), p. 42.

3. An annotated list of some of these resources appears at the end of this chapter.

4. Alfred North Whitehead, *The Aims of Education* (New York: Macmillan, 1929), esp. Chapter 2, "The Rhythm of Education."

5. See Maria Harris, "A Model for Aesthetic Education," in Durka and Smith, *op. cit.*, pp. 141–152, for one example.

out five years ago. Still, it is true that one penetrates deeper and deeper into the same ideas and the same experiences.[6]

If it is true that teaching takes place in the context of a rhythm, and if that rhythm is lifelong, the question most closely related to the activity is that of curriculum. This is because at root, one definition of the teacher is "one who designs appropriate curriculum." Thus, curriculum becomes a central focus and will need to be addressed in the church context by asking four questions: where, what, which, and why.

Where. The young spend a great deal of time in the building called school. When the agent of the teaching is the church as such, the decision may be to continue the patterns of learning established during school hours, and continue teaching on the basis of those procedures most appropriate to a school, which could be called "schooling." But it is also possible for the church to carry on teaching in many other settings: in the family, home, or some wider communal group; in political activity; in visits to job sites or work sites; in the religious activities of retreat; or in the recreational activities of play, art and sport. The teacher ought to consider, in view of the particular groups with whom she or he is working, which ones are the most valuable for these groups.

What. Wherever teaching goes on, however, the Youth Minister must be aware that any teaching ministry includes at least three specific curricula, each of which can be identified by an observer.[7] These are the *explicit* curriculum, the actual knowledge resources, ideas, activities and skills consciously addressed in the process; the *implicit* curriculum, or what is taught by such elements as the organizational structure, the pedagogical rules, the furniture, the patterns of authority. The implicit curriculum is equivalent to what the church teaches by the kind of a place, the kind of a community, the kind of a body *it* is. And third, there is the *null* curriculum—everything that is left out. The null curriculum can be further specified to center around two features: the intellectual processes emphasized, and the subject matter or content. Thus we need to ask what thinking capacities we are encouraging and developing as we teach the young, and what areas of life we are

---

6. Quoted in Sister Bernadette Vetter, *My Jouney, My Prayer* (Villa Maria, Pennsylvania: The Center for Learning, and New York: Sadlier, 1977), p. 15

7. Elliot Eisner, *The Educational Imagination* (New York: Macmillan, 1979), pp. 74–92.

designating as unimportant or outside the church's concern, by reason of their exclusion.

Which. Youth Ministers will also have to decide on the purpose of their teaching, given the setting and the subject. Is the aim of teaching, for example, the development of abilities to infer, deduce, speculate, analyze, make judgments about their faith? Is it, on the contrary, the learning "how to": how to pray, how to get a job, how to raise a family, how to be a good Christian, how to avoid child abuse. Or is the point of curriculum a kind of self-actualization, a move toward self-understanding so that the person being taught learns how to grow, to break bonds, to change, to be a better self. A fourth, and still different possibility is social reconstruction: teaching directed to the social issues of the day, to understanding the gospel in order to create a new human and political order. Or, finally, is the curriculum one that focuses on cultural transmission, assisting young persons to live in the world by gaining knowledge of the culture and tradition that has brought them to where they are. I would affirm each and all of these as legitimate choices for the teaching ministry[8] and urge Youth Ministers to name those that are theirs in actual practice.

Why. The teacher's final question regarding curriculum will be an examination of why this choice instead of that, why here instead of there, why include this and leave out that? Thus teachers will need to be skilled in examining different materials, drawing conclusions on the basis of evidence for one possibility rather than another. To do so, a community is needed, and the teacher is wise never to act alone in asking the questions that help uncover the assumptions behind choices, such as why, on what grounds, who decides, and who is to benefit? For ultimately, the ministry of teaching is a ministry of the entire church and never of the Youth Minister alone; it is based on the decisions of a corporate body, not of an individual.

ECCLESIAL TEACHING

I turn now to those characteristics that distinguish the church in its teaching and provide the ministerial dimension. Why and on what grounds is teaching a *ministry?* In what sense can it be considered *ecclesial* activity? Biblical scholar James D. Smart has writ-

---

8. These five options are the ones discussed in Elliot Eisner and Elizabeth Vallance (eds.) *Conflicting Conceptions of Curriculum* (Berkeley: McCutchan, 1974.

ten, "We must not forget that the primary function of the priest in pre-exilic Israel was ... instruction of people in the knowledge of God."[9] *Didache,* then, is one of the priestly elements in ministry, since religiously, it is a priestly function to give Torah, or instruction in sacred things. More precisely, it is instruction in Word, and it is instruction in Sacrament. One of the most hallowed definitions of the church is that it is that Body which is present where the Word is preached and the Sacraments duly administered. What I wish to do here is explain how these might be understood in our day, especially with reference to young people and the Youth Ministers who are their teachers. Speaking very generally, the Protestant emphasis in teaching—and even in Christian identity—is probably more toward Word than Sacrament; the Catholic emphasis is usually the opposite. My argument is that for *didache* to be whole and complete both are necessary.

WORD

In the Christian tradition, the primary meaning of Word is a person—the Word of God made flesh, and visible in the person of Jesus of Nazareth. A first access to that person is through other words, these the words of the people who lived with him, from whom he came, and who subsequently spoke to others about him. These words are of course the Bible: the Hebrew scriptures and the Christian story or New Testament. A third word completes the tradition. This is the word, or story, of the followers of Jesus through the centuries; obviously, the story did not stop with the death of the last apostle. The line is a continuous one, forward from Jesus to the present, and backward through Jesus to the men and women from whom he came, and whose journey is described in the holy books of ourselves as a people. In Psalm 78 (77) it is written:

> Mark my *teaching,* O my people,
> listen to the words I am to speak.
>
> I will tell you a story with a meaning,
> I will expound the riddle of things past,
>> things that we have heard and known,
>> and our parents have repeated to us.

---

9. *Op. cit.,* p. 59.

Ecclesial teaching, then, is primarily about a Word and about a story. It begins with Jesus, stretches back into the past of the Jewish people, and then moves forward in time through the New Testament, the early church, the Middle Ages, the Reformation, and into the present age. It is not, however, a bloodless story; it is one of flesh and blood, the story of the real lives of real men and women. As such it continually moves through polarities, all of which need to be shared with the young if they are to know the story in its entirety. I speak here of the polarities of love and hate, life and death, good and evil, remembering and forgetting. Fundamentally, what is handed on in the *tradition* is not a body of doctrine but the life of a people. This life is sedimented in the flesh and psyches of the young people of today, whether they know it or not. It can become apparent in what they accept and in what causes them to rebel. Even to understand themselves, it is necessary that they know the story.

In the act of teaching, the Youth Minister bears witness to tradition. This is particularly evident when the teacher/minister recalls for students that tradition is the gift of a people who while dead "in Christ" (to use Paul's phrase) are nevertheless companions with those living in the present. Many young Christians today are studying with Eastern teachers, with guru or swami or yogi, and this can be of great benefit. But it can also be ironic if the search of the young for a genuine religious life is due to ignorance of the giants of their own tradition: Bernard, Julian of Norwich, Angela of Foligno, Teresa, John of the Cross, as well as Pierre Teilhard de Chardin, Corrie ten Boom, Thomas Merton, Ernesto Cardenal and Dorothy Day in our own time. On the other hand, the teacher/minister needs to keep faith with the young by admitting that just as not all in the present are saints, not all in the past were giants. Indeed, the time may have come where an ecumenical climate exists that is warm enough for the differences, chasms, sins, lusts and infidelities of our ancestors to be named out loud, and perhaps in some sense exorcised.

In the vast and extensive story stretching back to Jesus, and through him to his Jewish roots, young people need to know that their own stories form an integral part. This is the place for the teacher to realize that *didache* is not only engagement with others *about* a Word; it is engagement with others *through* a Word. Teaching goes on in the myriad forms of word and language, beginning with the telling of one's own story.

I suspect that, because of the immediacy and "presentness" of experience in the young person's life, the best entrance toward the Christian story is by gathering young people together to tell their own stories. This can be an exercise in narcissism and in self-love, but in the hands of a skillful teacher, it can also be an entrance into human biography, human journey, and human religious life.

The purpose of a story, whether it be the narrative of an historic happening or a homey anecdote drawn from everyday life or a parable, is not to transmit information. Stories are told as a way of sharing experiences with one another. The language is plain, the actors ordinary people ... Story is one of the features that distinguish religious language—the idiom of evangelization and catechesis—from theological discourse.[10]

What the teacher needs to do here is build an environment of trust where stories can be shared and life themes identified, so that the young can come to "match" their own stories with their contemporaries in the present and with Christian companions of the past.

Teaching, however, cannot be limited simply to the telling of stories. Young hearers need the chastening intellectual accompaniment that comes through realizing how much the *form* of the story affects the content. John Dominic Crossan offers a typology of such story-form in writing that at least five exist: *myth* is the form of story which establishes world, *apologue* is the story-form defending that world, *narrative* investigates the world, *satire* attacks it, and *parable* is the peculiar story-form which subverts world.[11] It seems to me that the young could be brought to a far more profound understanding of their own religious story if it could be approached from each of these viewpoints. In what ways, for example, is the Christian story mythical? How have apologists defended the story, and how might today's Christians engage in apologue? Is it even appropriate that there be apologists for the faith, as there were in early Christianity? Can the narrative stand on its own and can the young phrase the story in a form that makes sense today? Is the story strong enough to be attacked—can it withstand criticism, and if so, how? And finally, what *is* a parable, and why did Jesus use them

---

10. Berard Marthaler, "Evangelization and Catechesis: Word, Memory, Witness," in *The Living Light*, 16, 1 (Spring, 1979), p. 43.

11. *The Dark Interval*. (Niles: Argus, 1976). See Chapter 1.

so often? Do our young people know the rich heritage they have not only in the content of the story but in its form?[12]

One other element in teaching the Word, which I would advocate especially with the young, is the act of *naming,* which is integral to the ministry of *didache.* I use the word not in the sense of labeling but in the sense of initiating the other into acquaintance with reality. I know of no passage in literature more apt to describe this than Helen Keller's description of her own teacher, Anne Sullivan:

She brought me my hat, and I knew I was going out into the warm sunshine. This thought, if a wordless sensation can be called a thought, made me hop and skip with pleasure. We walked down the path to the well house, attracted by the fragrance of the honeysuckle with which it was covered. Someone was drawing water and my teacher placed my hand under the spout. As the cool stream gushed over one hand she spelled into the other the word water, first slowly, then rapidly. I stood still, my whole attention fixed upon the motions of her fingers. Suddenly, I felt a misty consciousness as of something forgotten—a thrill of returning thought; and somehow the mystery of language was revealed to me. I knew then that w-a-t-e-r meant the wonderful cool something that was flowing over my hand. That living word awakened my soul, gave it light, hope, joy, set it free! There were barriers still, it is true, but barriers that could in time be swept away.[13]

Such initiation is particularly appropriate for the Youth Minister working with those for whom so much reality is yet to be named. For the skill to be exercised to the fullest, however, the Youth Minister must know his or her young people well enough to understand *when* such naming is desired and when it is best to hold off. Probably what serves the Youth Minister best here is studious attention to the *connections* words have: the connections of words with gesture so that the teacher/minister reads body language accurately; the connection between words and touch—when touch is called for, when it is unwanted; and the connection between words and si-

---

12. For further development, see Maria Harris, "From Myth to Parable, Language and Religious Education," in *Religious Education,* LXXIII, 4 (July–August 1978), pp. 387–398.

13. *The Story of My Life* (Garden City: Doubleday, 1936), pp. 23–24.

lence. Knowledge of such connections pushes the teacher/minister in the direction of wisdom and choosing the time, paraphrasing T. S. Eliot, to name and not to name, and the time to sit still. "Teach us to care and not to care, teach us to sit still," he wrote.[14] The Youth Minister's prayer is similar: "Teach me to name and not to name: teach me to wait in silence until my word is needed."

SACRAMENT

Ecclesial teaching is not only a teaching *about* the Word *through* the vehicle of language. It is also a teaching about sacrament through an attitude or quality best named sacramentality; this is its second component. I use the word "sacramental" in two ways. First, it is the affirmation that bodily, material, physical reality can be the place where divine and human meet. Second, it is a way-of-being integral to the life of the Christian churches, with the sacraments of the church understood as the heart of church life, and their ritual enactment absolutely necessary for the Christian person.

To arrive at such an understanding, several negative attitudes to sacramentality may need to be met and overcome. A faulty or incomplete catechesis can sometimes make these attitudes quite strong in young people. When they see sacramental life as equivalent to the "reception" of certain sacraments or as limited to moments of formal ritual, ecclesial teaching must be directed to correcting such notions.

Four negative attitudes stand out. The first is a view where the young person understands the sacraments as *static:* stopping places, stations, once-only or occasionally repeated engagements in ritual activity. Here, Baptism will be viewed as an occurrence "way back there"; Penance as a ritual where one "goes to Confession"; the Eucharist as "going to communion"; Confirmation as "entrance into adulthood." In such a view, connections will not be made, indeed cannot be made, with the young persons' present lives. In this instance a teaching is called for which points out that sacramental life, far from being static, is ongoing and continuous or it is not going on at all. Far from being an event that was "way back there," the young person's Baptism is presently occurring; she or he was

14. *Collected Poems* (New York: Harcourt, Brace, Jovanovich, 1963). The prayer is the concluding prayer of "Ash Wednesday."

and is baptized into life, and is continually baptized throughout life; she or he will eventually be baptized into death. The young are called to be forgiving and forgiven persons in all circumstances, not just when they participate in the sacrament of Reconciliation. They are continually moving into and entering adulthood, a journey that will take them a lifetime, and in need of continual confirmation of their young lives. And, as created beings, they are always in communion: with other people, with a Creator-God, and with the universe itself, not just when they receive the sacrament of the Lord's Supper.

What can make or break this attitude with the young is a style of teaching, an attitude by the teacher/minister that is sacramental. Thus, in the teaching role, the teacher/minister needs not only to present sacramental life as a subject-matter for study (though that is needed), but to demonstrate a sacramental quality in his or her teaching. Such teaching would be characterized by the Youth Minister's "being there" in a way that is continual and ongoing, and not just when the young person is receptive to teaching; by forgiveness and reconciliation when needed; by realization that the young person is destined to leave and be baptized into newer forms of life throughout life. The attitude would be demonstrated by the Youth Minister's view of the young person as someone destined for a particular, unique vocation which—it is hoped—will eventually be confirmed, but which at this time needs the confirmation of the Youth Minister acting in the name of, and as agent for, the whole church.

A second negative attitude lies in the assumption that sacraments are "spiritual," nonbodily realities, which one must be "angelic" and especially nonsexual to truly appreciate. The attitude can come from a childish and immature association with the out-of-time character often tied to church ceremony, especially the "First" Communion, and the purity, whiteness, and spotlessness often linked to the innocence of children at that time. But it is false to view the sacraments as nonbodily. They are, on the contrary, *rooted* in human bodiliness. Youth can be taught, through observation, an awareness that the ritual sacraments include the body through anointing, feeding, blessing, touch, eating, smell, and the clasp of hands. From such awareness, the young person can then move toward understanding sacramental life as intimately associated with the body. This *begins* with an affirmation of their own bodies, once immersed in baptismal water, and now burgeoning with a new understanding of sexuality and bodily strength. If truly sacramental, it opens wider to a sense of building the Body of Christ in the church as a whole, and on to the healing of the real bodies of real people in need of clothing, food, housing, legal justice and advocacy. Here we see the relationship between sacramentality and the prophetic areas of ministry. Those who would argue against instructing the young about such issues as outside the purpose of ecclesial teaching might need to be reminded that the *kerygma* is concerned with a Word, yes, but a Word who became *flesh,* and who, in his first teaching at Nazareth where he was brought up (and from which he was put out, I might add—Luke 4) spoke of proclaiming release to captives, liberty to the oppressed, and sight to the blind.

From this perspective, the sacramental will appear in the Youth Minister's teaching style through a willingness to address issues of bodiliness and sexuality with the young, not as adjunct considerations to their "religious" lives, but as integral manifestations of those lives, seen as sacramental. It will also be demonstrated through the minister/teacher's use of other teaching procedures than verbal presentation of material: procedures involving the body such as drama and theater arts, dance and sport, painting and sculpting, games real and simulated, and play, song and celebration.

A third attitude, if not negative, is certainly a misconception of sacramental activity. This is the idea that sacraments "belong" only to certain of the church's ministers, an idea undoubtedly traceable to the ordained being the chief ministers, and ad-ministers, of the ritual sacraments until very recently. Basically, however, sacramental activity is ecclesial and communal and never administered alone nor in the name of an individual, but by, and for, and in the name of the church as a whole. Sacramental activity is corporate activity, in the name of a people. This communality, this companioned activity, has two major ramifications for teaching.

The first lies in teaching *about* the sacramental, where the Youth Minister must point out that human life, if it has a sacramental dimension, is a life in companionship, but not only with other people. It is a life in companionship with the nonhuman as well and with the ordinary "things" of our everyday life. This is mirrored in the ecclesial sacramental "use" of such elements as fire, flint, candles, beeswax, bread, wine, cups and dishes.

The second ramification is a need for teaching to be toward the young person's own personal engagement in sacramental activity, from the more obvious roles of minister of Communion and sponsor in Baptism and Confirmation, to the healing, forgiving, praying, visiting the sick, counseling, comforting, instructing, affirming roles that they must exercise themselves in daily life. This too must be "named" in teaching if the fullness of the young person's baptism is to bear fruit in a personal and truly sacramental ministry so as to be entitled to be called "minister."

A final negative attitude toward sacrament is that it is somehow magical, a trick or ritualistic act. This is one of the oldest negative attitudes, embedded in our language in the term "hocus pocus" that first came from misunderstanding the words "*Hoc est enim corpus meum*" (this is my body) at the consecration of the Mass. It shows up in the notion that if only one receives a sacrament, some kind of grace is automatically granted and no need exists to live a grace-full life intentionally. The truth is that although sacramental activity is not a movement into *magic,* it is a growing into *mystery,* the paschal mystery which is the life, death and resurrection of the Christ.

One of the major aims of any teaching is to direct others toward growth. Ecclesial, sacramental teaching is a reminder of a twofold growth. First is the teaching that as one grows, he or she is involved in the mystery which life itself is; that not all of life can be explained but is, instead, paradoxical, ambiguous, inexplicable, mysterious; that the young persons themselves are, in a real sense, mysteries, as are all human beings. But secondly, sacramental teaching is an opportunity to explore with the young that their own lives are going in the direction of death, and that they will meet with many deaths along the way. They already know the death of childhood; they will soon face the death of adolescence. They need to be taught of other deaths possible in any human future: the deaths of hope, dreams and possibly even relationships not only now but in the years to come. No teacher can spare her or his students this knowledge; indeed, it is often good to speak of it. But what the teacher as ecclesial minister can explain is the entirety and breadth of the paschal mystery. It is not only life, nor death, that is the focus of sacramentality in the church. Ultimately, it is the fullness of resurrection.[15]

---

15. These ideas are explored in Maria Harris, "Catechesis as a Kind of Sacrament," in *The Catechist,* 12, 1 (September, 1978), pp. 14–15, 23.

CHAPTER THREE

CONCLUSION

In writing this chapter, I have attempted to say some general things about teaching and to specify Word and Sacrament as the essential components of *didache,* the ecclesial ministry of teaching. I want to point out in these final paragraphs that in order to teach, the Youth Minister can and ought to do several very particular things, requiring very precise attention, which might serve as criteria and checklist if the teaching ministry is to be concrete. Contrary to the view that all Youth Ministers need to do is make themselves available, I submit the following as essential to their teaching ministry.

The first task is to create an environment—physical and psychological—where learning can take place. It is *not* possible to teach in all settings and on all occasions, and details such as furniture, rugs, too much or too little space, air, and light are details that must be addressed. Similarly, any group with whom the Youth Minister meets should be allowed time to become "unfrozen" psychologically, to get to know one another, to establish bonds of trust that *do* take time, and to feel the security that comes from knowing they will not be judged, probed, interrupted or manipulated.

The second task is to provide a language that opens up the religious world to the young at the same time it touches their own. Teachers must reflect upon and ask colleagues to observe them in their attempts to do this. Ideally, they should be able to judge whether the words that operate most in their instruction and the images most prominent in their presentations are appropriable by their students, or simply technical jargon foreign to the language system of the young. (I remember observing one volunteer teacher, just before Easter, explaining to a group of fifteen-year-olds the "majesty of the Great Triduum which precedes the Paschal Event"!) Put more simply, are teachers able to hear their hearers hearing them? The complement of this skill is the teacher's ability to listen to the young, practicing that progression of abilities which begins with *listening* ("applying oneself to hearing something, paying attention, giving heed"), goes on to *hearing* ("listening attentively and *learning* by the speech of others"), and results in *communication*, the interchange of thoughts and ideas. The opposite of this is a situation described by several of Konopka's inter-

viewees: "All you did was sit around and listen to the leader talk
. . . it got boring . . . it was the same old thing."[16]

In that speech, moreover, the Youth Minister must teach the
young to question assumptions and to do their own thinking. This
will mean that in the teaching role, the Youth Minister has a very
clear conception of what thinking and questioning are—how else
can she or he know whether a certain "line of thinking" challenges
or leads to a dead end? It will also mean, especially in the area of
religion, that the teacher/minister has frames of reference and can
name them, can analyze and interpret, can draw out implications
and see relationships, can offer explanations, and can teach the
young to do the same. When the subject is the teaching of ideas, it
is not a service to the young to present them in packages to be accepted whole and intact. Rather, for a "learned ministry" to grow
in the next generation, teaching has to be critical, thorough, and often tough.

Another way of saying this is that in the teaching role, Youth
Ministers should stop apologizing for engagement in serious intellectual search as part of that role. If any one characteristic stands
out in the religious education of the young today, I fear it is this:
a failure to take the human thirst, hunger and passion to *know* seriously; an insulting of the young by not demanding discipline, rig-
or, and hard work from them as they search for wisdom. Of course
we need to be warm and caring and loving people, but this does not
automatically exclude the sweat and toil of study. Until we admit
that, however, Youth Ministers will be subject to the criticism that
while "strong in the heart" they are "soft in the head."

This means, finally, that the Youth Minister must himself or
herself be informed, intelligent, aware of ideas, a rigorous and serious student. Too many teachers prepare and conduct sessions
with the young by the seat of their pants or off the top of their
heads; too many rely on discussions based on shared ignorance; too
many simply do not know what they are talking about. That, when
it exists, is an intolerable situation for persons responsible in large
part for the religious knowledge of the next generation. Perhaps
the reason why this state of affairs occurs at all is the Youth Minister's occupational temptation to seek results far too quickly. We
might remind each other in such instances that quick results are
antithetical to a genuine education. Parker Palmer provides a view

---

16. Konopka, *op. cit.,* p. 131.

here on what might stand, in the final analysis, as the teacher's guide: "Authentic education is not necessarily quick in achieving results, nor are its results predictable. Education suffers when we keep uprooting the plant to see how well it is growing."[17]

During youth, let us recall, seeds are still being sown and the plant still being watered, pruned and nurtured. But let us also be aware that we do not, in the teaching role, have to be responsible or take responsibility for all the dimensions of ministry. While we engage in *didache*, others address *leiturgia, koinonia, kerygma* and *diakonia.* It is to the next of these, *leiturgia,* or the ecclesial ministry of prayer, that we direct our attention in the following chapter.

---

17. "How We Teach Is More Important Than What We Teach," in *Religion Teachers' Journal,* 11, 3 (April, 1977), p. 44.

Chapter Three
STUDY AND PRACTICE

ACTIVITY 11
Examining Resources for Teachers

The following is a basic list of books for teachers. Those in the teaching ministry would do well to spend several sessions examining, discussing, and experimenting with suggestions found in them.

Curwin, Richard and Fuhrmann, Barbara. *Discovering Your Teaching Self.* Englewood Cliffs: Prentice-Hall, 1975. This book contains over 100 different suggestions for observation, evaluation and analysis of the activities of teachers. It can be used by an individual, with a partner, in a small group, or with a large body of teachers. Ideal for beginners and for those introducing others to teaching, as well as for the more experienced.

Flanders, Ned. *Analyzing Teaching Behavior.* Reading, Mass.: Addison-Wesley, 1970. This book explains in detail the procedure and philosophy of interaction analysis, assisting teachers in naming ten basic happenings in all teaching situations.

Harris, Maria. *The D.R.E. Book.* New York: Paulist Press, 1976. Chapters 7, 8, and 9 of this book give a philosophy of teaching and religious education, and strategies and questions for teachers to ask either alone or in groups.

Kilgore, Lois. *Eight Special Studies for Senior High.* Scottsdale: National Teacher Education Project, 1976. A detailed set of units for older teens, with directions for planning and execution. Religious themes with meaning for today's youth are used.

Koch, Kenneth. *Wishes, Lies and Dreams.* New York: Random House, 1970. Koch's description of how he taught poetry to young people provides an excellent demonstration of how a teacher can work in order to evoke expressions of beauty from students.

Moran, Gabriel. *Religious Body.* New York: Seabury, 1974. See Chapter 5 for a developed understanding of teaching, as well as ways to distinguish it from giving information and counseling/therapy—two activities with which it is often confused.

RESPOND. Valley Forge, Pa.: Judson Press, 1972+ Five volumes directed to those who work with high-school age people. Every step is outlined, from materials needed and preparation, to completed session. Innumerable number of themes, thoroughly presented.

Swartz, John. *The Electric Bible I and II.* New York: Sadlier, 1974. Although certain updates are needed, this approach to teaching biblical themes through the use of media (film, recordings, TV) has extraordinary appeal to teen-agers.

Warren, Michael (ed.). *Resources for Youth Ministry.* New York: Paulist Press, 1978. Description and detail, by those working with youth in numerous situations (e.g., Young Life), with suggestions on how to do the same—what helps, what does not.

Weil, Marsha and Joyce, Bruce. *Information Processing Models of Teaching; Social Models of Teaching; Personal Models of Teaching.* Englewood Cliffs: Prentice-Hall, 1978. A thorough presentation, for experienced teachers, of three central families of pedagogy.

ACTIVITY 12
Understanding the Ministry of Teaching
(Sue Olmstead)

The purpose of this activity is to introduce the participants to the effectiveness of learning through doing. "I hear, I forget; I see, I remember; I do, I understand."

PROCEDURE:

1. In advance, divide the participants into two groups. Have the first group come earlier in order to be instructed in a skill by doing the particular skill. The skill chosen for this exercise was cleaning the grill in the kitchen of the school cafeteria. The same basic procedure can be used for any other skill.

2. Have the second group come later. They should be instructed by lecture without visual aids. Discussion follows with both groups

together. Ideally, there is a chance to perform the skill again with the two groups together to test the different models.

3. It is important to keep instructions and lecture the same. It is advisable to pick a skill that is very detailed in description and one that no one knows prior to the discussion. The skill of grill-cleaning is one of these. Other examples might be threading a sewing machine, changing a flat tire, baking bread, creating a liturgy, and so on.

4. The discussion that follows is directed toward reflection on how often we rely on verbal instruction in the teaching ministry, rather than teaching by actually doing. Because we are largely visually oriented, we often tag visual images to our verbalizations. When we can't find sufficient images, we are often confused. How much better the teaching of religion would be if we could "do" lessons or, for example, parables, creatively, rather than just listening to them or hearing them.

ACTIVITY 13
Young People Engage in the Ministry of Teaching

This activity is for young people who are planning to do teaching in the church. It is designed to help them explore their present attitude toward teaching.

PROCEDURE:

1. After the group has assembled, have each participant write the answers to the following:
   1. List three times you taught another person (or a group).
   2. List three times you were taught by another person (or group).
   3. List five circumstances or conditions necessary for teaching to go on.
   4. List five circumstances or conditions that block the possibility of teaching.

5. When you have your classes, what do you hope your students will say about your teaching?

2. Follow the completion of the questions with group discussion.

ACTIVITY 14
Drama: An Alternative Approach
to Teaching and Telling My Story
(Diane E. Root)

A creative drama program, when skillfully used, can be a very effective approach to Youth Ministry. It necessarily establishes a concerned, cooperative community. It also builds a structure and excuse for young people to discover, explore and express their own lives from behind the safe masks of literary characters and settings. Very often young people who are otherwise shy and self-conscious are able to act out their feelings and concerns if they know their emotions and actions will be attributed to their characters rather than to them personally.

A director can expand on these inherent benefits of drama by using theater exercises and creative dramatic techniques as a part of the rehearsal process. These focus on building acting skills, but can also reveal and develop personal resources. Script situations can raise issues and concerns of immediate relevance, and allow opportunities for useful discussion. Not only can the youth benefit from these interactions, but an alert leader might learn something of their world.

The rehearsal schedule for this kind of program may be quite unlike the more traditional type that teens usually find at school. Rather than progressing from stage movement through learning lines, and finally to character, the first step could be to explore the outer limits of meaningful interpretation. The cast should try on a variety of unlikely and extreme types for their roles, gradually selecting qualities that seem to work for them. Initial rehearsals could encourage experimentation with different physical environments and actions. Only after this would the director finally set the blocking and continue with the more usual aspects of production. This is a long and indirect approach to performance, but should support an increased sense of ensemble and greater participation by cast and crew. Ideally, it can leave the players with increased confidence and a method for working at their craft.

On the following page is a sample plan for the initial rehearsal of the one-act play "Aria da Capo," by Edna St. Vincent Millay. The play opens on a gay Harlequinade. The flighty Pierrot and Columbine are playing their farce when Cothurnus, the masque of tragedy, enters and announces that his scene will not be played. Pierrot and Columbine leave under protest, and two shepherds enter. They object that their scene cannot be played in such a merry set, but Cothurnus insists that it makes no difference, and the actors begin. The shepherds play a game of building a paper wall, to see what each might find on his side of the wall. They soon discover that they lack the trust to end the game, and eventually one is poisoned with an imaginary root, while he strangles his partner with a paper chain. Columbine and Pierrot enter, but claim they cannot play the farce with two dead bodies. Cothurnus instructs them to hide the corpses under a table, assuring them that the audience will soon forget them. They do so and again begin the opening scene, as the curtain closes.

"ARIA DA CAPO"
First Rehearsal

1. READTHROUGH. Having cast the parts, the first thing that must be done is a complete reading of the play, with all cast and crew members present. This ensures that all will have heard the entire play, and not only their own parts. Technical workers can begin to gather ideas for design.

2. CHARACTER EXPERIMENTATION. Exercises that begin to open up possibilities for interpretation and invite the cast to try the outrageous are useful. To begin, all should think of real or fictional characters they have seen who might fit their roles. Begin with extremes, and realize that at this stage characters may be as incongruous as possible. Pierrot and Columbine might be "cool" types from school or escaped lunatics. Cothurnus could be an undertaker or politician. The shepherds could be almost anyone, even a

television character such as Archie Bunker, John Boy Walton or The Fonz. After each person has selected a type, the cast should improvise the situation several times, with different approaches each time. Lines should not be worried about at all.

3. SITUATION OPTIONS. Next the group might suggest different settings for each scene and play them that way. The farce might find its way into a cocktail party or a pot party, for example. These improvisations should be done as slowly as needed, and played for reality.

4. PHYSICAL IMPROVISATIONS. If there is time left, physical interaction often suggests different interpretations. The two shepherds might try reading their parts while playing tug of war. Cothurnus might do his while manipulating the shepherds as puppets. Pierrot and Columbine might try their parts while continually moving about the room, backs touching.

5. TIME. The actual running time of this play is thirty minutes, but reading time should be shorter. It is difficult to guess how long improvisational work will take, but each of the exercises should be allowed at least half an hour.

Session Schedule for Drama Project

1. Introduction and play selection (e.g., *Aria Da Capo* by Edna St. Vincent Millay).
2. Readthrough and improvisation.
3. Experiment with blocking. (This is the assignment of specific actions to each character throughout the play. It is helpful to connect each such move with a specific verbal or visual cue.)
4. Experiment with blocking.
5. Set final blocking.
6. Lines memorized; begin character work.
7. Character work.
8. Character work; begin polishing.
9. Polishing.

Evening performances. Select plays for the next production (e.g., two or three short plays from *The Angel that Troubled the Waters,* by Thornton Wilder).

10. Read through; improvisations.
11. Experiment with blocking (groups work independently).
12. Set final blocking; lines memorized.
13. Character work.
14. Character work.
15. Polishing.

Evening performances. Select major play for final production (e.g., *The Journey with Jonah,* by Madeleine L'Engle).

16. Readthrough; organize.
17. Improvisations.
18. Improvisations.
19. Experiment with blocking.
20. Experiment with blocking.
21. Set final blocking.
22. Half of lines memorized; work scenes.
23. Work scenes.
24. Work scenes.
25. Work scenes.
26. Second half of lines memorized; character work.
27. Character work.
28. Polishing.
29. Technical rehearsal.
30. Final dress rehearsal.

Evening performances. Terrific cast party!

Resource List

Creative Dramatics:
Cheifetz, Dan. *Theatre in My Head.* Boston: Little, Brown and Company, 1971.
Heathcote, Dorothy. "Three Looms Waiting." Time-Life Films, 1972.

Slade, Peter: *Child Drama.* The University Press, Ltd., 1954.

Ward, Winifred. *Creative Dramatics.* Appleton-Century-Crofts, Inc., 1930.

Acting Theory and Philosophy:

Boleslavsky, Richard. *Acting: The First Six Lessons.*

Brook, Peter. *The Empty Space.* New York: Atheneum, 1968.

Growtowski, Jerry. *Towards a Poor Theatre.* New York: Simon & Schuster, 1968.

Stanislavsky, Constantine. *An Actor Prepares.* Tr. by Elizabeth Reynolds Hapgood. New York: Theatre Arts Books, 1936.

————. *Creating a Role.* Tr. by Elizabeth Reynolds Hapgood. New York: Theatre Arts Books, 1961.

Plays

Kozelka, Paul (ed.) *Fifteen American One-Act Plays.* New York: Washington Square Press, 1961. (This collection includes "Aria Da Capo".)

L'Engle, Madeleine. *The Journey with Jonah.* New York: Farrar, Straus and Giroux, 1967.

Wilder, Thornton. *The Angel that Troubled the Waters.* New York: Coward-McCann, Inc., 1928.

ACTIVITY 15
Teaching the Sacramental Life

For young people who are studying the meaning of sacramentality, the following activities are personally involving, but can be shared with the entire church as well. Each person should be given a period of two weeks, after which the ceremonies will be shared, either by explanation, presentation, or a "dry run".

1. *Plan the baptismal ceremony for your first child.*
   a. Decide on naming.
   b. Decide on godparents—why are they chosen?
   c. Decide on who should be present in/at the ceremony.
   d. Prepare a short homily, describing your wishes for the child.
   e. Prepare a short invitation to the whole church, explaining what you wish from them.

2. *Plan a ceremony/ritual of forgiveness or penance* for a (hypothetical or real) young person who wishes to rejoin the group.
   a. Decide on elements you wish to include.
   b. Decide on roles of forgiveness.
   c. Decide on reasons for such a ceremony.

3. *Plan the ritual/ceremony for your own funeral.*
   a. Decide the time of day.
   b. Decide the kind of service.
   c. Decide the symbols you wish present that can represent you and your life.
   d. Decide whether or what kind of music is needed.
   e. Decide whether or what kind of comments should be made.
   f. Compose the words of blessing or interment to be used at the conclusion of the ceremony.

ACTIVITY 16
Changing the Setting for Teaching

The purpose of this planning exercise, which is to be followed by its execution, is to discover how the "where" of teaching, the environment where it occurs, influences the activity of teaching.

PROCEDURE:

1. With a group of young people plan a ten-week teaching series. Except for the first and last sessions, each week the teaching setting should be a different place. Some suggestions are given below, but each group should select their own settings.
   SESSION ONE. Home base.
   SESSION TWO. The job-site of one of the members of the youth group.
   SESSION THREE. The job-site of the parent of one of the group members.
   SESSION FOUR. A local newspaper (religious affairs editor's office).
   SESSION FIVE. A local TV station (religious affairs editor's office).
   SESSION SIX. A local synagogue.
   SESSION SEVEN. A local theater for a play (stage, not movie).

SESSION EIGHT. A local prison.
SESSION NINE. A local college.
SESSION TEN. Home base.

2. Some other possibilities for teaching environments might include boarding school, children's shelter, state or county legislature or seat of government, mayor's office, police or fire department, and so on.

Chapter Four
LEITURGIA: THE MINISTRY OF PRAYER

Often, a Youth Minister working with persons of junior-high or high-school age will wonder if schooling is the most appropriate form for ministry with young people. Most often, that question is answered by the characteristics of the persons and environments involved. However, in recent years, the ministry of prayer has often taken precedence over schooling as the best way to educate the young religiously. The purpose and aim of prayer is not, of course, teaching or learning: it is centered on the worship of God and on the relationship between human and divine. However, it may be the vehicle through which one does learn best at one or another time of life. In any event, it is a necessary component of ministry at all times and for all ages.

Prayer is a subject that is both extensive and complex, and the plethora of books and publications currently being printed is an example of the renewed interest recently given it. Because this chapter is on young people and prayer, however, I have chosen to emphasize two issues that are of particular concern to Youth Ministers. The first is research in faith development and religious experience. I choose this because of the help it is to those in prayer ministry to have at least a general sense of age-related religious data where such is available. The second is a naming of four areas integral to all prayer, but particularly important to the young at this time and in this culture: the imaginal, the companioned, the political and the comic. I will begin with an overview of the work of Fowler, Westerhoff and Robinson, and then proceed to the four areas named.

FAITH DEVELOPMENT

Since the early seventies, in work similar to Lawrence Kohlberg's, James Fowler has been attempting to see if a structural, developmental theory of faith could be refined and elaborated.[1] His basic question is whether there are patterns of thinking, feeling and valuing that underlie the growth of what he calls "faith." In his view, although not synonymous with religion or belief, faith is closely allied to them. ("By faith," he writes, "I mean a dynamic set of operations, more or less integrated, by which a person construes his or her ultimate environment.")[2] Fowler's interest is not with content as such, but with uniformities and patterns that might be described in a sequence of stages. Here, stage means a "typical set of integrated operations, a structural whole, available to and employed by a person to construct, maintain and orient him/herself in the world."[3]

To say too much about this work is difficult, because it is so recent; the first of Fowler's interviews seeking to understand faith development were conducted in1972-74.[4] Sam Keen has criticized the work in a friendly way as predominantly cognitive, intellectual, institutional and symbolic, in contrast to an emphasis on fantasy, feelings and the sensual elements necessarily present in faith and trust.[5] More serious may be the unintended implication in Fowler's work that given stages, "higher is better." Fowler has demonstrated sensitive awareness of such limitations; at present, it is far too early to make definitive judgments about his work.

Nevertheless, while keeping such limitations in mind, Ministers helping the young to pray can benefit from the tentative findings with reference to the young person's time in life. Fowler has described six stages, but three are especially pertinent. The first one is what he refers to as Synthetic-Conventional Faith, which often coincides with a person's entrance into the teen-age years. At this stage,

---

1. "Faith Development Theory and the Aims of Religious Socialization," in Gloria Durka and Joanmarie Smith (eds.) *Emerging Issues in Religious Education* (New York: Paulist, 1976), pp. 191 ff.

2. *Ibid.*, p. 192.

3. *Ibid.*, p. 194.

4. James Fowler, "Stages in Faith: The Structural-Developmental Approach," in Hennessy, *op. cit.*, pp. 181–182.

5. Jerome Berryman (ed.) *Life Maps: Conversations on the Journey of Faith* (Waco: Word, Inc., 1978), Chapter 3.

The person's experience of the world is now extended beyond the family and primary groups. There are a number of spheres or theaters of life; family, school or work, peers, leisure, friendship, and possibly a religious sphere. Faith must help provide a coherent and meaningful synthesis of that now more complex and diverse range of involvements. Coherence and meaning are certified at this stage, by either the authority of properly designated persons in each sphere, or by the authority of consensus among "those who count." The person does not yet have to take on the burden of world synthesis for himself/herself.[6]

The description is undoubtedly one that resonates in the experience of many Youth Ministers, and their association with young people confirms it as fairly accurate. With reference to prayer, the emergence of "a number of spheres or theaters of life" may present a need for synthesis and reconciliation as activities within prayer. In the religious sphere, possibly, the young person now becomes conscious that a way formerly understood as the one, true path to God is only one of many different and parallel ways. The other issue is the authority and influence of "those who count." These may include the Youth Minister and the person's parent(s); but it is also quite likely that "those who count" may be the person's peers. Thus it is likely that prayer and exploration of spirituality can occur among groups of young people as well as alone or one-to-one.

The stages on either side of this one might also be taken into account. Prior to Synthetic-Conventional Faith is what Fowler calls Mythic-Literal Faith, where the person takes on the stories, beliefs and observances of his or her community, and where moral rules and attitudes are one-dimensional and literal. *If* it is true that this stage is prior to Synthetic-Conventional Faith, and that the latter builds on it, then care must be taken that The Story is presented and known, providing a base for a deeper and more complex faith. Hence the importance of Word and Sacrament as described in Chapter 3, and for some prayer based on the story in scripture. Fowler describes the stage succeeding Synthetic-Conventional Faith as Individuating-Reflexive, where the "late adolescent or adult must begin to take seriously the burden of responsibility for his/her own commitments."[7] Thus, much of the ministry of prayer at the time

---

6. Fowler, in Durka and Smith, *op. cit.,* p. 196.
7. *Ibid.*

of later youth may need to be toward achieving responsibility and commitment. In this instance, care must be taken (a) not to rush growth in prayer, and (b) not to assume the Youth Minister's prayer issues are the same as those of the young to whom they are ministering; for often, the Youth Minister is the one experiencing Individuating-Reflexive faith.

The impossibility of any one of us moving through these or any other still-to-be-discovered stages of life by ourselves is, in my judgment, apparent. Thus, the work that Youth Ministers might find both complementary to and an enlargement of Fowler's theory is the description by John Westerhoff not of *stages* of faith, but of *styles* of faith.[8] Westerhoff's work is helpful because of his stress throughout on the role of the community. He suggests that we begin our religious lives with *experienced* faith as a result of interactions with other faithing selves in our childhood and early adolescent years; go on to *affiliative* faith through most of adolescence, where we experience belonging to a community; begin growth into *searching* faith in late adolescence; and eventually if all goes well and we are supported, arrive at *owned* faith. However, he points out that each style of faith is whole and complete in itself, like the rings of growth in a tree. Because people are at very different points in their religious journey, no *single* educational program is therefore valid, and a pluralism of possibilities is needed. Nevertheless, he does make some important suggestions for adolescence, such as the need for a communal ritual to affirm persons in searching faith, instead of keeping them moored to a single vision,[9] the postponement of Confirmation until adulthood, exploration of religious alternatives, and serious study of the story, especially in the movement from affiliative to searching faith.

In order to move from an understanding of faith that belongs to the community, to an understanding of faith that is our own, we need to doubt and question that faith. At this point the "religion of the head" becomes equally important with the "religion of the heart" and acts of the intellect, critical judgment, and inquiry into the meanings and purposes of the story and the ways by which the community of faith lives are essential.[10]

---

8. In *Will Our Children Have Faith?* (New York: Seabury, 1976), pp. 89 ff.

9. *Ibid.*, p. 102.

10. *Ibid.* p. 96.

Reflecting on this passage, the Youth Minister may consider schooling as one option to address such searching, and it may indeed prove the most effective. Another possibility, however, and one many Youth Ministers engage in, is a time of retreat when young people come together in an environment that is safe but searching. Here they might entertain the serious religious questions, considering them over an intensive two or three days (and nights), a procedure that could be repeated periodically.

Anyone familiar with the nature of mystical, numinous or religious experience[11] knows that the divine does not always break in on the time schedule humans set up. Therefore, understanding religious development, religious growth, or religious life solely on the basis of styles or stages of faith can do the young person (or anyone else) a great disservice. For this reason, I urge Youth Ministers to inform themselves about the work of at least one more source that provides a superb balance to the theorists just mentioned. This source is the Religious Experience Research Unit at Manchester College, Oxford, England, where, again for a decade (about the same length of time as Fowler's studies) researchers have been collecting accounts from thousands of persons. These latter are men and women who felt that their lives had in some way been affected by a power beyond themselves, and who in response to a public, publicized invitation, have shared accounts of their experience and its effects with researchers at the Unit. *The Original Vision,* one of four books describing the research and also the most striking of the volumes, is an account of the religious experience of childhood.[12] It is not written, however, by children. Instead, the accounts quoted (accounts of meeting a Power, or a Presence, or Someone, or Something) are from that 15 percent of the to-that-time four thousand who responded, who started by going back to events and experiences of their earliest years. The obvious point in this is that many people have a profound sense of the religious from the first years of life but often have never shared it until, as in these cases, researchers provide the opportunity for its recollection.

---

11. William James, *The Varieties of Religious Experience* (New York: Modern Library edition, 1902), is probably still the definitive work in this area.

12. Edward Robinson, *The Original Vision* (Manchester College, Oxford: Religious Experience Research Unit, 1977). The other three are Edward Robinson (ed.) *Living the Questions, op. cit.;* Timothy Beardsworth (ed.) *A Sense of Presence* (Manchester College, Oxford: Religious Experience Research Unit, 1977); *This Time Bound Ladder* (Manchester College, Oxford: Religious Experience Research Unit, 1977).

Remarking on this fact, Edward Robinson writes that his first concern, given so many accounts, was to learn "more about how children think and feel, how they experience the world."[13] While maintaining that as a primary interest, however, he soon came to realize that a number of fundamental issues had surfaced as a result of the material, leading him to several conclusions based not only on particular examples, but on the general tendency of the collected material as a whole. Some of these conclusions had to do with the "original vision" of childhood as a form of knowledge; others with the obvious fact that many people have mystical experience but never name it; still others to the persistence of the power of the vision over a long period of time, and to the self-authenticating nature of the experiences described.

My concern in taking time to describe the work here is to point out to Youth Ministers that among our young people are those who have undoubtedly met the divine, just as these other persons did. Moreover, the experience is so strong, and often so self-authenticating, that it would be foolish to push them into a religious mold where they are certain—with an inner certainty—they do not belong. In addition, Youth Ministers could learn from such research that if they are to engage in a ministry of prayer with the young, they must take the following into account:

(1) As a group, Youth Ministers, in their studies, have far more access to the results of developmental research and stage theory than they do to findings such as those just described. In such a circumstance, it is only natural that their work is informed by developmental approaches. This, in turn, can lead to an overreliance on the as yet inconclusive data of that research, and a bias toward looking for, and therefore finding and judging, certain behaviors as typical at certain ages. The nature of religious experience is to bring one up sharply in the realization that the Spirit is never bound by time, place, or age.

(2) Much of what we do as Youth Ministers, whether in a school *or* retreat setting, is tied to what can be said. The accounts from the Religious Experience Research Unit give ample evidence that, although they cannot always articulate their experience, young people often have remarkable sensitivity toward the "divine" while conscious they do not have the linguistic skills or vocabulary to talk about it. Facility in speech is not the same as *capax Dei*.

(3) The accounts affirm those Youth Ministers who see the de-

---

13. *The Original Vision*, p. 11.

sign of secure environments and the creation of places and zones of quiet as central to the ministry of prayer. Two examples of the need for this are found in *The Original Vision*. One is the comment of an adult who said that as a child in school, "I would willingly have talked of the inner life if the setting had seemed right, but it wasn't."[14] The other is the story of a little girl who used to hide at unauthorized times in the school library in order to find some quiet, and only discovered years later that one teacher had known all along and put out books especially for her.[15]

(4) In assisting the young to work out their relationships with formal religion or organized church, Youth Ministers will need to accept the reality that although the young persons are going to God, not all will take the route of the established church, and it is still a ministry to help these young persons. We may need to entertain the possibility that God will call people to the divine Self in ways unknown to us and that if a person decides to "leave the church" this is not synonymous to "leaving God." How much we have vested in institutional or self-preservation as ministers may be revealed in precisely such a circumstance.

SPECIAL ISSUES

In our day, initiating and educating the young to rich lives of prayer (which is one definition of the ministry of *leiturgia*) has taken on the complexity of modern life itself. Thus, to securing as much information as possible about religious development, and to studying ways of designing appropriate prayer environments, Youth Ministers must attend to four additional elements. Each of these is related to sociocultural factors less pressing in other times, but vitally important today. I will comment on each in turn.

The Imaginal. Our time is characterized by an extraordinary sensitivity to language. The impact this has on the Youth Minister's prayer involvement is that he or she must attend to whether the God-images presented, used, and referred to are appropriate *to* the divine and appropriable *by* the young person. Our words when applied to God ought to convey a hesitancy, a tentativeness and a sense of the impossibility of ever completely naming the Name. Actually, in the tradition, this is one of the first revelations we have of God: when Moses asked what the Name was, the response was

---

14. *Ibid.*, pp. 79–80.
15. *Ibid.*, p. 80.

at best enigmatic: I am Who I am; I will be Who I will be. The point I am making is that appropriate to any images for the divine the Youth Minister chooses is the accompanying sense and suggestion that the image is only an approximation—a sense and suggestion to be shared with the young. In this context, and *only* with this context established, we can proceed to sharing the images most cherished in the Tradition; that God is Father, as Jesus taught; that God is Creator, by whom all things are made; that God is Spirit, to be worshiped in spirit and truth; that God is love, and those who abide in love abide in God and God in them. However, other possibilities for naming God will also need to be shared: images such as those in the *Veni, Sancte Spiritus,* the Sequence for Pentecost, where the Holy One is invoked as "Rest in labor," as "Cool respite in heat," as "Comfort in weeping"; and images from the Hebrew and Christian scriptures of God as rock; God as hen; God as mother. Such images, personal and beyond-the-personal, remind Youth Minister and young person that even "person" is an image, a metaphor. The inexpressible God is not the same as the-image-of-God.[16]

Deserving special attention from the Youth Minister is the understanding that the relationship the young person has to God in prayer is necessarily mediated by the images used. Thus of central importance is the not-so-quiet-Christian question: how does the continued and exclusive use of the pronouns he, his and him to refer to God, or the exclusive use of masculine metaphors (Shepherd, Lord, Master, Father, King) affect the relationship of young women and young men toward God? How do they thus *appropriate* God's image? Most Youth Ministers would agree that God is beyond gender (Jesus of Nazareth was of course *a* man) but the questions for prayer are these: How is the divine-human relationship experienced if it is always spoken of as male-male (for boys) and male-female (for girls)? As adults, will these same people come to a rejection of God because of this usage? Is the exclusively male image capable of appropriation by persons who more and more are being educated to a feminist consciousness, both males and females? Is it true that the words convey that God is male, or is it possible to separate the words from the reality? I am not arguing here for the extension of God images to female ones (Mother, Lady, Queen, Mistress—note the negative connotations embedded in almost all

16. For development of this point, see Phyllis Trible, *God and the Rhetoric of Sexuality* (Philadelphia: Fortress, 1978), pp. 20–23.

language referring to the female!)—although speaking of God as the Great Mother is a very beautiful practice. Instead, what I do ask is that Youth Ministers be concerned about the effect of all images on the life of prayer, and be aware that we live in language as do fish in the sea. Nowhere are such truths so important as in our feeble attempts to articulate a language that refers to the ineffable God.

Although prayer is often in community, it is the *private* nature of much religious experience that underlies imaginal issues. Writing of his work in this area, David Hay has reported, "My enquiries indicate that the commonest situation in which people report numinous or mystical experience is when they are alone or in silence, and they feel it belongs to the most private and secret core of their existence."[17] Perhaps what the Youth Minister can do, given such circumstances, is explore not only nonhuman images, but images that are common to both human and nonhuman nature. Thomas Clarke, for one, has done this in probing the meaning of the Center. Commenting on the recently rediscovered symbol for God as the sphere whose center is everywhere and whose circumference is nowhere, Clarke writes:

When, as a modern Christian, I yield to the attraction of journeying to the center of my being, my faith tells me that this center is both my own human self, the image of God that I am, and the Self of God.

. . . I as a Christian affirm (and as a praying Christian I act on the affirmation of) this unfathomable mystery of the Holy Spirit dwelling within my spirit, as the divine Self selfing my human self: and hence as transforming Center of my center.[18]

God as Center is beyond gender; here is at least one image where boys and girls are both obviously in the image of God. The Youth Minister could search with them for others.

The Companioned. The search for community among the young is not new; each generation of young people eventually comes to un-

---

17. In "Religious Experience and Education," *Learning for Living* 16, 3 (Spring, 1977), p. 160.

18. See his essay, "Finding Grace at the Center," in Thomas Keating *et al. Finding Grace at the Center* (Still River, Ma: St. Bede Publications, 1978), pp. 52–53.

derstand that it does not go to God alone. However, in our times, community has been spurred by the ecological movement to include not only companionship with other humans but with the nonhuman universe as well. This attitude spills over into prayer understood as *companioned,* that is, the recognition that relationship with God is incomplete unless it includes relationship to that which is "other" than our own selves. The Youth Minister approaches this by stressing attitudes of community and of contemplation.

Caryll Houselander once commented that a child has no difficulty realizing that clouds are God's thoughts. The ministry of prayer as companioned is one that assists young people to reclaim this vision of childhood by seeking to *see* God's thinking expressed in the world around them. One spiritual director I know helps her retreatants do this by instructing them to go outdoors and "Pray a tree." I agree with her that this is a powerful way to engage in companioned prayer, and I would urge Youth Ministers to teach retreatants not only to pray trees and clouds and hills and moonlight but the less obvious companions of their earthly journey as well. Perhaps they could pray earthworms and sidewalks and dogs and highways too, as exercises designed to make them sensitive to the vast company of God-made and humanly made co-inhabitants of their world.

If the Youth Minister would attempt this, it could create the possibility of community, even communion with the nonhuman universe. Then the young might move not only to the practice of communion, but to the attitude of communion, and then, when practice and attitude are together, to the prayer of communion. My hunch is that the poets are the ones most alert to this possibility, the poets and the mystics. As part of the ministry of prayer, Youth Ministers can introduce poets to young people and point out how rich a resource they are: not only Rod McKuen and Kahlil Gibran, but William Wordsworth, Walt Whitman, Anne Sexton, Thomas Merton and Daniel Berrigan, too. A woman who is a poet-mystic in our day (as Anne Morrow Lindbergh was several generations ago) is Annie Dillard, who opens her book *Holy the Firm* with this description of waking into community with time under the aspect of the day itself:

> Every day is a god, and holiness holds
> forth in time. I worship each god. I
> praise each day splintered down, splintered

down and wrapped in time like a husk, a husk
of many colors spreading, at dawn fast over
the mountains split.

I wake in a god. I wake in arms holding
my quilt, holding me as best they can
inside my quilt.[19]

Some among the young (and among the ministers!) might see calling a day a "god" a form of idolatry. However, I think it more likely
that with their sensitivity to the land, the earth, and the water,
young people already realize that God is found not only in community with humans but everywhere: in the day, in time, and in the
depths of the ground.

The more obvious companionship, however, even more than
with nonhuman nature, is with other people. Without community
prayer, spiritual and religious life leans dangerously toward narcissism or individualism. In Chapter 1, I spoke of the community
prayer of liturgical worship and named some important emphases
for the church's ministry in that area. Here I would fill out the idea
of prayer as companioned-in-community by pointing out some
things the Youth Minister might do. He or she can bring the young
together to pray, even briefly (often *especially* briefly) at beginning
and closing of events, can offer opportunities to pray regularly as
"prayer groups," can revive the custom of asking for and giving
blessings to each other at special times such as birthdays, commencement, or leaving or returning from journeys; and can always
include the remembrance of those less fortunate and beyond the
gathered, present community. In addition, the Youth Minister can
challenge young people to that dimension of spirituality where *they*
minister to one another, relying not so much on someone older or
in a position of authority but on their own inner gifts. In many circumstances, they find themselves in the role of listener, healer,
comforter, minister. Such roles have communal as well as personal
value, since, as Henri Nouwen comments, "Our society seems to be
increasingly full of fearful, defensive, aggressive people anxiously
clinging to their property and inclined to look at their surrounding
world with suspicion, always expecting an enemy to suddenly ap-

19. (New York: Harper and Row, 1977), p. 11.

pear, intrude and do harm."[20] In these instances, what the young would be moving toward is their own ministry of prayer, which is part of the Christian vocation "to convert the hostis into a hospes, the enemy into a guest and . . . [to create] the free and fearless space where brotherhood and sisterhood can be formed and fully experienced."[21]

An entirely different but related dimension of community prayer can be included by inviting the young to join adult communities at prayer. One of the most moving instances of this I know is a high-school faculty that invites seniors to its community liturgy every Thursday evening. We forget, sometimes, that the young need role models not only for their exterior, vocational lives, but for their inner lives as well. Seeing adults taking a life of prayer seriously is one of the richest ways to learn its importance as adult, companioned activity.

One last element in a companioned vision of prayer comes as the young discover and experience the presence of God as Companion. "The limits of every community teach the person the meaning of human limit and give intimation of some greater community. The communally based person finds that the way to transcend finiteness is not to go out of the world but to go through the world. The individual is flipped upside down to continue a journey toward the center of the earth."[22] The journey is made with, in, over, and through the created world and other humans, already spoken of. Paradoxically, it is made not by moving but by being still; not by speech, but by silence; not by turning away, but by turning within; not by holding on, but by letting go. The companionship experienced here is with the Holy Itself—a Companion Who is not one more in the series of companioned relationships, but the Ground and Depth and Being of all Companionship. *Contemplation* is often the name given this Companionship which is, quite simply, everything. Dorothee Soelle tells a story of "a pious old man who, in his last years was of sound mind but feeble in speech. All the old man could say—and he said it repeatedly—was 'Everything, everything, everything.' He died with these words on his lips."[23] Soelle comments that this repetition of a word, a classic practice in contem-

---

20. In *Reaching Out* (Garden City: Doubleday, 1975), p. 46.

21. *Ibid.*

22. Gabriel Moran, *Education Toward Adulthood* (New York: Paulist, 1979), p. 72.

23. *Op. cit.*, p. 138.

plation, is a kind of formula for the confirmation of totality. "Everything here means simply that nothing can separate us from the love of God."[24] Such an assurance is one due all young people by those who minister among them.

The Political. A third element is essential in the ministry of *leiturgia.* This is an awareness of political, societal and global issues in any prayer life that is complete. Gregory Baum writes that the ethos and milieu in which a person grows and develops shape that person's religious vision.[25] Thus, Youth Ministers can contribute to a world vision that is basically erroneous if they concentrate on the imaginal or the communal to the exclusion of the social order. I have seen this demonstrated in slide-and-tape shows that often accompany "prayer services" for the young, where all of the slides are of peaceful, tranquil settings with no allusion to human beings or to the realities of social existence. The missing element here is the relationship to society, to the *polis,* and what I suggest is a critique within prayer itself that is directed to "effort to transform the structures of the dominant society so that a greater currency of human love can be lived in and through them."[26] Rosemary Ruether notes that "the youth of today do not struggle against mere flesh and blood, but against powers and principalities, against cosmic forces so huge and so deeply entrenched that their removal by any puny efforts of mere humans seems impossible."[27] Part of ministry with youth thus becomes an involvement in this struggle, and at this point, prayer ministry is not only priestly, but prophetic too.

The political can be incorporated many ways. One is the inclusion of the ancient discipline of fasting as training the body to meet powers and principalities, a discipline closely related to abstinence from drugs. Youth must be helped to see the spiritual dimension of this bodily activity as organically related to prayer just as it is to sport. For just as one "trains" for athletic activity, one "trains" for prayer and contemplation. A second possibility is choosing retreat themes that are not about the self in relation to inner dynamics (Who am I?) but about oneself in relation to the cosmic order (Who am I *in this world?* How can I be *for* this world, a man or woman

24. *Ibid.*

25. In *The Social Imperative* (New York: Paulist, 1979), p. 129. See especially his essay, "Spirituality and Society," pp. 129–147. See also his essay, "Prayer and Society" in Gloria Durka and Joanmarie Smith (eds.) *Emerging Issues . . . Op. cit.,* pp. 18–28.

26. Rosemary Ruether, *Liberation Theology* (New York: Paulist, 1972), p. 34.

27. *Ibid.,* p. 35.

for others?) Still another possibility is the institution of all-night prayer vigils, combining discipline, solitude, rigor and social awareness, where the idealism and strength of the young can be marshaled to face social evil in a religious setting.

The resources for a Youth Minister wishing to include the political are enormous, from the writings of such people as Thomas Merton,[28] Daniel Berrigan[29] and Dorothy Day[30] to the work of such organizations as *Bread for the World*[31] and *Theology in the Americas*.[32] The greatest, and sometimes most difficult resource to discern, however is a community that models political concern by its way of life, and persons whose life-styles are prophetically inspiring to the young. The difficulty of this aspect of the political is that it cannot be a modeling consciously aimed for, but one demonstrated over the years, in season and out, without pretension. The undersong for any such human living, however, is not the human alone. Rather, it is a Divinity who proclaims release to captives, sight to the blind, hearing to the deaf, food to the hungry, and hope to the despairing. No ministry of prayer is complete without it.

The Comic. With the threat of nuclear disaster hovering over them, many young people no longer ask "Why *this?* or "Why *that?*" but, "Why anything at all?" Living in this century posits the issue of absurdity in ways that will not go away. In the face of this, Youth Ministers are often brought to the point of either being asked to explain or being met by an attitude that assumes the God question has no meaning at all.

---

28. Merton's work is extensive. See, for example, his *Conjectures of a Guilty Bystander* (Garden City: Doubleday, 1966); see also *The Asian Journal of Thomas Merton* (New York: New Directions, 1973).

29. See *Consequences; Truth and . . .* (New York: Macmillan, 1967); *The Geography of Faith: Conversations between Daniel Berrigan, while underground, and Robert Coles* (Boston: Beacon, 1971); *Lights on in the House of the Dead, A Prison Diary* (New York: Doubleday, 1974); *Uncommon Prayer: A Book of Psalms* (New York: Seabury, 1978).

30. See *The Long Loneliness* (New York: Harper, 1952); see also William Miller, *A Harsh and Dreadful Love: Dorothy Day and the Catholic Worker Movement* (New York: Liveright, 1973).

31. Arthur Simon, *Bread for the World* (New York: Paulist, 1975), is the best introduction to the work and ideals of this organization.

32. *Theology in the Americas* has its office at the Interchurch Center, 475 Riverside Drive, New York, New York 10027, and is headed by Sergio Torres, an exiled priest-theologian who also staffs the new Ecumenical Association of Third World Theologians.

In view of this, a final element that might shape the ministry of prayer is recognition of the comic as residing in the midst of the Holy. My point is not blasphemy; instead, I direct attention to the comic as a narrow escape, not from the clutches of the serious, but out of the jaws of the solemn, the pretentious, and the explicable. Christopher Fry calls it such an escape, "not from truth, but from despair; *a narrow escape into faith.*"[33] If it is true that Youth Ministers wish to help the young "into faith" one possibility lies in asserting, with Fry, that there is an angle on experience where the dark is distilled into light, either in this world or another, either in or out of time. It is this angle of experience I mean in speaking of the comic and urging it as a critical element in prayer.

I believe that many young people could agree with John Dominic Crossan that if one has been taught or taken it for granted that reality shows some great or overarching pattern of meaning, and then comes to doubt the existence of such plans, it is easy to claim the world lacks meaning and is filled with absurdity.[34] However, most young people also have a glimmer of insight that another reading of the situation would be that the world simply *is*—comic, yes; ambiguous, yes; paradoxical, yes; puzzling, certainly. But not absurd. ("O God, forasmuch as without Thee/We are not able to doubt Thee,/ God, give us the grace/ To convince the whole race/ We know nothing whatever about thee" might be their prayer in this instance.) Not knowing anything whatsoever about God, in the final analysis, means that in all circumstances, the creature must allow the Divinity, the Holy, the Sacred to be Itself. "I am Who I am; I will be Who I will be." To make this point, Crossan writes:

Consider four assertions. First, the Holy has a great and secret master plan for the Universe in process of gradual but inevitable realization. Second, this overarching scheme is known only to chosen initiates. Third, alternatively, the cosmic plan is a mystery and thus inscrutable to all human intellect. Fourth, the Holy has no such plan at all and that is what is absolutely incomprehensible to our structuring, planning, ordering minds.[35]

---

33. John Dominic Crossan, *Raid on the Articulate* (New York: Harper and Row, 1976), quotes Fry on p. 17.

34. *Ibid.* See especially, "First Variation: Comedy and Transcendence," pp. 9–54.

35. *Ibid.,* p. 44.

Such recognition of the comic preserves the autonomy of the Divine. If the end of a life of prayer is eventually adoration, perhaps the comic, more than the tragic, provides the possibility of genuine prayer because the structural security of one's human world is shattered by it, and the divine is then able to touch the human heart. Adoration, or the human being brought to final genuflection and reverence is, I submit, the hope all Youth Ministers have for those to whom they offer a ministry of prayer, of *leiturgia*. In adoration, the temptation to give answers, to be an oracle, and to shield from hurt is swept away from the Youth Minister, and she or he realizes the essential ministry is to be quiet and recede into the shadows. His or her care is no longer necessary when the young are settled into the Care of God.

Chapter Four
STUDY AND PRACTICE

ACTIVITY 17
Questions on Youth Spirituality

This activity focuses on youth spirituality and is for groups of youth ministers. Have the group consider the following questions as individuals and then discuss their ideas as a group.

1. You are planning a youth retreat and have two options with reference to its direction. (a) It can be a recreational, "fun" retreat with many games and activities, or (b) It can be a retreat centered on prayer, silence and worship. What direction do you choose, taking into account the young people on the retreat?

2. Your youth group is planning a worship service for the Sunday after Easter. How do you go about assisting them in setting it up?

3. You wish to have a session on prayer with your youth group. How do you begin?

4. The question of images of God arises in your youth group. What is your own way of speaking about God, and how do you articulate the problems of explaining images of God to young people?

5. Two persons in your senior youth group are considering vocations to what they believe is a religious or spiritual life. How do you advise them?

ACTIVITY 18
The Prayer of the Spoken Word
(Brian Benoit and Meg Curran)

The following prayer activity is one that many young people have discovered to be comfortable for them and comforting to them.

At root, each person is asked to choose only one word as his or her prayer, to speak it aloud as part of the community, and to join with others in silent affirmation as they speak their words.

PROCEDURE:

1. Sit in a circle, quietly.
2. Leader asks the group to take a few minutes to be quiet, still, and to "collect" themselves.
3. Silently, each person is requested to choose *one* word, which sums up his or her prayer.
4. Beginning with the leader, the word of each person is then spoken out loud.
5. It is not necessary to go around the circle more than once; however, the group may wish to do so.

SUGGESTED THEMES:

1. "In a moment, I will ask each of you to speak aloud the name of a *place* upon which you wish to ask God's blessing ..."
   (Sample answers as we move around the circle: "Israel ... Ireland ... Lexington High School ... Main Street ... Mexico ... Leadville ... "
2. "In a moment, I will ask each of you to speak aloud the name of a *person* upon whom you wish to ask God's blessing ..."
3. "In a moment, I will ask each of you to speak aloud the name of a *grace* you wish to ask for upon the world and its people ... "

ACTIVITY 19
The Great Rewrite:
Prayer as Spoken Word
(Karen E. King)

As I have come to struggle with definitions, concepts, expressions and methods of conveying an understanding of spirituality, I have become more and more convinced of the emptiness of abstract and academic approaches. How can one talk about spirituality and prayer if one is not a spiritual being or does not have a prayer life?

I am sensitive to the multifaceted problems one can and does encounter when two or more are gathered in the Lord's name and try to come to a consensus on how one prays. Nonetheless I have come to a more recent understanding of spirituality and prayer. Prayer is relating to God. Spirituality is the style in which a person relates, and the living out of that relationship.

In exploring "prayer as spoken word," I see *The Great Rewrite* as a part of a larger teaching unit of spirituality.

The objective of this activity is to explore the idea of prayer as spoken word. After completing the exercise, individuals will have experienced the unity yet diversity of the spoken word as prayer.

MATERIALS NEEDED:

Newsprint and markers, or a blackboard with chalk and erasers

Paper and pens or pencils for each participant

Bibles for each participant

PROCEDURE:

The room should be comfortable with chairs scattered around as well as open space to sit on the floor. The title, *The Great Rewrite,* should be displayed, yet should not reveal anything of the nature or content of this exercise. As people enter the room, hand them a sheet of paper with the following question on it, "What is prayer?" The session should then proceed according to the following steps.

1. After participants are seated, ask them to think about the question for a few minutes without discussing it with one another. They should then write their answer on the sheet provided.

2. When everyone is finished (more or less) call attention to the newsprint in front of the room. Ask the group, "What are your expectations of prayer?" Jot down responses as they are offered. As a starter, you might suggest they use their own definitions which they have just written. Encourage them to see a variety of expressions of prayer. The important concept to keep in mind is not to convey the ONE way to pray or the ONE experience of prayer, but to convey the variety and diversity of prayer.

3. After jotting down the ideas of the group, shift to a more traditional exploration of prayer. Look over the text of the Lord's Prayer (Matt. 6:9–13). Have one group member read the text while the others follow along in their own copies. Depending upon the lev-

el and experience of the group, you can go into the history and background of the Lord's Prayer. Some questions to be raised might include: What does this say to me? How do I view my debts and debtors? What kind of temptations do I endure? How does the Lord's Prayer fit into my expectations of prayer?

This portion of the activity may be expanded or shortened as the needs of the group dictate. The important concept to realize is that the Lord's Prayer is not the static, dull "thing" we repeat each Sunday. Rather it is a spoken word, a commandment alive and fresh to each individual.

4. Display a copy of the traditional Lord's Prayer on newsprint. Refer participants also to Matthew 6:9–13. Ask each of them to do *The Great Rewrite* of the Lord's Prayer. This should be done in a way that fulfills their expectations of prayer and with the assumptions that have been explored and questioned. Allow for and encourage sufficient time, a minimum of ten minutes, for this activity.

5. Have two or three volunteers read their versions of the Lord's Prayer. In comments, make sure to affirm the variety of interpretations yet the unity of purpose. A variation here is to have participants write their versions anonymously and then let someone else read it.

6. Have all, in unison, recite their version of the Lord's Prayer while you recite the "traditional" version. Reaffirm the unity yet diversity of the spoken word as prayer! (Variation: have people write item down anonymously and let someone else read it.)

RESOURCES AND REFERENCES:

Buttrick, George A., Harmon, Nolan B., *et al.*, eds., *The Interpreter's Bible.* 12 vols. New York: Abingdon-Cokesbury Press, 1951, vol. 7: *New Testament Articles, Matthew, Mark.*

Beers, V. Gilbert, *Patterns for Prayer.* Old Tappan, New Jersey: Fleming H. Revell Co., 1972.

Corbishley, Thomas, *The Prayer of Jesus.* New York: Doubleday & Co., 1977.

Harner, Philip B., *Understanding the Lord's Prayer.* Philadelphia: Fortress Press, 1975.

Hein, Lucille E., *I Can Make My Own Prayers.* Valley Forge: Judson Press, 1971.

STUDY AND PRACTICE

ACTIVITY 20
Prayer Retreat
(Barbara Gianino)

The following is a sample outline for a twenty-four–hour prayer retreat for high-school seniors. The retreat should seek to provide an opportunity to share personal images of God and to offer experiences that will hopefully help to expand those images leading to a more meaningful relationship with God.

Many have erroneous ideas of God. God needs and wants to be real to us. This retreat is designed to broaden ideas about God through relationships, nature and Scripture.

MATERIALS NEEDED:

Bibles for each participant
Magic markers
colored construction paper
film or films (such as ones mentioned below), 16mm. film projector, screen and any necessary extension cords

PROCEDURE: (The following is an outline for a prayer retreat.)

FRIDAY:

7:00   Arrival, settling-in

7:45   Brief orientation
        Ground rules and purpose of retreat

8:00   Name tags. Tear a piece of colored construction paper into a shape symbolic of you, for example a heart, a butterfly, or a symbol of your own choice. Write your first name on it and around it write a few adjectives that best describe you. Punch two holes in it and wear it on a string around your neck. (*Serendipity,* p. 77)

8:30   Getting to Know You Better. In small groups of four, explain and share about yourself using your name tags.

9:00   Film. *Who is God?* and *Do You Ever Talk to God?* or another film with a similiar theme.

105

9:15   Response to film. In large group, allow for individual sharing and reaction to the film.

10:00   Worship

10:30   Free-for-all (snacks and singing)

12:00   Sleep

SATURDAY:

9:00   Breakfast/cleanup

10:00   Worship

10:15   (Leader) "Our God Is Too Small"
Each of us has false (positive and negative) ideas of God. The "Testing God"—wants us to suffer; it is more pleasing to God when we suffer; watches us to see if we are faithful to the test (what would we think of a husband/wife who tested the relationship in this way?); life is a series of tests. The "Judging God"—an old man; big book; checks good and bad deeds; good bookkeeper; makes no allowances for a bad day. The "Vending Machine God"—impersonal; floating around somewhere, benevolent at times, drop in coin, ask for our need, receive an answer; it's a bargaining relationship; leave the machine when needs are met. God wants to be real to us. Needs and wants to be more than a Word; need to meet him and discover who God is for us. (Share experiences when God first became real. Leader may want to share his/her experience(s) first.)

10:30   Response (small groups of four)

11:00   Break

11:15   (Leader) "Your feelings and God"
Feelings are often conditioned by false images and injunctions:
—need to remove restrictions of certain feelings—sharing

106

angry/hurt feelings can often lead to a deeper relationship;
—God knows those feelings, but wants us to tell
—no feeling is unacceptable to God
—paradigm of human relationship—sharing feelings is important to relationships that we want to deepen and that we cherish.

11:30   Response (small groups of four)

12:30   Lunch

1:30   "Nature and God" (Nature walk) directions given by leader:—allow yourself to wonder as you wander—let God speak to you through nature—find something that speaks to you of God and let it tell its story—bring your treasure back to the group

2:00   Response (small groups of four)

2:30   Break (snack, singing)

3:15   "Scripture and God." Bring together the whole group. Using selections from Scripture in which Jesus interacts in a protracted way, encourage each participant to look at God as God really is and is revealed through Jesus. Give each person a copy of the following:

1. Look at God. What is God like?
2. What is God doing?
3. Tell how you feel about what God is doing. (Either you like it or you don't.)
4. Look with open eyes at the Person of Jesus.
5. What does he say? Do? How does God relate?
6. What manner of relating?
NO REACTION IS EVER WRONG!!!

RESOURCES

BOOKS

Coleman, Lyman. *Encyclopedia of Serendipity,* Los Angeles, Ca.: Serendipity House, 1976.

Ignatius, Keith L. *Respond.* Vol. I. Valley Forge, Pa.: Judson Press, 1971.

Jacobson, David C. *Clarity in Prayer.* Corte Madera, Ca.: Omega Books, 1976.

Nelson, Virgil and Lynn, *Retreat Handbook, A Way to Meaning,* Valley Forge, Pa.: Judson Press, 1976.

FILM

Franciscan Communications, 1229 S. Santee, Los Angeles, Ca. 90015
Who Is God? An abstract discussion of God is undercut by visuals of suffering and the question, "Would you know God if you saw Him?" (3 min.)
Do You Ever Talk to God? A-man-on-the-street interviewer asks about God, gets varied answers, then waits for the viewer to answer. (3 min.)

NOTES

Doherty, Robert, S.J. "Spiritual Direction," course, Weston College, Cambridge, Ma., 1976.

ACTIVITY 21
Learning to Pray:
"Moving Beyond Memorization to
Creativity and Personal Involvement"
(Chuck Ericson)

The purpose of this activity is to help young people to understand the meaning and importance of prayer in Christian religious life, and to help them realize that their thoughts and beliefs are *valuable* and *worthy* of being shared in the context of prayer. Also, to make them feel comfortable and familiar with the various styles and methods of prayer.

Aside from being able to recite the Lord's Prayer (hopefully!), many young people—and even adults—are often unfamiliar with or uncertain about prayer. This activity is intended to relieve them of this uncertainty—to help them feel more capable of offering prayers in any setting, from an informal vesper service at camp to participation in Sunday morning church worship. They should realize and feel supported that their talk about God *is important*—that they have something special to offer in proclaiming their Christian faith through prayer. This is not a lesson in memorizing existent prayers, but of creating and forming prayers—of expressing personal concerns to God in a way that will be meaningful to other worshiping Christians.

The activity is designed for junior or senior high youth groups; but all ages from approximately fifth grade to adult could benefit from it. There are people in all age groups who need to feel more at ease with prayer.

Time: Allow an hour and a half to two hours for the program.

Materials: paper, pencils, chalk-board or newsprint, copies of a few selected spirituals and folk songs, piano, guitar or other instrument suitable for accompaniment.

PROCEDURES

1. Begin the session with group singing. This helps to create a spirit of fellowship and unity, whereas starting off with one person (the leader) talking or giving instructions tends to create a less-inspiring atmosphere. One or two contemporary folk songs followed by a more spiritual song (e.g., "They'll Know We Are Christians By Our Love") should suffice.

2. Following the singing, have the young people sit down and meditate/reflect silently for three to four minutes about their conceptions of God. Provide them with some stimulating ideas and themes: Who is God? How does God work in our lives? Does God help us when we ask? Have them each find a spot in the room to sit by themselves (alone) so there will be less temptation to talk or create distractions. Also, a room environment that does not have many physical distractions (e.g., magazines, playing cards, sports equipment, etc.) would be desirable.

3. Now have the young people think specifically of things about which they would like to pray. Leave the subjects open to them. After they have been thinking for a minute or two, pass out pencils and paper and ask them to write down those concerns about which they would wish to pray. They need not write their names on the paper—this is a gathering of ideas, not a test.

4. When they have finished writing, make four columns on a chalk-board or a piece of newsprint, and write one of these headings at the top of each column: Thanksgiving, Praise, Intercession, Pe-

tition (do it *in this order*). Briefly explain what each of these terms means. Then collect the papers and copy down their responses on the chalk-board or newsprint, arranging them in the columns under the proper heading (e.g., a prayer that asks God for strength to resist temptation would be included under the "Petition" column). Notice the pattern into which the responses fall: very often the great number of responses will fall into the two columns on the right, with very few in either the "Thanksgiving" or "Praise" columns.

5. Discuss the pattern of responses for ten minutes or so. Why do we tend to ask God for many things, but neglect to thank or praise God enough? What things are we thankful for? How can we become more aware of the need to praise God?

6. Now have the young people write down *titles* or names we call God (e.g., Heavenly Father, Eternal God, etc.), and also the ways in which we *describe* God (e.g., Creator of Heaven and Earth, Father of our Lord Jesus Christ, etc.). If the group seems receptive and comfortable with this exercise, you may want to have them offer their responses verbally this time instead of anonymously on paper. Keep a record of the responses on another section of the chalkboard or on another piece of newsprint.

7. Discuss for a few minutes why we have the titles and descriptions we do for God and what they mean. Do these titles describe both the respect God deserves as well as the more personal nature God has revealed to us? Are the titles fitting to God? When we use these titles at the beginning of prayers, do they help us to center our thoughts upon God?

8. Now have the young people construct a prayer of their own that is based upon the ideas and thoughts they have contributed. Use the following formula:
(a) Title (e.g., "Most Holy Giver of Gifts"); (b) Description (e.g., "Creator of Heaven and Earth"); (c) Body of the Prayer—based on ideas from the four columns on the chalk-board or newsprint. For example:

"Most Holy Gift-giver, who has made the heavens and the earth,
    (title)   (description)

we thank you for the beauty and glory of your creation . . . "
    (body of prayer, with a "thanksgiving" theme)

Guide the process, and help the young people to assemble their ideas in a meaningful, flowing order, but let the ideas and thoughts be their own.

9. When the prayer is completed, copy it down on the chalkboard or newsprint and have the young people stand to form a semicircle in such a way that they can all see the prayer. Ask them to join hands and then read the prayer together as a group. After they have finished reading it, emphasize to them the community effort they have made and affirm the value and worthiness of their prayer. You also may want to suggest that they offer their prayer as part of the liturgy in an upcoming church service (this should first be arranged with the pastor). In suggesting this, the young people will (hopefully) realize the importance of their special prayer— because it has been deemed worthy enough to be included in the liturgy. They can read it as a group during the service, or they can make copies for all the congregation and ask them to join in the reading, or they can be even more creative and transpose it into a litany format. The church organist might even be requested to play softly a tune of their choosing in the background as the prayer is read.

10. Conclude with a song or two—of the same nature as the songs used in the first section of this activity. Another possibility is to conclude by having the group sing the Lord's Prayer, then read their own prayer once again, and then depart in silence. By concluding on a quiet note, the young people will have the opportunity to reflect further upon the thoughts they have had and the prayer they have written.

Concluding Remarks: In doing this activity, keep the following basic goals/objectives in mind: 1) The activity should help the young people to understand the meaning, importance and basic construction of prayer; 2) It should encourage them to realize the special value and worthiness of their personal thoughts and words about God as they are expressed in prayer. They should begin to feel comfortable with prayer. If these two goals are accomplished, then you have been successful.

RESOURCES:

A. For terminology related to prayer see:

Weidmann, Carl F. *A Dictionary of Church Terms and Symbols.* Norwalk, CT: The C.F. Gibson Co., 1974.

—defines terms such as: intercession, thanksgiving, prayer. There are numerous other dictionaries of church terms that can also be helpful.

B. For texts that help you become more familiar with the style, mood and language of prayer. These are not "how-to" books but rather they provide many examples of popular as well as relatively unknown prayers that will acquaint the leader/teacher with the variety of prayer language and style that she or he can share with the young people.

American Bible Society. *The Psalms for Modern Man.* New York: Pocket Books, 1972.

Doyle, Leonard J., trans. *St. Benedict's Rule for Monasteries.* Collegeville, Mn: The Liturgical Press, 1948, especially p. 41.

Niebuhr, Reinhold. *Justice and Mercy.* Edited by Ursula Niebuhr. New York: Harper and Row, 1974. A collection of excellent prayers on many topics by one of the twentieth century's greatest religious thinkers.

The Pilgrim Hymnal. Boston: The Pilgrim Press, 1931. Some very good prayers and litanies suitable for worship are found in the back.

von Trapp, Maria. *When the King Was Carpenter.* Harrison, Arkansas: New Leaf Press, 1976, especially pp. 77–95, which contain several prayers and benedictions that existed in the time of Jesus, and that Mrs. von Trapp believes Jesus might have recited as a young man.

The Bible. Read the Psalms in King James and Revised Standard Version for comparing the old and more "modern" styles of the Psalms.

Also:

Most denominations have pamphlets/booklets of various kinds or worship services and liturgies that include examples of prayers for various occasions.

Talk to your pastor and/or R. E. Director!

Chapter Five
KOINONIA: THE MINISTRY
OF COMMUNION

Esse est co-esse.
To be is to be with.
—Gabriel Marcel

Often, when *koinonia,* or community, is spoken of as ministry, the assumption is made that community equals the church. Ideally, a church *is* a community of people, but to make them coextensive prematurely offers a narrow and rarefied understanding of *koinonia* as starting point. Therefore, in this chapter, I will speak first of *koinonia* as participation in and communion with *Being,* with all of being. From the moment of my birth, indeed from the moment of conception, I am at once in relation to all being. The reality of my life is neither *I am* nor *I think.* The reality of my life and of my existence is that *we are.* "We are": this is the religious, metaphysical, essential and primordial affirmation that assists our understanding of community and communion, and therefore unlocks the mystery and ministry of *koinonia.*[1]

In the pages to follow, I will address *koinonia* from three perspectives. First, I will speak of those elements essential for the self-to-self and self-other people relationships: I will call this "I and We." Then, I will move to two major groups in which young people live communally, the family and the church: I will call these "Us," and point out the need to include the "Not Us" here as well. Finally, I will sketch a vision that takes into account communion and

---

1. Most of this first section is obviously indebted to the work of philosopher Gabriel Marcel. I hope the ideas presented here stimulate others to go to his works as rich sources for understanding communion.

community with the "Less than Us" in nature and with the "More than Us" of Divinity. In each section I will attempt to offer practical and concrete suggestions to the Youth Minister.

I AND WE

One of the major aims of any Youth Minister is to help young people understand themselves. For this reason, we tend to include, as a matter of course, opportunities for them to ask "Who Am I?" in terms of growth, sexuality, church, values, dreams, family. My investigation here concerns this identity question. The lens I will take, however, is not a psychological one. It is, instead, a lens that sees identity independent of stages of growth and development, and as true of human beings at nine months as at nine decades. It is a philosophical lens where the "Who Am I?" question is posed in terms of incarnation, presence, self-consciousness and intersubjectivity.

Incarnation. One of the most serious obstacles to the grasp of the Community of Being is the tendency we have to reduce our human bodies to the level of mere objects.[2] It is, of course, a natural tendency to think of my body as something I have, as an object (even a most important object!) among other created objects in the universe. The point that I wish to make here, however, is the unreality of such a view. Incarnation, bodiliness, or corporality is not an added-on dimension to prior existence, something I have or get, but that quality of existence that inserts me into the world of real existence. But one of the greatest tendencies of young people is to have an object relationship to their bodies rather than a subject one. Spurred on by advertising, an individualistic society, burgeoning sexuality and their own heightened self-awareness, they view their bodies as something to look *at,* to get things (clothes, hair conditioners, cosmetics) *for,* even to be traded or offered. What the Youth Minister must insist on here is that the body is not something outside of or external to me but that *I am my body.* Everything, literally everything, that any one of us contacts is met through this body; everything in the world comes to me through this body; indeed, the only way I can be in this world is as a bodily creature. Thus, the first of my human communions is this one: I am in communion with my body.

Incarnation can be illuminated and understood by stressing

2. Vincent Miceli, *Ascent to Being* (New York: Desclee Company, 1965), p. 49.

two related points. These are feeling and environment and the young person's attitudes toward them. In our meetings with youth, much talk is directed to the feelings they have, to naming them, to "getting them out." But again, prior to this and far more fundamental than *having* feelings, *feeling* is the way that they participate in being. "Feeling is not an act of receiving; it is a further participation in being in an immediate way."[3] Therefore, it can be a false emphasis to stress the feelings young people *have* or do not *have* as a primary concern. To *be* is, for incarnated beings, to feel. A similar relation exists with the attitude a young person has to environment; it is not something, primarily, which I am *in*—far truer is the realization that I *am* my customary environment.

Presence. These three—incarnation, feeling and environment—are critical to the idea of human presence. To be incarnate is to be able to be in the world in a spatial way, to sense the world around me by feeling, and to be receptive to that world as the environment I am. To be such a receiver is not possible if I am an object, or if I think of myself as an object. But if we can understand that we are incarnate subjects, not only addressing, acting on, and going outward toward the rest of the world, but receiving it, and being addressed by it as well, we become capable of human presence, and eventually, of human communion.

Presence in the world is by spatiality, but for communion. To be alive is to be open to reality with which I must enter into some sort of commerce. Thus, presence denotes something far more comprehensible and real than just being there. Objects ... are never strictly speaking present. They are there but have no experiences. And presence depends on irreducible, vague experiences, on the sense of existing, of being in the world. Only human beings have this consciousness of existing.[4]

I would argue that young people are especially sensitive to the absence of human presence. It is manifested in their repeated cry, "You're not listening," either to one another or to parents; to the sinking feeling they often experience of not being seen and heard; perhaps even to the prevalence of teen-age suicide. I would further argue that one of the causes of such situations is the emphasis in our culture on spatial presence alone, where the body is viewed, touched, seen as an *it*, and as something one *has*, and our lack of

---

3. *Ibid.*, p. 52.
4. *Ibid.*, p. 54.

emphasis on human presence, where I am there as a subject, as a person, as the *imago Dei,* as one capable of communion.

It is an undeniable fact, though it is hard to describe in intelligible terms, that there are some people who reveal themselves as "present"—that is to say, at our disposal ... There is a way of listening which is a way of giving, and another way of listening which is a way of refusing, of refusing oneself; the material gift, the visible action, do not necessarily witness to presence. We must not speak of proof in this connection; the word would be out of place. Presence is something which reveals itself in a look, a smile, an intonation or a handshake.[5]

Self-Consciousness and Intersubjectivity. To help young people understand themselves as capable of presence, Youth Ministers need an attentiveness to self-consciousness, a characteristic often associated with the young. Our role as Youth Ministers is to distinguish between the obvious and to-be-taken-seriously self-consciousness that is part of post-pubertal physical awkwardness (acne, weight gains/losses, gangling legs, voice changes), and the growing capacity to be conscious of the self as that which a person can take into her or his hands and give to another. In the French, this latter capacity is *disponibilite.* In English it is the spiritual condition of availability, or the willingness to be with another with the whole of the self when the other is in need. Indeed, putting oneself at the disposal of the other in the deeper and richer sense of self-consciousness might, in the beginning, involve some of the discomfort of the first meaning of self-consciousness, but it is the latter that will bring the young person to the possibility of communion with others. Consciousness of what it is to be a self enables one to stand in the shoes of, perhaps *in the skin of* the other, and thus experience intersubjectivity. Marcel writes that to be incapable of presence is to be in some manner not only occupied but *encumbered* with one's own self;[6] such encumbrance will get in the way of genuine communion. In contrast, the practice and attitude of availability leads to the ministry of *koinonia.* For when the young person truly engages others, he or she begins to whisper communion and then to speak it loudly and clearly. Availability and intersubjectiv-

---

5. Gabriel Marcel, *Philosophy of Existence* (New York: Philosophical Library, 1949), pp. 25–26.

6. *Ibid.,* p. 27.

ity are the criteria signifying this point has been reached. Shared existence is now felt as preferable to isolated existence; and relationship to other people is known in terms of the contrast between fullness and emptiness of being.

The Youth Minister's role in encouraging growth toward this vision of communion is twofold: (a) the role itself must be an exercise of communion with the young person; and (b) the role must be directed toward the young person's becoming a minister of *koinonia*, an agent as well as a recipient, a subject and not an object of ministry. Some of the emphases that can help this occur are:

(1) An emphasis on *hospitality*, perhaps a "ministry of hospitality," as integral to the ministry of communion. "If we devote our attention to the act of hospitality, we will see at once that to receive is not to fill up a void with an alien presence, but to make the other person participate in a certain plenitude."[7] Here hospitality is a gift of what is our own, that is, of ourselves.

(2) An emphasis on *listening*, directed to creating opportunities for human presence. Responding to the question why she calls young people "voiceless ones" since they seem to make a lot of noise, Gisela Konopka writes: "Noise does not mean voices. It is a din that frequently hides feeling and thoughts, and it is a din that the adult world often shuts out by closing two opposite doors: One is marked, 'Dangerous, Nuisance,' the other 'Marvelous, Ideal, Hope of the future.' Both doors spell 'Keep Out.' Both keep us from listening."[8] Her position is that any such predetermined labels will make impossible the hearing of what it is the young are actually saying.

(3) An emphasis on *waiting*, manifested in the Youth Minister's refusal to spend inordinate amounts of time trying to figure out what makes *this* young person tick, in the conviction that it takes time for every human person to forge an Identity.

(4) An emphasis on *partnership* as the way to engage in the ministry of *koinonia*. A young person may say to the Youth Minister the equivalent of "I belong to you," a declaration of love that might be answered by "You are *my* youth group" or "Yes, you do belong to me." This answer is a very real, concrete temptation for ministers in responding to the affection and affirmation the young can give. But the appropriate response is different: "I welcome you

---

7. Gabriel Marcel, *Creative Fidelity* (New York: Farrar, Straus and Company, 1964), p. 28.

8. Konopka, *op. cit.*, p. xiv.

as a participant in my work, in the ministry to which I have given myself."[9] In this way we become co-ministers, for *esse est co-esse;* to be is to be with.

US

Whenever a local church engages in the ministry of *koinonia* it does so toward people in their individual, specific, concrete living situations. Thus, since I have spoken to this point of communion only in terms of the young person, my vision is as yet incomplete. To flesh it out, I turn to what the church might do in its ministry toward the family, which is the basic communal unit where young people live. If there is anywhere where participation, partnership and hospitality are called for, it is in the church's ministry to the families and communal units in its midst. The local church itself, despite rhetoric to the contrary, is not a family, although it may have familial qualities. However, in the religious lives of young persons and their families, it is a powerful partner, which can enhance the reality of family life. Its major contributions are as catalyst, as source of support, and as resource and sounding board for families and young people as they seek to grow together.

I indicated in Chapter 1 that the local church needs to recognize the plurality of situations in which people live. Single-parenthood, divorce, separation, death, even young people with no adult house member are almost as common as the father-mother-children unit. These individual differences need to be taken into account as the local church as a whole, or acting through its Youth Ministry, engages in communal ministry with families. It can offer itself as a place, a physical facility where familial units can meet together. One way to do this is by providing the setting for specific programs such as P.E.T., Al-Anon and Family Counseling. Essentially, however, the church is a religious group, and if community agencies perform social services, it does not need to repeat them. What it does need to do is minister to familial units as they address those religious situations primarily located in the family. It will be such a ministering church if it helps these units deal with solitude, with failure, and with commencement.

Solitude. "Loneliness," writes May Sarton, "is the poverty of

---

9. Marcel, *Creative . . .* , p. 40.

self; solitude is the richness of self."[10] Solitude is also very difficult for the poor to achieve; it is a luxury of the wealthy and the middle class. Nonetheless, the church ought to encourage families to strive for an ideal where all young people have pockets and spaces in their lives to enjoy solitude, to be by themselves, to take time for laziness, and to make the siesta (in whatever form) the center of their spiritual, religious lives.

Loneliness, isolation and abandonment can be genuine terrors for a young person, just as they are for adults, but so too can smothering, which in the teen-age years is a stifling possibility, as the parent feels the young person growing more independent. Genuine solitude provides the opportunity for the young to be "watchers," observing life without judging it, getting the feel of it, and sensing its flow and its rhythm. The bombardment of noise, often coming from stereos, and the drug-like quality of much television are certainly not conducive to solitude; more often they are rivals or enemies of the possibility. To counteract them, families might be encouraged to have designated "quiet rooms" or "quiet spaces" where the family members could explore the stillness and silence within and outside themselves.

The Youth Minister could help by offering one hour a week, or one evening, or one-half-day a month devoted to exploring family solitude. This could be done in the church's facility/space, or if families are interested, in individual homes. It could provide a structured, planned opportunity for "Us" to be "Us" in silence; for "Us" to explore solitude together rather than creating the impression that one must always "go away on retreat" in order to find stillness. It could also be a chance to develop the privacy so often necessary for genuine religious experience, since that privacy is basically found in the midst of the small community where persons live their everyday lives.

Failure. No community can move to communion unless it is a place where failure is tolerated; communities are made up of sinful human beings. In this instance, Robert Frost's memorable verse is apt: "Home is the place where, when you have to go there, they have to take you in."[11] Even with, *especially* with, failure: Home is

---

10. In *Mrs. Stevens Hears the Mermaids Singing* (New York: Norton, 1965), p. 183.

11. The line is from "The Death of the Hired Man," in *North of Boston* (New York: Henry Holt and Co., 1914), p. 20.

the place where it must be met; people live too closely in families in the physical sense to hide failure when it occurs. The attitude to failure—in school, in games, in sport, in work, in love—that the family expresses has a great influence on the power young people will have to distinguish between trying, losing, error, mistakes, sin, and genuine evil.

If it is true, as suggested in Chapter 4, that the comic is a narrow escape into faith, one of the times for making that escape to faith comes when young people experience failing others, failing self, being failed. The loss of innocence may even need to happen (*o felix culpa*) if the young person is to come to a deeper understanding that the presence referred to as necessary for communion is a presence that remains even when she or he is unworthy. In the Christian tradition where death and resurrection are the kerygmatic center of the gospel message, acceptance of failure is essential to a grasp of the paschal mystery.

Families, especially the adult members, can make this a possibility for their young people if they themselves are able to accept failure. But because this is often difficult to do without a community, it is an instance where the church, through its Youth Ministry, can offer many opportunities to help. Its first offering can simply be to *be there* as a communal organism saying to isolated families, "You are not alone." In addition, Youth Ministers can sponsor forums at periodic intervals on parent-teen disagreements where all voices are heard, can hold intergenerational meetings where all ages act on failures owned by the whole community (racism, sexism), can raise the problem of parents' desire to experience success through their children's lives, rather than through their own, can publicize the existence of pregnancy counseling not only for teen-age girls, but for teen-age boys and for the families of such teen-agers, so that if that situation arises, families know there is a caring place to go. In conjunction with these, they can offer liturgical and paraliturgical penance ceremonies and rituals—at church, and/or in homes—where reconciliation is the theme and the healing of family hurts is accomplished as prelude to family communion. Such activities can encourage a family to be a real world of real humans where mistakes are made, where messiness and ambiguity are never far, where lost tempers are admitted and found, and where failure is acknowledged and faced. In such families, the seeds of forgiveness, redemption, resurrection and communion may be buried for a while, but eventually, they will flower from hard and bitter ground.

Commencement. By referring to the family as a place of commencement, I intend this description: it is, uniquely, a place that succeeds if its members can leave it. A family is a community that can let go. To understand how difficult this can be, one need only ask any parent what it is like to send a child out alone to the first day of school, to "give away" a child in marriage, to watch a child choose a path different from the one the parent thinks best. The pain in the situation is that raising children, when it is lovingly done, is in the direction of a dependent independence. It is helping the young, as they grow older, choose and make their own decisions. It is enabling them to discover their own unique gifts, thus no longer needing yours in the way they did as children.

Commencement is the act of starting people on the adult journey that life itself is. To assist young people and families move in the exploratory way of such journeys, churches can make sure they know the stories of the great religious travelers: Abraham and Sara, Naomi and Ruth, Paul, Jesus of Nazareth. The church can encourage families to be places of exploration where new things are tried. They can be urged to be the settings for brief, initial journeys, for short forays, before the larger, longer adult journey claims its time. But when that moment comes, the way the family is the place of commencement is by letting go.

The church's major contribution in the event of commencement is to affirm it as a normal and natural occurrence, indeed as a precondition and prelude to communion. Ministry here is accomplished through designing commencement or "journey" rituals, where the community gathers together and in ceremonial fashion affirms all that has been in the past, all that has led up to this day, all that is hoped for the young person beginning the journey, all that is desired for its completion. Often, the young person leaves home, but the *leaving* is not faced because going to college, or marrying, or military service is the focus. What I am suggesting here is an acknowledgment of this important time in the human, communal journey, where the family communion is strengthened by being named, confirmed by being seen as integral, and sacramentalized by public, symbolic action.

Another way of describing commencement is to say it is the time a person knows that it is all right to leave. A strength is given in such a time, especially if publicly acknowledged, for the young person to say then of her or his family, "These people trust me. They aren't saying a lot, they aren't giving me orders, but they hear me, they care, and they believe in my own eternal beginning of the journey to which I am called. They think I can make it." The poetic irony in the situation is well known: Once the vision beyond the family, the going out, the exodus, is allowed, it is possible to come back; indeed, it is the only way to assure return. The end of all exploring is arriving at the place from which we started and knowing it for the first time. If, from the beginning, both church and family have indicated "God is where you are going," the irony will not change. If the family has allowed for solitude, and has tolerated failure, then wherever the journey takes the young person, now grown, it will be in the direction of home.

NOT US

I have spoken of human communion thus far as incarnate participation in Being with those who are closest, which for the young person is usually the family. However, if *koinonia* is genuine, and if community and communion mean relationship with all of being, the young person needs a larger social fabric, which while including the family, is not limited to it. By the phrase "not us," then, I mean those other people who though unrelated in familial ways share our condition of creatureliness.

The social fabric of humans is diverse, and one of the realizations a minister of *koinonia* carries is that not everyone does belong to those who are "us," not everyone wants to belong, not everyone could belong, not everyone is invited to belong. That realization is on the one hand an acknowledgment of ethnic, racial, value, age and socio-economic differences; and on the other hand, a recognition of sin: some original wound in human creatures keeps alive possibilities of hatred, evil and division. But the realization is also of the complexity of the term community as meaning at the very least (a) the smaller unit that shares common interests, values, history, and geography; and (b) the universal ideal toward which humanity tends, but which humanity has not yet realized. We are not a global community, but the seed of possibility for that is with us, a seed that can be nurtured. I assume here that acknowledgment of *koinonia* as an element in the church's ministry *impels* the minister to engage in such nurture. I further assume that the way of nurturing lies in (1) recognizing diversity and (2) providing opportunities to face, and if necessary, overcome it.

The church's ministry of advocacy and outreach toward others grows directly from *koinonia,* and I will speak of those elements in succeeding chapters. Here I want to note that the ministry of *koin-*

onia in relation to "not-us-es" is at least threefold. First, there is awareness of other family groupings, whose traditions, practices and values may be quite different from but just as valid as those of our young people. (There will also be those which are not, in our judgment, as valid.) In addition, there are other communal forms, and acknowledgment is needed of the infinitely diverse ways in which people live: alone, in institutions such as asylums, hospitals and military service, in religious orders, in nonmarital pairs, in homosexual arrangements. Here, the church can engage in teaching about *koinonia* simply by examination and exploration of such forms. Not all young people are moving in the direction of marriage and family, and this truth should be pursued. The church can also arrange its own programs so that the congregation is not assumed to be a group of, for example, 200 homogeneous "families." In doing so, it can help keep families, as well as other groupings, *from* being isolated and overburdened and *in* touch with each other.

Second, the last part of the twentieth century brings unprecedented awareness of religious groupings that are ecumenically diverse. The young need to be aware of and in touch with not only other Protestant denominations or other Christian churches such as the Orthodox, but with Muslim, Jewish, Hindu and Buddhist groups as well. The point today is not so much *that* such groups exist, but in what ways they are going to encounter one another in an increasingly shrinking world. One of the most effective moves Youth Ministers are already making here is arranging opportunities for activities such as joint retreats, reciprocal visits to each other's "home" turf, sports encounters, sharing diverse foods and styles of eating, and participation in each other's rituals such as Mass, Sunrise Ceremonies and Seder. Local ecumenical clergy associations are especially helpful here.

Third, the ancient and hallowed tradition of the "Communion of Saints" in Christianity is a reminder to Youth Ministers that community is not only with contemporaries, but with those who have lived before and who are to come afterward. To insure this vision, family histories and biographies ought to be studied. So too should the biography of the local church, neighborhood and community, often accomplished via interviews with the oldest residents. This can lead to a deeper understanding of each person's "roots"; and, by engaging in such interviews and reporting, the young may begin to realize their own role in being bearers of tradition toward the generations to come after them. Certainly, they should be encouraged to think of themselves in this way.

It is not at all clear that awareness of those who are "not us" will impel young people toward a care for those outside their immediate circles. In the present "Me" age, where narcissism is spoken of and written about as a "culture" of its own,[12] such concern may be very difficult to muster. The situation is compounded because isolation from those not like oneself is accompanied by a paucity of experiences which are, by their nature, communal. Writes one commentator on today's youth:

The "me generation" child can't direct much interest or energy outside his or her individual boundaries ... I discovered this lack of community when I taught in a fine small, suburban liberal-arts college; my otherwise delightful, intelligent students were almost illiterate in group experience. They had participated little in any organization which might have demanded loyalty or submission of one's own agenda for the achievement of a whole greater than the sum of its parts. An amazing number of them had never been part of an orchestra or a band, a chorus or a theater group, a political campaign or even student government.[13]

Nevertheless, a ministry of *koinonia* will be one that attempts to provide such experience, and a natural possibility exists when a group of young people come together in the church. In calling them together, the Youth Minister becomes a crucial person, not just for the sake of the young people, but for the sake of the world—the *polis,* or *oikumene*—in which they live.

LESS-THAN-US AND MORE-THAN-US

The ministry of communion—with oneself, with those closest to oneself, and toward a universal sisterhood-brotherhood with all peoples—takes a lifetime of growing into. In these final comments on that ministry, let me suggest two companions who can help us achieve it. The first is that created reality which is unlike us in being nonhuman, yet with us in being part of the journey. I refer here to the animals and the trees, the ground and the sky and their in-

---

12. Christopher Lasch, *The Culture of Narcissism* (New York: Norton, 1978).

13. Joanna Bowen Gillespie, "Meditation of a Middle-Aged (Upper) Middle-Class, White, Liberal Protestant Parent," in *The Christian Century,* XCVI, 26 (August 15–22, 1979), p. 793.

habitants: that which is Less-Than-Us. The Other is precisely that: the Other, God Who is the Ground of all Being, incarnate among us in the person of Jesus, yet More-Than-Us in every imaginable way; More-Than-Us, but at the same time, in the Christian tradition, revealed in the divine inner life not only like communion, but *as* communion or what we call Trinity.

Less-than-Us. Our major efforts in the ministry of communion will be with other people, as I have indicated in this chapter. What is less obvious is that our attitudes toward others—of presence, participation, incarnation, availability—will not make sense if turned only toward the human in creation. For communion to be complete, it must rise from awareness of partnership with *all* that is. This religious understanding of creation has been changing in recent years in the West, so that we now tend to rebel toward and resist a Genesis interpretation that says "Subdue the earth; master it; dominate it." Exploitation of the earth's resources has taught us how dangerous and destructive that attitude has been and can be.

Because our attitudes and actions toward the nonhuman can mirror our attitudes and actions toward people, the ministry of communion ought to include some practice and work with the less than human. In my own teaching, I have found artistic activity the most powerful vehicle for such religious partnership.[14] The aesthetic is one way to establish relationship with world-stuff: clay, paint, water, color, earth, trees, sky. One of my students described a session where we tried such activity thus:

The process required that I go outdoors, perceive something in nature thoroughly enough to get some relationship with it, and then, through the disciplined structure of a poem, express what I had encountered. The "something in nature" turned out to be the strong bark of an oak tree, which I attempted then to express in the following:

> Fibre
> Rough-layered,
> Stretches, routes, contains,
> Tough, enduring shell of life.
> Bark.

---

14. See Maria Harris, "A Model for Aesthetic Education," in Durka and Smith, *Aesthetic . . .* , pp. 141–152.

It may not be great poetry; on the other hand, I surely know more about the subject than I would through many other processes, and not only more about it, but know it, in itself. When I was with the bark, it gave itself to me, and through the poem, possibly to others.[15]

Others, of course, have discovered different possibilities, and Youth Ministers can let their imaginations soar as they try to engage in communion and companionship through care for animals (how many young people *first* come to a sense of communion through the companionship of a dog?); through creation of meals (starting with the baking of bread and the making of butter together), even liturgical meals; through the early morning joy of bird-watching; through the careful, intricate and profound engagement of astrology; and through activities of building, carpentry and stonemasonry (Francis of Assisi, take note!) which are all possible ways of rooting us to the earth and its inhabitants.

MORE THAN US

The Touchstone and Ultimate Symbol of Communion is, for us, God, that "Sphere whose center is everywhere and whose Circumference is nowhere."[16] Engaging in, working with, joining together with the human and the less than human, we come to the discovery at their centers of *The* Center. To those in the ministry of communion, it is indeed comforting to realize that the mystery of God in its oldest Christian rendering is of an Other, More-Than-Us in every way, who still chooses to walk among us, a Divinity called Emmanuel, God-With-us, very early in the story. God wrestles with us, pitches a tent among us, dwells among us from the beginning. If our theologians are correct, such being-with-us is part of the divine essence, for God as Trinity is a Community of Being. Saint Thomas writes that what is in common possession by the Trinity is precisely this, their very being or existence. "Only those things can be said to be of one essence which have one being. So the divine unity is better described by saying that the three persons are of one essence."[17] The Trinitarian formulation is open to new explanation in every age. This one, however, seems to transcend the centuries, this

---

15. *Ibid.*, p. 148.
16. Clarke, *op. cit.*
17. *Summa Theologica.* Tr. by Fathers of the English Dominican Province. (New York: Benziger, 1948), I, q. 39, a.2, ad. 3.

symbol for the divine not just as Being, but as Being-in-Communion. If it is true that we humans are in the image of God, then the symbol might also be ours—at least as a desired dream and hoped-for destiny. We too are called to be beings-in-communion, and a ministry of communion, *koinonia,* is born, dies, and rises in the heart of the mystery of God.

Chapter Five
STUDY AND PRACTICE

ACTIVITY 22
Experiences of Listening

This activity focuses on experiences of listening. Each group should be provided with a marker and some newsprint. Individuals should have paper, pencils and a copy of the four questions given below. Instruct the participants to spend about one hour on the questions. They should allow fifteen minutes for individual reflection, thirty minutes for group sharing, and fifteen minutes for arriving at a consensus on questions 3 and 4. Each group's response to questions 3 and 4 should be written on newsprint and brought back to the whole group for discussion and comments.

1. What were three times when you had the experience of being listened to?

2. What were three times when you had the experience of genuinely listening to another (or others)?

3. Upon reflection, what conditions need to be present for listening to go on?

   If possible, place these conditions in priority order (1. most important, etc.).

4. Upon reflection, what conditions are hindrances to listening?

   If possible, rank these hindrances in priority order (1. worst, etc.).

ACTIVITY 23
Family Koinonia: Twenty Questions

This questionnaire is a discussion starter. It is intended to spark conversation about family experience and to discover how (a)

128

complex and (b) diverse families are. Thus participants will be led to preclude "blanket" approaches to family ministry that assume homogeneity of experience. The activity can be used alone, with groups of Youth Ministers, and/or with groups of young people.

PROCEDURE:

The group moderator should ask each question in turn, giving participants time to jot down answers. Ask participants to comment on which questions struck them most. Participants should be encouraged to share whatever they find most important or interesting, and to keep private whatever they choose not to reveal.

1. What were your parents' ages when you were born?

2. How many of your grandparents did you know? Remember?

3. What is your birth order among the children in your family?

4. How many siblings do (did) you have? Of what sex?

5. How many aunts, uncles, cousins do you have ? Are they on one side of the family or on both?

6. What was (is) the economic situation of your family?

7. When did you receive your first accurate information about sex? From whom?

8. What was (is) the attitude toward work in your family?

9. Were you (are you) an ethnic, racial, religious minority?

10. What was (is) the attitude toward authority and/or power in your family?

11. Was (is) anger openly expressed in your family setting?

12. Did you move a great deal as a child?

13. In what kind of dwelling(s) did (do) you live as a child?

14. When did you leave (or do you plan to leave) the home of your parents?

15. What was (is) the family attitude toward sports? Toward art?

16. Were boys and girls treated differently, or raised differently in your family setting?

17. Were you held, caressed, touched as a child?

18. In your family, were (are) church and religion the same?

19. What is your family's attitude toward God?

20. What is the single most positive recollection you have of your childhood?

ACTIVITY 24
Toward Communion:
Families Below the Poverty Level

The accompanying chart shows some facts about the poverty level in the United States in the late 1970's (from *Healing Family Hurts*, New York: Paulist Press, 1979). Using the statistics given, individuals or a group might want to do the following exercise.

Imagine that you wish to teach the relationship of Christian *koinonia* to the issues raised by these statistics. Given (a) the Youth Minister; (b) the group of young people involved; (c) the need to understand the effect of poverty on families; and (d) the environment in which you are ministering, would you:

1. Plan a presentation on the relationship between *koinonia* and family poverty geared to helping young people think (infer, speculate, question assumptions, gather evidence, etc.) about the issues?

2. Plan to involve the youth in an outreach situation where their learning would be "on-site" involvement?

Facts on Poor Families
FAMILIES AND TOTAL INCOME

Total Yearly Income	Millions of Families	Percent
$25,000 or more	12.8	22.4%
$15,000 to 25,000	18.1	31.7%
$10,000 to 15,000	10.6	18.4%
$5,000 to 10,000	10.4	18.1%
$5,000 or below	5.3	9.3%

FAMILY RELATIONSHIPS

Total number of poor families........................ 5,311,000
Families with husband and wife...................... 2,524,000
Families with male head, no wife.................... 177,000
Families with female head, no husband 2,610,000

NUMBER OF CHILDREN AND POVERTY

Percentage of families that
are poor having ....Number of children
under 18

	Number of children under 18
12%	0,1,2
17%	3
23%	4
36%	5
49%	6

RACE AND POVERTY

Number of Poor (Individuals)	% of all poor	% of total pop.
7,726,000 Blacks	29%	12%
2,700,000 Hispanics	10%	6%
16,416,000 Whites	61%	72%

3. Design a prayer retreat centered on the need to include these issues in one's spiritual concerns?

4. Study ways in which the young are themselves involved in situations such as those cited, either as participants or as fellow citizens—and then move to social action?

5. Teach the Christian tradition, from the scriptures on, to indicate the attitude of the Christian churches to the inequities caused by poverty?

6. Other?

ACTIVITY 25
Toward Understanding an Intergenerational Community:
Older Meets Younger
(Nancy Pearl Adams)

This is a program to assist young people (junior-high age) to become more aware of the needs, problems and joys of aging. Some preliminary questions to consider are: What are our attitudes toward growing old? What are some of the things we are afraid we will not be able to do as we get older? What are issues for the elderly in our community? (e.g., survival, living on fixed income, loneliness, death/dying, separation, illness, and so on). (Resource: *Ministering to the Aging: Every Christian's Call.* Laurello, Bartholomew J. New York: Paulist, 1979.)

In most churches and/or communities there is a good representation of both older people and junior-high–aged young people. What follows is a design for providing an intergenerational exercise involving both groups. It is an evening of fun, fellowship and sharing that will encourage further interaction. Background:

Many small rural communities do not have senior citizens' projects, meals-on-wheels, free public transportation for the aging, or other senior citizens' benefits. Such a setting is quite different from a large city. The setting will influence the ways of contacting senior citizens. One can check with the community at large, nursing facilities and members of local church congregations to discover older people who might be interested in the design.

It is important for the Youth Minister and the community to be enthused and eager to help the junior-highs in this ministry. It begins with the junior-highs extending personal, written invitations (with RSVP requests) to some of the older citizens, preferably but not exclusively from the congregation. It would probably run more smoothly if the young people know something about those invited, though this is not essential. The plan is for a nostalgic evening of partying, approximately two hours long. In some cases, other adults may need to provide transportation. It is important to have a leader who can co-ordinate the activity and who realizes the necessity of everyone's participation. Activities must be planned with the physical limitations of the senior citizens in mind.

Song. Before the party night, the junior-highs should practice some of the oldtime favorite songs such as, "Oh My Darling Clementine," "Oh Susanna," "Tie a Yellow Ribbon," "Tipperary," "Don't Sit Under the Apple Tree," etc. Numerous others will do, but the song and song leader are most important. The leader must be able to get everyone involved and perhaps sing some rounds. Playing favorites on a record player may take up some of the slack; it may be helpful and/or necessary to have a microphone and speaker depending on the size of the facility chosen.

Upon arrival, seat *pairs* of old and young together at small tables (four to six at a table). On each table place materials for games and banners: pens, paper, crayons, markers, tape, crepe paper, large paper bags and song sheets. Begin by playing some games. These should be something both young and old can do together. The following are examples, to be done in teams. (Teams insure that no one feels threatened or embarrassed at not knowing the answers.)

State Silhouettes: Cut out of colored paper the silhouettes of about twelve states and mount them on a white background. Walk around the room giving each table ample opportunity to view and guess them. Table with the most correct answers wins.

Alphabetical Treasure Hunt: Ask each group to select any four letters of the alphabet. Now ask the group to write down on sheets of paper as many visible articles in the room as they can whose names begin with any one of the letters selected. Suggested time for this activity is five minutes.

Holiday Game: Take the name of the nearest holiday and ask each group to come up with four or more three- or four-letter words found in the holiday name. Suggested time limit is five minutes. (Resource: Herdic, James F. *Organizing and Programming a Suc-*

cessful Senior Citizens Club. Manchester, Ct.: Superintendent of Recreation Division, 1963.)

Next, take a refreshment break from the games. The junior-highs and their leaders will have made cookies and punch (or something more elaborate). It does not really matter what the refreshments are, but the manner in which they are served is important. While the refreshments are being served, the song leader can lead a hymn sing. This time, let the participants request the hymns.

By this time, the groups of four to six (equally divided between younger and older) have had the opportunity to get to know one another a little better and to work as a group. At this time, on the banner paper, ask each group to draw two scenes. One can be the center of town as it used to be years ago; the other the center of town—or the neighborhood—as it is now. Almost anything can be suggested, as long as it shows changes from past to present. Allow about twenty to thirty minutes for this activity. Encourage everyone to participate in the banner-making exercise. If they were not present in town until recently, allow the participants to make educated guesses.

After the banners are finished, have the young people in each group hang them on the wall. Explain to the groups they have just decorated their own environment. Allow the groups to share a little about their banners with one another.

Finally, ask the members of the group to take the large paper bag in front of them and to decorate it with their favorite activity or hobby.

Conclusion: Draw the evening to a close. Have each group stand up and hold hands in a circle. Sing "We are One in the Spirit" or some other appropriate hymn/song. Conclude with the reading of Psalm 90: 1,2 or Isaiah 40:28–31. Let the closing prayer center around the theme of thanking God for the opportunity to be with one another. When the evening comes to a close, make some plans for follow-up in the community. Possibly, the young people will agree to make a commitment to provide a service project for and with the older people. Perhaps each youngster would be willing to visit with his/her "partner" one-half hour a week to share experiences, talk, do some shopping, or help in light housecleaning. The possibilities are unlimited.

ACTIVITY 26
Communion with the Less-than-Us

Cinquains can be used in many ways: as discussion starters, as exercises to explore a particular subject matter, as concluding or summary activities. In this case, it is suggested they be used to probe the nonhuman environment, the less-than-us.

FORM ONE: (origin unknown)

Directions:
Line 1: Give a one-word name, which is the subject of the poem.
Line 2: Give two words to describe the first line.
Line 3: Follow this with three action words.
Lone 4: Create a phrase descriptive of the subject.
Line 5: Summarize in one word.

EXAMPLE:
Fibre
Rough-layered
Stretches, routes, contains
Tough, enduring shell of life.
Bark.
                    —Eric Bascom

FORM TWO:

Here a cinquain is a five-line poem in which the first line has two syllables, the second line has four, the third line has six, the fourth line has eight, and the fifth line ends the poem with two syllables.

The caution here is to urge young people to continue the search for the precise word. They should not choose a word just because it has a certain number of syllables, or add a nonessential word just to fill the count. The challenge is toward authenticity.

EXAMPLE:
(2) Morning
(4) Comes on the night
(6) like a robber stealing

(8) something precious from a big house.
(2) Morning.
                                        —*Ellen, age 11.*

Information on this form can be found on pages 47 to 57 of *A Celebration of Bees: Helping Children Write Poetry,* by Barbara Juster Esbensen (Minneapolis: Winston Press, 1975). The author credits the origin of the cinquain to Adelaide Crapsey (*Verse,* New York: Alfred A. Knopf, 1938). Esbensen cites the cinquain as a forerunner to understanding the Japanese form called Haiku.

ACTIVITY 27
Where We Grow Up Makes Us Who We Are
(Karen Moeschberger)

Activities 27 and 28 are designed to show the influence that environment exerts on youth. The activities should be done together. Activity 27 describes growing up in a rural setting, while activity 28 addresses growing up in a city. Ask the participants to read each section. When the reading is completed, ask each individual to do one of the following activities:

1. Write an autobiographical account similar to the one in activity 27.
2. Engage in the actions suggested in activity 28.
3. Create a new design, based on their special "place."

Introduction:
The purpose of this design is to reflect on my own experience as a youth within the church in a rural situation. My major interest is in the way I was shaped by the environment of a small town and the role that the church played in forming my present conception of the role of the church in the life of a rural adolescent. At some points within this design I will contrast my rural experiences with my urban experiences. Until recently, little material has been published on the rural church outside of denominational periodicals occasionally featuring a rural congregation. It is easier to find material on the urban situation.

Environment: To speak of one's environment is to speak of communities, one's family, peers, friends, one's employment, one's school, church, and all that surrounds one's self. None of us escape the effect that our environment imposes on us. By changing environments, we change the type of influence upon ourselves.

My home town is in northeastern Indiana, thirty miles south of Ft. Wayne and twelve miles from the Ohio border. Monroe has a population of 700. The majority of the population works in local industry and in agriculturally related enterprises such as the grain elevator and fertilizer plant. The downtown area consists of a gas station, grocery store, furniture/hardware store, beauty parlor, pool hall, liquor store, reupholstery shop, and a pizza parlor. When I was living in the town the pool hall, liquor store and pizza parlor were not in existence. I feel the changes are a result of changing attitudes within the community.

Adams Central Community School is housed within a one-story building that encompasses kindergarten through twelfth grade. At the time I was in high school there were approximately 400 students in the high school. The majority of students were bused from outside of town as they lived in the country. Few students lived in town. Most of the students were white, middle and upper-middle class. During the summer and early fall there was an influx of Hispanic migrant workers. The town had no black families living there.

There is no mass transportation in the area so it is necessary to have a car or have access to a vehicle of some kind. Most students drove to school once they had acquired their license, rather than take the school bus. Extracurricular activities that were scheduled after school included rehearsals for band and choir, sports, drama, language clubs and art club.

The religious scope is broad in the surrounding community. Within the town limits there is a United Methodist Church, an Evangelical Brethren Church and a Friends' church. Numerous sects such as Amish, Mennonites, Jehovah's Witnesses, are included in the profile of the community. Mainline denominations exist as well. These include the Roman Catholic church, the United Church of Christ, the Lutheran church, and the Presbyterian church.

My own affiliation is with the United Church of Christ. As I was growing up my church was affiliated with the Evangelical and Reformed Synod. The Sunday School curriculum was from the

Moody Publishing Co. For a brief period in the 1960's the U.C.C. curriculum was used.

My parents were and are active in the church. Both of my parents taught Sunday school and participated in church organizations. As an adolescent most of my extracurricular activities were within the sphere of the church. I attended catechism every Saturday morning for a year when I was in eighth grade. During this time I was required to memorize the Heidelberg Catechism. Most of my concepts of church doctrine were learned then. The Youth Fellowship was a large part of my life. For the most part, the church was the center of all activities outside of school or work.

The Youth Fellowship that I attended was made up mainly of senior-highs. St. Luke's was yoked with St. John's, a church in a neighboring county. The students who attended St. John's went to a school in the city of Bluffton. We thereby had a varied group of farmers, townspeople and small city people. Our meetings usually were two hours in length with the first hour being a worship service led by one of the group, which included a lesson/discussion of some type. The second hour was spent in playing games and eating refreshments. The meeting gave the youth a chance to learn leadership skills and provided the opportunity for social growth. This is true for most youth groups whether the group is an urban or rural setting.

Through participation in the Youth Fellowship I gained skills and found a place where I could belong. I worked on an association and conference level youth board my junior and senior years. This provided me with the opportunity to meet youth from the entire state of Indiana. It also exposed me to youth from larger cities. When I was in junior high I visited several major cities, such as Chicago, Detroit, Louisville, etc., with my youth group. On these visits we learned what our national denomination was doing missionally. The trips included sightseeing as well.

A rural congregation has less competition from secular activities than does an urban or suburban church. For many people living in a rural situation, the church is the only place where there is involvement outside of their working environment. City living provides a person with options other than attending a church activity more so than in a rural area. This being the case, persons planning activities for city youth need to have a program that will be able to compete with other activities. This is true of rural programs, too, but if there is nothing else to do but attend church, youth will probably attend just to have something to do.

With the exposure of the world that television has brought, the rural youth is no longer isolated from events and foreign places. The impact of actually visiting a city like Boston or Chicago still lingers in my mind. The size of the buildings, the number of people, the traffic, the mass transit and many other facets of city living were new for me. I had heard of them, but to experience the city made it a part of me. Having grown up in a small town I was naïve. I trusted people and thought that the majority of people belonged to a church and were active members. How much I learned by visiting cities! I learned of the hurts and the joys of the city.

I feel it is important for youth from cities and the country to meet each other and interact; therefore, I think that any type of church activity that can bring the diverse groups together is crucial for their development. It is meeting other people and visiting where they live which makes youth aware that the people who live in the city or country are *real* live people who have questions about faith and their futures. Programs such as area youth rallies, exchanges of youth groups from one church to another for a period of time, or a week-long excursion to a city or farm are all options for helping the city and the rural youth to exchange ideas and meet new people.

RESOURCES

Cole, Larry. *Street Kids.* New York: Grossman Publishers, 1970.

Havighurst, Robert. *Growing Up in River City.* New York: John Wiley and Sons, Inc. 1962.

Hollinghead. A.B. *Elmtown's Youth and Elmtown Revisited.* New York: John Wiley and Sons, Inc., 1949, 1975.

Pettitte, George A. *Prisoners of Culture.* New York: Charles Scribner's Sons, 1970.

ACTIVITY 28
Life Together in the City of God
(Stephen Fisher)

This activity is designed for use with Activity 27. Suggestions for using the activity are found at the beginning of Activity 27.

Presupposition: The predominant view of the city in American society at present is that urban life is undesirable, inferior, dangerous, and to be avoided if possible. The goal of every urban dweller is therefore to escape the city. These views are due in part to the "return to nature" movement, in part to "white flight" and the development of self-sufficient suburban communities, and to the negative images of American cities presented by the media. This phenomenon has two results that are the concern of youth ministry. First, this negative attitude contributes to the decay of cities by engendering an attitude of apathy and hopelessness in urban people, rendering as meaningless any attempt to revitalize our cities from within, and by allowing the rest of the nation to write-off the cities as "lost causes," thereby diminishing any sense of responsibility of the nation toward its cities. A youth ministry that takes seriously the demands of love and justice must recognize that youth needs an environment that is sustaining, growth-producing, and positive in its self-understanding. Such a ministry has as one of its responsibilities the kind of education and concrete action that seeks to actualize the best possible environment for urban youth.

Second, the condition of American cities can contribute to a negative self-image in urban youth, but more importantly, the commonly held negative image of the cities contributes as significantly, if not more so, to the negative self-image of urban youth. If young people are told by the media and the segment of society represented by media (i.e., the society comprised by middle and upper classes, to which poor people and working people are taught to aspire) that their environment is hardly fit for human habitation, their self-understanding will necessarily be low and self-abasing. Self-image is critical during the developmental years of adolescence, and youth ministry must be concerned with helping young people to develop a positive self-understanding. It follows then that urban youth ministry must engender a more positive view of city life and the urban environment among young citydwellers.

Theological Assumptions: The city has always been a powerful symbol in Christianity, whether in the Bible or in later tradition. St. Augustine used the symbol of "the City of God" to describe the anticipated Kingdom of God. In the later sections of the Hebrew Bible, Jerusalem is seen as the locus of the Holy. Jesus also speaks about the city as a symbol of the Kingdom of God, and uses it as a metaphor having a positive connotation (cf. Matt. 5:14). In Luke 19:41–44 Jesus weeps over the city of Jerusalem because of what it had become, in contrast to what God had intended it to be. The Revelation of John also refers to the Holy City of Jerusalem repeatedly. In Christian tradition, then, the city is seen in positive terms as a way of life that is blessed and instituted by God.

STUDY AND PRACTICE

Purpose: To help young urban dwellers develop a sense of pride, joy, and hope about their environment, and to cultivate a sense of community and cooperation among urban people.

Preparation: The leader should become familiar with some references to the city in biblical material and should bring along some art supplies such as newsprint, markers, stuff for banners.

Format: Discussion, games and art.

Location: If possible, this session may be held in a park or other city neighborhood center such as Shawmut Square in South End, Castle Island in South Boston, the Fens, Bunker Hill Park in Charlestown, Government Center Plaza. It should be in the neighborhood of the young people's residence.

Discussion:

A. Read and discuss some biblical images of the city:
   1. Salvation of Nineveh—Jonah 3
   2. Restoration of Jerusalem—Nehemiah
   3. "A city on a hill"—Matthew 5:14
   4. Jesus weeping over Jerusalem—Luke 19:41–44
   5. St. Augustine's City of God (the leader should just introduce this symbol and stimulate discussion)

B. Your Own City

   1. Who are the people who live in your city? Neighborhood? What do they do for work? For pleasure?
   2. How do the people in your neighborhood work together to make it a better place in which to live?
      How would you go about getting people together for this?
   3. What do you like best about your city/neighborhood?
      What do you like least?
      What would you do to change those things you do not like?

C. The Presence of God in the City

   1. Do you see God at work in your city/neighborhood?
      Where? How? When?
   2. How do people try to serve God in the city?

How do they work together to do this? (Youth minister should be aware of community programs and ministries.)
3. How can this group experience more fully the presence of God in our environment and *do* the will of God in our city and our neighborhood?

Images: List films, songs, and television programs that present images of city life. Are these images fair? Why do people often have distorted images of the city? If you were making these films or songs, how would you change the image of the city in each to reflect more accurately your image of your home? What are positive images of the city that people hold? What are negative ones? What images do you have of the places where other people live? (Leader should bring music and pictures that contain images of the city.)

GAMES:

A. Design Your Neighborhood: (Using newsprint and markers) Students should break down into groups of four and draw plans of their neighborhood as they would ideally like to see it. They should include all of the basic necessities, but be imaginative in their inclusion of features that they would like to see. How could these designs be realized? Leader may bring in some imaginative city designs, such as Paolo Soleri's *City Book* or Arcosanti (cf. *Boston Globe*, April 30, 1978), or some drawings by Buckminister Fuller. The students' drawings may be displayed in the parish hall.

B. Banners: Construct some banners for worship that celebrate the city, using biblical images and scenes from your own city.

C. City Mouse and Country Mouse: If your cousin came from the farm to visit you, where would you take him/her? Plan a program that will show him/her the finest aspects of the city, but make sure your visitor sees the city that you experience, not the one in the travel brochure.

Further Involvement: The group may be interested in participating in a community project, such as a regular park clean-up, getting to know and assisting elderly in the neighborhood, etc. A valuable ministry for the group itself to perform would be to compile a list of various resources, medical, legal, educational, recreational, for youth in the city.

Chapter Six
KERYGMA: THE MINISTRY OF ADVOCACY

Ad-vo-cate n. 1. A person who argues for a cause; supporter or defender. 2. A person who pleads in another's behalf; an intercessor. 3. A lawyer.

In this chapter, I turn to the first of the two more obviously prophetic elements of ministry, advocacy. In Chapter 1, I explained its derivation from the ecclesial work of *kerygma*, highlighting its meaning as word enfleshed in speech. Obviously, advocacy is not the total meaning of *kerygma*, and in some cases may not even be the most important. However, in ministry to youth, I believe it is central and is a place where the Youth Minister will have to take on the prophetic task of pushing back boundaries, taking on unpopular positions, and often speaking the word that no one wishes to hear.

Ideally, advocacy is (as is all ministry) the work of the church. A Youth Minister as *an* advocate may be doomed to fail if her or his advocacy is not eventually part of the church's ministry. In the meantime, a Youth Minister will need to see that advocacy in its entirety is at least fourfold: (1) It is a speaking to institutions, first the church itself, and secondly, those of the wider society, on behalf of young people; (2) It is rooted in conversation with and among young people, which obviously involves being silent in order to hear them speak ("Advocacy in youth ministry means *listening*, caring, interpreting");[1] (3) It is an offering of opportunities for young people to speak about themselves to the church and the wider society; (4) It is an offering of opportunitites for youth to speak for other young people.

---

1. "A Vision of Youth Ministry," *op. cit.*, p. 11.

The areas for such advocacy are manifold, although obviously the primary area for advocacy is the cause of youth as a whole. "An advocate for youth shows dedication by interpreting and speaking for youth before the Church and secular community. Advocacy 'gets down' to the everyday practicality of being a buffer, an intermediary, a broker. It is a call to be a true listener who can then accurately represent the position of youth in the public forum."[2] In general, the Youth Minister engaged in advocacy alerts others to what concerns youth have, defends their capabilities, and argues for their access to knowledge and skills. To get to this point, a minister must take seriously one of the cardinal principles in Youth Ministry, "Be ready to hand over true responsibility to the teens."[3] This means starting not with general areas, but with very specific areas that are primary concerns for young people. By focusing on the specific and particular, actual advocacy takes place.

It is my contention that handing over true responsibility occurs with reference to three areas, and these form the substance of this chapter. They are sexuality, power, and resources. I would note immediately the choice as far from arbitrary; in a true sense, they are kerygmatic as well. For close examination shows that in addressing them we are attending to what from earliest times was the object of the traditional evangelical or gospel counsels. Poverty was directed to resources, especially economic resources; chastity directed to human sexual encounter; and obedience, directed to the human expression of power, will and authority. As human beings grow into adulthood, these are central issues, and if the church takes the lives of its members with seriousness, cannot be ignored. My own work with Youth Ministers over the past several years indicates that in addressing sexuality, power and resources, we are able to act prophetically for and with the young, and ultimately toward the health and well-being of society as a whole. In presenting my arguments, I will be drawing largely from such work.

SEXUALITY

A year ago, one of my students who works as an adolescent probation counselor and spends weekends in her home church as a

---

2. *Ibid.*
3. Richard Costello and Michael Warren, "Principles and Procedures in Youth Ministry," in Michael Warren (ed.) *Youth Ministry: A Book of Readings* (New York: Paulist, 1977), p. 117.

Youth Minister, walked me back to my office after class. The class had been on adolescent sexuality, conducted by a young woman who has been working with teen-agers in that area. My probation-counselor-student's comment to me was, "Whew! If I tried to do any of that in my parish, I'd get put out. It's necessary, sure, but nobody will touch it."

In raising the issue here, and telling this story at the beginning, I intend to make two points. (1) It is naïve to think we will be able to address sex and sexuality with teen-agers without people getting upset, often very upset; and (2) Not everyone is qualified, able or comfortable enough to try. Nevertheless, I want to speak of it here and advocate that it must be addressed in Youth Ministry. If we are not yet qualified, or able, or comfortable, we will have to work at it until we are. It is simply too important and too vital to evade in our churches. Young people may be fortunate enough to receive thorough, adequate and complete information in schools, but often do not. In either case, they need places where their private questions and concerns can be raised at leisure with trusted adults. They need to know how sex and sexuality are viewed in their own religious communions, and be liberated from the equation of morality with sexual morality so many of their parents and grandparents still entertain. And they need opportunities to deal with the extraordinarily wide range of issues related to human sexuality such as pregnancy, contraception, abortion, homosexuality, sterilization, frigidity and the changing concepts of maleness and femaleness in this society.

Many fine resources exist which can help Youth Ministers with adolescent sexuality; I will list some of them at the end of this chapter. However, I want to write here of those areas where a ministry of advocacy is most important. (1) *Advocacy must go on with the young people themselves.* Here, the Youth Minister can speak for the young in several ways. The first is by offering a place where simple—or complex—information and attitudes can be shared. Young persons' failure to act responsibly is often directly attributable to their not being adequately informed. To discover what information teen-agers seek, and which topics they most need to explore, the Youth Minister does well, before any more formal program in sexuality, to ask the young people, perhaps in small group conversation, more usually through a checklist questionnaire, which areas they want to address. Where a young person may not easily *say* "Masturbation," or "Homosexuality," or "Incest," the anonymity of a form to be checked and handed in can insure some

145

awareness on the minister's part of what the young people are asking about. It is important that the Youth Minister not generalize or take for granted that the young are adequately informed. Nevertheless, questions and concerns will probably be different and may need to be handled differently depending on the age of the group. Junior-highs, for example, will differ from late adolescents. The benefits for all of the young people are many: the first one is knowing of a safe and open atmosphere where sexuality and sex are neither embarrassing nor taboo subjects. The second is the surprising discovery on the young person's part that he or she is not alone in her or his questions. Often, because sex/sexuality *is* so often hushed, a young person gets the impression that he or she is the only one filled with concerns; because *it* is not discussed, *it* is not on anyone else's mind. Opening up the area can dispel this false assumption.[4]

A second side-benefit in such advocacy is that the Youth Minister is able to offer young people a language in which to speak of the sexual area of life. Price and Morrison's fine handbook, *Values in Sexuality,*[5] suggests several exercises under the heading "Vocabulary Brainstorming" where the basic procedure is to give a word such as penis, vagina, homosexuality, impotence, and to ask the young people, either alone or in a group, to share words they know that are synonyms. Their categories are: the language of science, childhood language, street language, and common discourse; and they instruct the group, as soon as a word is given, to write synonyms from any one of the four languages.[6] (I have met other Youth Ministers who use other categories—Patrick Ryan told me he tells his teen-agers there are barroom words, living-room words, classroom words and bedroom words!) One of the most poignant comments I have heard is from one sexuality educator who commented that in years of doing this exercise both with teen-agers and with adults, the word "intercourse" had drawn the synonym "making love" only three times.

(2) *Advocacy must go on among parents.* Parents generally want their sons and daughters to be informed about sex and sexuality, es-

4. Nancy Elder has given me invaluable assistance, based on several years of work with adolescent sexuality in the church, in understanding this area. I acknowledge my debt to her here.

5. Eleanor S. Morrison and Mila Underhill Price, *Values in Sexuality* (New York: Hart, 1974).

6. *Ibid.,* pp. 31, 32ff.

pecially toward the basic facts of reproduction and toward values. However, people in the parental role often do not have opportunity to discuss their own sexual issues any more than do their teen-age children. For this reason, a set of advocative activities with parents are: (1) Offer to parents similar exploratory sessions to those given the young people, prior to any program of sexuality. Invite them, too, to name the information, areas, and attitudes they believe most important for their children, but also for themselves. (2) Ideally, offer a follow-up program. Because the basic advocacy is for the teenagers, the Youth Minister could take direction here from what DRE's do prior to First Eucharist.

Among the most successful Eucharistic preparation programs for families in many local churches are those that offer a role to parents prior to reception of the First Communion. The best DRE's I know conduct five or six sessions with parents alone, where religious issues are addressed as a complement to the instruction being given the children. The issues are raised as related to the child, but almost always, when groups are kept to eight or ten or twelve adults, move quickly to adult concerns in connection with religion. A similar procedure should be going on with sexuality advocacy. If the young people of a local church are being offered the opportunity to explore questions related to sex in a free, open, and relaxed atmosphere, the adults should be given a related opportunity.[7] The program has a natural beginning in its connection to the young, but often has a subsequent flowering in adult questions and concerns.

(3) *Advocacy must go on with Youth Ministers themselves.* Most Youth Ministers work under the auspices of a local church with directions, principles and guidelines given by national, diocesan, and/or judicatory bodies. Although projected training for Youth Ministers is described in detail, and recommendations made that they be competent in scripture, doctrine, psychology of adolescence, and educational procedure, the area of sexuality is sometimes not even mentioned. Yet in listing the preoccupations of U.S. adolescents, especially early adolescents, Jerome Kagan names uncertainty over sexual adequacy first.[8] *Whether* it is first or not is debatable,

---

7. Robert Grinder, *Adolescence* (New York: John Wiley, 1973), p. 444, quotes research indicating that because the majority of adults have an overwhelming fear of sex and numerous inhibitions about it, meaningful cross-generational dialogues can take place only if there is a broad adult sex-education program too.

8. Jerome Kagan, "A Conception of Early Adolescence," in Kagan and Coles, *op. cit.,* p. 100.

but *that* it is a central preoccupation is not. The advocacy I call for here is that Youth Ministry training take the area of sexuality centrally and seriously. This raises the need for a second advocacy: Youth Ministers must deal with their own sexuality and with sexual issues to the extent that they can be comfortable with this area in ministering to the young, and/or if they are not, be sure they have backup among other persons as ministerial resources. The hidden curriculum conveyed if this is not done is that sexuality is irrelevant, unimportant, and unrelated to religion. The contrary is actually true, and a reason for including sexuality advocacy in ministry.

Sexual questions have an inevitable religious dimension. The Christian heritage contains not only a plethora of teaching concerning sexual morality, it also bears great theological themes of sexual relevance. What we believe about human nature and destiny, what we believe about sin and salvation, about love, justice and community, all these and many other basic beliefs will condition and shape our sexual understandings.[9]

(4) Advocacy must be directed to eliminating sexual stereotypes. During the teen-age years, what it is to be male and what it is to be female become important questions. Obviously, they are closely related to how young people feel about themselves sexually. But they are also related to larger social and cultural views of male and female that are undergoing considerable revision today. Many Youth Ministers find a useful starting point in this area an exercise where boys and girls are separated and each group asked to list the advantages and disadvantages of being a male and/or a female.[10] The groups then come together and share lists, preconceptions, assumptions, and inevitably, stereotypes.

The issue is complicated by the use Youth Ministers make of adolescent psychology, which as I noted in Chapter 2, is admitted by psychologists to be based on the psychology of adolescent boys.[11] (One of the schemata most in question here is the stage theory of Lawrence Kohlberg; recall, his original work was done entirely with adolescent males.) Ironically, a male bias turns out to be destructive in the case of boys on many occasions. Persons working in

9. James B. Nelson, *Embodiment* (Minneapolis: Augsburg, 1978), pp. 14–15.
10. See Morrison and Price, *op. cit.*, pp. 67–94 for several such exercises.
11. Adelson, *op. cit.*, "Generalization Gap . . ."

pregnancy-counseling clinics comment that girls often receive an hour of a counselor's time; boys, five minutes. Culturally, boys of any age are still expected to be sexually knowledgeable in a way girls are not, although how they are to gain such knowledge is rarely explained. A more complicated issue is the historically devastating evidence of religious groups' inhumanity toward females, especially in the Christian tradition, from ceremonies designed to wash away the "uncleanness" of menstruation and childbirth, to the systematic genocide of women in the burning of so-called witches, to the still tolerated second-class status of women, by both sexes, in too many of our churches.[12] A Youth Ministry that includes advocacy in the area of sexuality will have to include this as part of its agenda.

POWER

The second area for Youth Advocacy is power. I use the word here to mean the ability or capacity to act or perform effectively, especially to exercise control or authority.[13] If a Youth Minister is to act as advocate for the young, such work is toward assuring others that young people are in the process of developing abilities and capacities in many areas and need opportunities to do so. The areas of power imbalance for the young are many. Some experience lack of access to information that concerns them (from parents and school personnel); others lack knowledge of their civil rights. Most lack any substantial opportunity to exercise leadership in churches, especially where their own lives are concerned. The issues I wish to address here are related to these areas and ought to involve all Youth Ministers. I choose them with the awareness that in other circumstances, Youth Ministers may have different priorities, but I urge at the least their consideration.

(1) A first focus for a ministry of advocacy is the sharing of data with young people concerning their civil and legal rights. In our society, "law" is so narrowly associated with criminal activity that many persons go through life unaware of the protection given them

---

12. See Mary Daly, *Gyn-Ecology* (Boston: Beacon, 1979), for description of Indian suttee, Chinese foot-binding, African genital-mutilation and U.S. gynecological practices for some documentation in this regard.

13. A more developed definition might be explored, such as that in Michael Parenti's *Power and the Powerless* (New York: St. Martin's Press, 1978), especially pp. 12–13 ff.

in local, state and federal statutes. Needed information is often un-available until serious crises occur, and even then not always of-fered because of ignorance. Nonetheless, an extraordinary body of law exists for the protection of minors, often designated as "juve-niles," which can assist young people in understanding their rights.[14] Speaking to the Association for Supervision and Curricu-lum Development some time ago, Dwayne Huebner asked that group,

Why have the court cases for racial equality, to permit long hair and dress options in schools, freedom of high school people to print po-litically oriented papers sometimes critical of the schools, the rights of pregnant girls to be in school, and the rights of Amish kids to stay out of public school been pushed by a few parents and civil libertar-ians rather than ASCDers?[15]

My point here is that the same question should be directed to Youth Ministers. How many of us are versed in law regarding young peo-ple as we are in adolescent development? Is this not an equally im-portant area for us in ministry, and ought our concern be limited only to what might be called "spiritual"?

The areas where such law applies are many. Do our young peo-ple, for example, know the age of majority in their state and wheth-er it can be applied for early? Do they know what access exists for them with reference to medical care in general, and specifically in the cases of contraception, abortion and pregnancy? Do they have information about work, contracts, and the ability to own and keep money? What of police and pretrial procedures, courts and fact-finding procedures for those who are arrested, guilty and innocent? Are they aware of the existence of juvenile-court advocacy pro-grams when these do exist, and of agencies they can contact if in need of legal representation? Suppose they are subjected to abuse, neglect, or statutory rape: what legal recourse do they have in these instances? All of the information one needs to answer these ques-tions is easily and readily available.[16] My argument here is that

---

14. Among the most valuable resources are Alan Levine and Eve Cary, *The Rights of Students* (New York: Avon, 1977), and Alan Sussman, *The Rights of Young People* (New York: Avon, 1977), both published by the American Civil Liberties Union.

15. "Poetry and Power: The Politics of Curricular Development," in William Pi-nar (ed.) *Curriculum Theorizing* (Berkeley: McCutchan, 1975), p. 274.

16. See note 14.

all Youth Ministers should have such answers at their fingertips, but should also make sure it is placed in the hands of the young, where it is equally accessible to them should they find themselves on their own and in need of help.

As with sexuality, I know that sharing knowledge of legal rights with the young can draw criticism of the Youth Minister who does so. The question to raise here is whether one can speak of a ministry that withholds such information as moral and religious, a question for local congregations and individual Youth Ministers to decide in their own work with young people.

(2) A related area offers a second focus for a ministry of youth advocacy, but here the emphasis is on the young people's own roles as advocates. The area is child abuse and neglect (though the procedure is applicable elsewhere).

Last year, one of the Youth Ministers with whom I worked[17] began an advocacy program with his youth group, composed of people ranging in age from junior through senior high. In conjunction with the state of Rhode Island, which was then instituting a child-advocacy program, he worked with these young persons in understanding the state program and in developing one of their own.

The result was a five-step procedure. They began by (1) Studying the history of child abuse and neglect, finding out, for example, in the study, that in this country in the seventeenth century death was a punishment by law for "unruly children" in several places. (2) They next moved to research on the statistics concerning child abuse, and the reasons behind it, learning firsthand of such contributing factors as the youth of the parents, the absence of outside help, the physical expectations of children especially re: urination and defecation, and the part that drugs, especially alcohol, play in child abuse. (3) From this they moved to their first bit of advocacy, making slides and tapes and pictures from their studies that they put together for demonstration. (4) Their fourth step was a search for the scriptural and religious grounding for child advocacy, engaged in through reading and meditating on texts related to children. (5) Their last step was a discovery and description of the great number of agencies available to help, from Parents Anonymous and social services to the state hotline, the Child Welfare League, and the American Humane Association. Meeting them, I found myself in the presence of young people not far in age from children them-

---

17. Rev. Frank Armstrong, an American Baptist minister from Portsmouth, Rhode Island.

selves, but responsible, caring, informed and involved in a ministry of advocacy they had themselves discovered. Ideally, it would now be a short step for them to influence their own church to what it, in turn, could do, from offering child-care facilities to setting up a chapter of Parents Anonymous.

(3) The most obvious place for the advocacy of power is toward empowerment of the young in the church itself.[18] Here, the Youth Minister as advocate assures the congregation that the young people are acting in good faith, are qualified to act responsibly in the power structure of the church, especially with reference to what concerns them, and are willing to accept (a) responsibility, (b) the consequences of irresponsibility, (c) the privileges of power. Often what holds up such responsible activity is the separation and segregation of the young from the rest of the church. This may mean that a first step will be providing opportunities for all in the congregation to meet each other through intergenerational activities.

However, certain activities are natural places for youth participation. The first is the worship service itself, which may be addressed by a "Youth Sunday" monthly, bi-monthly, semi-monthly, or yearly, where the young persons are responsible not just for readings and guitar music but for the design of the entire service, from altar call to final blessing. Many churches are committed to doing this. What may be more difficult, but in the long run more healthy, is a conscious and sustained attempt to make young people participants in *each* service, responsible in cooperation with the adults of the parish in that church's worship.

Closer to their own group life, one of the most effective ways to call on the power of youth is in the choice of Youth Ministers and youth advisors. A striking example of such exercise of power was in the decision of one youth group to choose its own leaders. The associate minister went over a list of all church members with the young people, and they chose from that list the men and women they would like most as their advisors that year. When the choices were made, they asked the minister if he would issue an invitation in their name to those adults. The minister's response was no: they had made the choices; they would have to extend the invitations. They did so, going in twos and threes to the homes of the adults, and asking if they would be willing to serve as ministers to them for the coming year. The result was that each one said yes. Al-

18. For much of this material, I am indebted to the Rev. Stephen Wayles of South Congregational Church (UCC), Brockton, Massachusetts.

though some admitted later they were very pressed for time, the invitation had been so enriching and so flattering that none had either the heart or the desire to turn the young people down.

Perhaps the most striking sign of the church's sense of its attitude toward youth will come in the latter's participation (or nonparticipation) in ecclesial polity and decision-making, in the actual exercise of power. It would seem to be appropriate that if a church is making decisions about the young, in areas as divergent as their eligibility for ordination, their catechesis, the setting aside of funds for their use, or the encouragement of evangelization toward them, young people ought to be represented. But it would also seem appropriate that if they are to be responsible members of the church, they should be present as full members whatever the topic of consideration. The range of contemporary practice here is enormous, from those churches where only male clergy take part in policy, especially at national and international levels, to those at whose synods youth are fully represented with voice and vote. Where such national representation is encouraged, it appears to be highly successful. Where it is not even in the talking stage, the place of initiation would appear to be the local congregation and the initiating persons the Youth Ministers. Indeed, the initiating action might well be the ritual of confirmation. If that could be designed as a celebration preceded by a two-year service or educational program directed toward taking on full participation in church life, *as some churches have found,* others might also discover a generation of strong young women and strong young men empowered and eager to engage in their own ministries both to church and to world.

RESOURCES

In his work on child advocacy, *Birthrights,* Richard Farson begins his chapter on "The Right to Economic Power" this way:

Money is power. It's not easy to start an argument with most Americans on that statement. Almost everyone agrees that money and power just seem to go together. For that reason, the attempt to strengthen the rights of children without giving them access to economic power would surely be a futile exercise.

Economic power would give children the right to work, to acquire and manage money, to receive equal pay for equal work, to gain pro-

motions to leadership positions, to own property, to develop a credit record, to enter into binding contracts, to engage in enterprise, to obtain guaranteed support apart from the family and to achieve financial independence.[19]

Farson's argument is in reference to children, but it raises issues that are similar for adolescents. Often, the first reaction to a passage such as this is, "But that's impossible. Children and young people don't know what to do with money. They'll throw it away." The issue I wish to raise here is where, if we have it, we got such an attitude. Why the widespread assumption that the young must be denied economic power because they do not know how to handle it?

The first recognition that needs to be made is the recency of such an attitude in United States society. Until well into the twentieth century, as pointed out in Chapter 2, young people were crucially important to earning power. But with the advent of this century, the coalition of labor unions and humanitarians seeking to stamp out child-labor abuses moved us to a position where the young are excluded, by law, from most jobs and therefore from economic security, economic freedom, and economic independence. "Ending the tragic conditions of child labor was surely a noble achievement of (hu-) mankind. But history has left us with only the atrocious pictures of the abuses of children during that period and no genuine understanding of the meaning child labor had . . . in general, it was not considered dishonorable. On the contrary, it was thought of as both economically and ethically valuable—good for the family and good for the child."[20] If we are to be youth advocates, if we see this as part of our ministry, a first consideration will be to realize how largely our attitude toward young people earning along with adults is shaped by societal assumptions.[21] We cannot even argue, "We've always done it this way," since most families still have living members who remember the opposite. We will have to try to think of young people not just as "students," as many of us do, nor as dependent members of a family, but "as individuals who may need to achieve, to be productive, to gain necessary expe-

---

19. (New York: Macmillan, 1974), p. 154.

20. *Ibid.*, p. 158.

21. In *The Social Imperative, op. cit.*, Gregory Baum draws a thorough picture of what he calls Ethos I in this connection, and helps us see how narrow contemporary attitudes to work in the United States are. See pp. 130–132.

rience, to qualify for the next step in their plans for personal development."[22] That next step may be toward economic independence.

Another possibility, however, does exist and is receiving growing attention today. This is the view of the young person as one of the regular family wage-earners, a traditional view until well into our own time. Today, such a view is often attacked or at least viewed with suspicion, as a move toward erosion of the family. What is not acknowledged, however, is that it is viewed as an erosion of the middle-class, middle-income family. Economic issues are far more openly addressed and considered in poorer families. To begin with, when negotiations are engaged in about young people's financial responsibilities and rights, the learning potential in poorer families is greater than in middle- or upper-income families. In the first situation,

parents may refuse a child's request not because of some abstract principle, but simply because they do not believe they can afford the item being requested. When such rejections occur for the latter reason, children may still try to change their parents' mind, or work with the parents to devise some compromise ... There is no great incentive for the child to try to stimulate guilt in the parents. The essential cause for the denial is beyond the parents' control.[23]

For millions of families, even such situations as these are a luxury; in these latter families, the young must work if they are to eat, and young people necessarily attempt to get part-time jobs or quit school in order to get full-time jobs. At a time of growing inflation, it is these young people who become unemployment statistics or who turn to crime as a means of support. At the same time, they lose any benefit that may have come from schooling which could possibly enable them to achieve greater earning power at a later time.

Even such a brief overview as this surfaces many issues connecting youth and resources. Some of these are: (a) the young person as capable of financial independence and as having a right to economic resources; (b) the young person as contributor to family resources; (c) the importance of the resource of schooling to earning

---

22. Farson, *op. cit.*, p. 162.
23. Wynne, *op.cit.*, p. 35.

power; (d) the issue of unemployment among young people; (e) the causes and prevalence of juvenile crime. In face of these, what is to be the Youth Minister's advocacy?

(1) *An informed advocacy.* Just as Youth Ministers need to know those laws pertaining to the civil, legal and political rights of the young, they need to be aware of the origins, history and current state of labor practices among the young. It is not enough to know the financial situation of the individual young men and young women toward whom they minister; they need to know, in addition, something of the social and economic factors in the wider society that contribute to these situations.

(2) *A political advocacy.* When the Carnegie Council on Children issued its report in 1977, it discovered that the single most important factor that stacks the deck against tens of millions of United States' young people is poverty; it urged that, other things being equal, the best way to ensure that a young person has a fair share in the rewards of this country is to ensure they be born into a family with a decent income.[24] At least three political policies are presently needed to make this occur: full and fair employment, guaranteed incomes for all citizens below which no one could go by law, universal access to social services, especially health and legal service.[25] The Council calls for "public advocates" who will work toward achieving such policies, pointing out that families often blame themselves for their social and economic woes and insists that change "must be not just personal but also political. When they blame themselves, American parents define their family problems as somehow rooted in themselves. They thereby neglect basic questions: how to give parents more power outside the family, how to make the distribution of rewards in our society more just, how to limit the risks of technology."[26] What an informed Youth Minister might do is engage in the political questioning that asks not how to change the victims of the social order, but how to change those forces within the social order that are doing the victimizing.

(3) *An advocacy for alternatives.* Even for the young who are not battling poverty, the present access to economic resources may be inequitable because they are discriminated against solely on the basis of their age. Where young people are competent to earn and

---

24. Kenneth Keniston *et al., All Our Children: The American Family Under Pressure* (New York: Harcourt, Brace, Jovanovich, 1977), pp. 83 ff.
25. *Ibid.*
26. *Ibid.,* p. 214.

have passed whatever competency tests are required for a particular job, and where labor practices are such that the physical well-being of the young person is not in danger, a job may be a more appropriate use of time and personal gifts than schooling. When basic literacy skills are gained, some young people are equipped to do their learning far better in a job situation than in a schooling situation. For those young persons so geared, the alternative should be considered. There may even be youth advocates who work seriously to end laws of job prohibition and compulsory schooling, a movement that already has many serious supporters. The young are always delighted by tales of such famous dropouts as Sir Freddie Laker and Albert Einstein who give the lie to the demand our own society makes in this area; they can be helped by adults such as Youth Ministers who realize the social reasons for the law in former times may not be sufficient reason today.

I must candidly assert this particular issue is extremely complex. For there will be ministers and situations demanding an almost completely opposite tack. Among the greatest resources any society enjoys are its knowledge resources, and for some, these *are* most accessible and available through the schools. For those advocating this alternative, however, the need for political action is still critical, for schooling, when it is advocated, must be seen as the right of all who desire it—a public service for which a community must take responsibility, and an agency characterized by excellence. Youth Ministers who go the route of advocating schooling must therefore be concerned not only for the parochial and/or private schools of their own churches and denominations, where these exist, but for the quality of schooling available to all the young people of their community. Otherwise they risk the charge of a selective advocacy geared only to "us" and unworthy of the *koinonia* which is integral to all ministry, but especially to the ministry of advocacy.

(4) *A prophetic advocacy.* When Jesus returned to Nazareth as a public figure to read for the first time, he opened the scroll and found the place where it was written, "The Spirit of the Lord is upon me because he has anointed me; to bring good news to the poor he has sent me, to proclaim to the captives release, and sight to the blind; to set at liberty the oppressed, to proclaim the acceptable year of the Lord" (Luke 4:17–19). His association of the proclaiming of the good news, the *kerygma,* with the poor, with captives, with the blind, with the oppressed, is one of the pristine Christian exemplars of a prophetic ministry. For those Youth Min-

isters who would seek to be inspired by him, and who would even seek to imitate the ministry he described, the way is similar. It does begin, as his did, with the poor, with advocacy for them, with a call for help to them, although it is never quite clear exactly which way of exercising it is best. While I have tried to outline some possibilities here, I can make no claim for infallibility. The most I can predict is that whoever tries to face injustices and engage in the ministry of advocacy will undoubtedly face the same reception Jesus did at Nazareth. Many will want to throw them out, and some will try. I can also predict that deep in their hearts they will be convinced that whatever happens, it will be worth their effort.

Chapter Six
STUDY AND PRACTICE

RESOURCES
(Nancy Elder)

I.   Sexuality Education: Techniques, Methodologies, Curricula
     Morrison, Eleanor and Mila Price. *Values in Sexuality.* New
     York: Hart Pub. (1974.) An *excellent* book of exercises that can
     be adopted for use with junior high to adult groups.
     Sex Education: Teacher's Guide and Resource Manual
     Available from: Planned Parenthood of Santa Cruz County, 421
     Ocean Street, Santa Cruz, CA 95060—$10.00 + $1.00 shipping
     charge. Certainly a *must* for anyone involved in sexuality edu-
     cation. Includes factual information, teaching techniques, and
     bibliographies. If you get only one book, I would recommend
     that it be this one.

II. Factual information, background material for a teacher about
     sexuality:
     Boston Women's Health Book Collective *Our Bodies, Ourselves.*
     New York: Simon & Schuster, 1976. Good information as well
     as sensitive insights and feelings about sexuality.
     Collins, Gary, ed. *It's OK to be Single.* Waco, Texas: Ward Books,
     1976. Looks at the phenomenon of singleness in the twentieth
     century and the challenge it poses both to the individual and
     the church. A good book.
     Gearhart, Sally & William Johnson. *Loving Women, Loving
     Men.* San Francisco: Glide Publications, 1974. Gay liberation in
     the church. It has an excellent section on "Homosexuality: A
     Contemporary View of the Biblical Perspective;" a helpful
     book.
     The Sexual Adolescent, Gordon, Sol. New York: Duxbury Press,
     1974. A good book about communicating with teenagers about
     sex; it has information about the special problems of abortion,
     pregnancy, birth control, etc. for teenagers.
     Johnson, Warren. *Human Sexual Behavior and Sex Education*
     Philadelphia: Lea & Febiger: 1973. Historical, moral, legal, lin-
     guistic, and cultural perspectives on sexuality. A good book, but
     a little outdated now.

Fundamentals of Human Sexuality, Katchadorian, Herant. New York: Holt, Rinehart and Winston, 1975. A good basic informational book covering biology, sexual behavior, and sexuality in culture.

Mace, David. *The Christian Response to the Sexual Revolution.* Nashville: Abingdon Press, 1970. Beginning with Biblical reference to sex, the book examines Hebrew society and the early church to explain how some basic misconceptions about sex have become accepted Christian principles; it then considers the significance of the sexual revolution and Christian attitudes; extremely good book to have for background for a sexuality program in a church.

III. Books for Teen-Agers, Junior Highs, and younger
Kelly, Gary. *Learning About Sex.* New York: Barron's Educational Series, Inc., 1976. A sensitive, intelligent book about human sexuality; informational as well as dealing with issues of morality and values; excellent book for ages 14 up.

McBride, Will. *Show Me!* New York: St. Martin's Press, 1975. A controversial book of photographs explaining and illustrating sexual development from infancy to adulthood; should be carefully read and screened before use with groups; some people have objected to its explicit phtographs; others have thought they are great. Designed for young children, but helpful for all ages.

Mayle, Peter. *Where Did I Come From?* New York: Lyle Stuart, Inc., 1973. Excellent book for young children, covering everything from conception and birth to love-making and orgasm.

_____ *What's Happening to Me?* New York: Lyle Stuart, Inc., 1975. Presents facts of life during puberty and does it with honesty, sympathy, and a sense of humor. Great book for kids between ages of 8–14.

_____ *Will I Like It?* New York: Lyle Stuart, Inc., 1977. "Your first sexual experience: what to expect, what to avoid, and how both of you can get the most out of it." This is certainly a book that has long been needed as it deals honestly with something most books on sexuality avoid. Read it before you recommend it. I had some problems with its style (it seems flippant and casual, not as supportive as it could have been of the teenager who is struggling with the decision about whether or not to have sexual intercourse), but would still recommend it for older or sexually mature teenagers.

Nilsson, Lennart. *How Was I Born?* New York: Delacorte Press, 1975. A photographic story of reproduction and birth for children; has photographs of the fetus inside the womb—a fascinating book for all ages.

ACTIVITY 29
Abortion Role Play
(Charles G. Campbell)

The following role play is designed to (a) emphasize the five central elements of ministry; (b) investigate whether it is possible to interrelate all of them. Participants should be given their parts beforehand. Twenty to thirty minutes should be devoted to the role play. A debriefing session should follow, which allows participants and observers time for comments.

1. You are a woman with a harbored secret. In the not too distant past you chose to have an abortion. You are unmarried and hope to remain uncommitted until you settle your own career plans. During your first year of graduate school you became a statistic—that is, the pill failed to work and you found yourself pregnant. After much personal struggle you decided in favor of an abortion. In spite of the guilt that you feel, you know that you had made the right decision.

2. You are in charge of this group meeting. As a leader in the church, you have become increasingly aware of the issue of abortion. Several people have spoken to you directly, asking for some help in sifting the issue out and learning more about it. Sensitive to that spoken need, and acting on a hunch that there was more need than had been vocalized, you have drawn these people together to begin to talk. You will have about ten minutes in which to begin . . .

3. Abortion? No way! In no circumstance could you ever justify an abortion. In fact you firmly believe that the choice is so clearly wrong that you find it hard to respect those who have had abortions or seem supportive of the abortion issue. You are firm in your stance, although not abrasive in your presentation.

4. You are interested in abortion as a political issue. You have been excited by the issue and wish to find out more about it. At this point you are not sure where you stand and are very curious about other people and their views.

5. You are a young parent who has an unwanted child. You feel trapped with the responsibilities and, if you had it to do over, would have had an abortion.

Author's Note: This role play is designed to explore individual feelings and attitudes toward abortion without immediately taking a particular position. With young people, adults and Youth Ministers, it can be a way of helping persons sound out their own attitudes and can create the possibility of moving toward an intelligent moral stance. M.H.

ACTIVITY 30
Advocacy Toward the Rights of Young People:
Legal, Human, Christian
(Bruce Sandy)

This activity is designed to help junior-high-school students to adults to explore the rights of youth and to become more aware of and sensitive to the rights of (and resources for) youth. It is also designed to stimulate persons to advocate the rights of youth.
Background:
All human beings, regardless of age, have rights. Unfortunately when we think of "rights," we often restrict rights to only those who are seen as being adults; children are often seen as having no individual rights other than those that adults allow them to have.
This learning process can broaden our concept of rights from the legal aspect of rights to include the human and Christian aspects of rights. It can also remind us as Christians to continue in our nondiscriminatory practices within the Church as well as outside it.
Time: The minimum time suggested for the activity is one hour.
Materials: The room should contain a large blackboard and chalk. You will also need copies of "Jesus Loves the Little Chil-

dren" or some other similar hymn, or of a suitable scripture text. Have available handouts such as the *Directory of Youth Services* and so on. The leader should have an awareness of different areas, laws and resources within youth advocacy (see the Rights of Children Table).

PROCEDURE:

1. Begin by singing "Jesus Loves the Little Children" or some other related hymn. Introduce the topic of youth advocacy by reading an example from any recent newspaper article in which there has been a violation of a young person's rights. Briefly discuss the article.

2. Divide the blackboard into three equal sections. At the top label "Rights of Youth"; at the head of the three columns label "Legal," "Human," and "Christian," respectively. (See page 165.)

3. Ask the group to name *any* and *all* rights (and the column in which it goes) that come to mind.

4. When there are no further suggestions, review the existing suggestions for further clarification, elimination, amending, and/or re-categorizing. This step is a crucial part of the naming process. Feel free to suggest any omissions or clarifications; you are part of the class.

5. Open to discussion. This time is for further clarification, for giving opinions, for suggesting resources. Discussions, debates, and good arguments should arise over all or a few of the issues at hand. This is where the real evaluation of laws, agencies, philosophy, theology, others, and self take place. In brief, this is where the personal growth takes place.

6. Debriefing and Summation. While handing out directories and any other relevant material encourage (challenge?) the people to act within this area (youth advocacy) by being aware, assisting, and advocating on behalf of youth and their rights.

7. Close by singing "Jesus Loves the Little Children."

Lecture/Discussion: It would seem ideal to invite a city/regional/state child or juvenile advocate to come and lead the discussion.

Groups: 1. Break into three groups. Each group is given one area within youth advocacy (legal, human, Christian) to explore. Each group writes down its thoughts on large sheets of paper. Each group's paper is hung up for all to see, explained by the group, and discussed by all. 2. Divide into two groups: one group with the title

"Youth" and the other "Adults." "Adults" are to write down as many ways as possible to deny youth their rights while the "Youth" list as many rights as they see as being their rights. Regroup, discuss, and enjoy!

RESOURCES:

1. Children's Protective Service
2. Council for Children/Help for Children
3. Parents Anonymous
4. Police Department
5. School (Guidance)
6. Rights of Children Table
7. Bakan, David, *Slaughter of the Innocents*. Boston: Beacon Press, 1971.
8. Everyone in the class!!!
9. Sussman, Alan. *The Rights of Young People*. New York: Avon Press, 1977.

ACTIVITY 31
A.D.V.O.C.A.T.E.
Another Daring [and Determined]
Voice Of Christ Addressing Teens Everyday
(Susan E. Wilson)

Purpose: As one about to assume a position involving youth ministry, with special emphasis on advocacy in terms of legal and social services, I have formulated this design as an initial source of guidance for the new youth minister.

Background: The role of advocate for youth necessitates the establishment of two things: (1) credibility in the eyes of the young people; and (2) trust relationships. To develop these two characteristics the youth minister must be willing to invest a great deal of time in learning all he/she can about the community in which he/she will be ministering. Also, if the advocate is to be involved in legal matters or a more social work dimension it would be extremely helpful to have past experience in these areas and to be aware of social agencies for referrals and information. The person exercising the role of youth minister must be familiar with the "five cries of youth" as outlined by Merton Strommen (loneliness,

Rights Table		
Legal	**Human**	**Christian**
1. to be defined as "juvenile" (police department)	1. to information/education	1. to Christian Education (Board of Christian Education)
2. to be protected by statutory-rape clause (police department)	a. academic (guidance counselor)	
	b. special education 766	2. to receive sacraments regardless of age (?) (church by-laws)
3. to be provided with 766 Special Education (school guidance counselor or Council for Children)	c. sex education (?) (family planning, etc.)	
	d. nutritional (outpatient pediatric unit)	3. to vote on money-property related issues which are in church by-laws (anyone under eighteen years old cannot)
4. to be helped by Section 51 mandatory report of child abuse/neglect (Department of Welfare or Council for Children)	e. day care	
	2. to at least a minimum quality of life (Department of Welfare, ALA-TEEN, Children's Protective Services, etc.)	
		4. to be seen as a viable worthy member on decision-making boards—especially on boards dealing with youth (by-laws)
5. to have legalities invovling marriage (with and without consent), abortion, and access to medical help (any doctor)	3. to make mistakes or fail	
	4. to grow up	
6. to be aided in the area of child labor	5. to pursue happiness	
a. laws (any personnel office)	a. recreational services	
b. employment (CETA or job banks)	b. YMCA-YWCA	
	c. counseling services	

Note: Definitions, laws, age limits and so on have been purposely omitted from this table. It is my hope that the leader, by looking into the different resources that are listed, will become more knowledgeable of and committed to youth advocacy.

family trouble, outrage, closed minds, and joy) and have some concrete ideas about how to deal with such issues.

It is important right from the beginning to have a clear understanding that the definition of an advocate is, "one who pleads in favor of or on behalf of another; to recommend publicly." The issue of advocacy makes a firm demand on the youth minister to reach out, become personally involved, and when necessary, publicly stand forth as a witness and supporter of and for young people.

Intended Audience: This design could be used by all youth ministers as a source of suggestions of people, texts, organizations, and social services that can be found in most towns and cities and which can be of invaluable aid (morally, financially, supportive services, etc.). Such a list would be especially helpful to the new youth minister as he/she enters a new environment and feels the need for some type of "checklist" to assure gaining familiarity with key resources in the surrounding locale.

Time: The time necessary for initiating oneself to a new community will vary; however, the youth minister must learn to be patient. It is very important to take the time to: (1) acquire an open and varied sampling of opinions regarding needs to be fulfilled and problems to be dealt with; (2) find out where young people spend their time and visit these places; and (3) attend meetings in the community and personally visit many of the people listed below. If a youth minister is willing to do this (and it will be a gradual process) the rewards can be great: essential contacts are made, insights are gained which otherwise might have been missed, and a sense of direction will gradually emerge for this exciting mission.

MATERIALS NEEDED:

1. A sense of humor
2. Town and regional handbooks with listings of churches, social agencies, government officials, youth directors and activities, etc.
3. A tape recorder to maintain accurate records of information (especially helpful when initially meeting and discussing issues with many varied groups)
4. Music, books, banners, posters: all reflecting the interests of youth so as to make one's office or meeting place more welcoming and affirming
5. A telephone with a specific number for the Youth Minister (answering service would also be helpful in case of emergencies). This assures direct communication between youth and the Youth Minister.

STUDY AND PRACTICE

PROCEDURES:

1. My initial task upon entering a parish setting would be to have extensive meetings with the other pastoral assistants to (a) discuss and outline specific issues they see a need to deal with, (b) to set goals, and (c) to determine the amount of support and energy they are willing and able to give to youth-oriented programs. I would also like to get advice regarding which adults and youth in the parish to contact.
2. Look to the youth of the parish and community. Where are they? What do they do? What issues confront them? What problems are dominant? What are or have the churches offered them? What excites them? What talents can be drawn upon? Who are their leaders?
3. I would like to meet with other church leaders (possibly as a group and then later individually) to discuss their ideas and assess their support. Ecumenical activities can be quite important at this time.
4. I would also be constantly investigating community resources (as listed below).
5. With the above information, I would begin meeting with key adults and youth to implement specific programs utilizing the various contacts being made. These programs need not be equated with youth coming to the parish hall for a CCD or CYO type experience, but rather, they may be geared toward the prevention of delinquency, the making accessible of information regarding legal rights, the introduction of Christian social-service projects, the integration of youth and adults in parish activities, etc. All such programs would be aimed at confronting and helping young people resolve the many cries and frustrations they so often experience during these years.

RESOURCES:

Bell, Martin. *The Way of the Wolf.* New York: Seabury Press, 1970. Short, thematic stories helpful for small group work and personal enrichment.

Cavan and Ferdinand. *Juvenile Delinquency.* New York: J.B. Lippincott Co., 1975. Excellent general text on causes, preventive methods, and legal implications associated with the actions of youth.

Hollings, Michael and Etta Gullick. *It's Me, O Lord!* New York: Doubleday and Co., 1973. Prayers for ALL occasions. Very supportive for the youth minister himself/herself and quite popular with young people.

Kilgore, Lois. *Eight Special Studies for Senior Highs.* National Teacher Education Project, Arizona Experiment, 1976. 108 Learning Centers—an excellent resource text for all youth ministers. Also, many of the exercises can be used with adults and intergenerational groups.

Sussman, Alan. *The Rights of Young People.* New York: Avon Books, 1977. The most current text on the legal rights of youth. *Very* helpful appendixes are included and the question-answer format makes the text easily understood. A MUST!

Wilkerson, David. *The Cross and the Switchblade.* New York: Pillar Books, 1962. A popular true story of young people growing up in the ghetto and the problems they encounter. A good text to have available for youth—portrays Christian witness in an honest and radical manner.

Schur, Edwin M. *Radical Non-Intervention: Rethinking the Delinquency Problem.* Englewood Cliffs, New Jersey: Prentice-Hall Inc., 1973. Emphasis on de-institutionalization and the use of community-based programs to deal with youth in trouble. Alerts the reader to alternatives in juvenile corrections and the roles we can play.

Massachusetts Bar Foundation, One Center Plaza, Boston, Ma. 02108

Very helpful booklets; especially: "Your Rights If Arrested"

National Clearinghouse for Alcohol Information, Box 2345. Rockville, Md. 20852

Scriptographic Booklets by Channing L. Bete Co., Inc., Greenfield, Ma. Quite informative texts on various topics—especially good for young people;

Ex. "ABC's of Drinking and Driving"

"What Everyone Should Know About Alcohol"

Public Relations, Kemper Insurance Companies, Long Grove, Illinois 60049

This insurance company provides well-done pamphlets on alcohol and will send up to fifty copies free.

Four that would be effective with youth are:

"What About Drugs and Employees?"

"The Way To Go" by Kenneth A. Rouse

"Detour Alcoholism Ahead"
"Guide for the Family of the Alcoholic" by Joseph L. Kellermann

PEOPLE:

1. Juvenile Officer
2. Youth Coordinator for the town (if one exists)
3. Clergy in the town
4. Police officers in the town that the youth like and dislike and why
5. School officials: especially counselors
6. Civil official who is willing to support affirmative-action programs for young people.
7. Adults in the parish: Are there certain adults the youth gravitate toward? Who have talents that could be drawn upon? Who want to help?
8. Street workers in the town

ORGANIZATIONS AND MATERIALS:

1. Youth Commission in the town
2. Recreation Committee
3. Division of Employment Security: what type of outreach do they supply to youth who need jobs (especially important to those in trouble)
4. C.E.T.A.: many programs for economically disadvantaged youth; important to locate their regional office and to be familiar with what they have to offer
5. Town organizations and Women's groups often lend support and funding
6. Hotlines and their personnel: know specific areas of expertise of each and the services they offer
7. Much legal information in the form of pamphlets available from the county sheriff's office
8. Hospital resources—special divisions (i.e., alcoholism programs)
9. Booklets on area social services and family services available from one's state Mental Health Division or town government offices
10. Big Brother–Big Sister programs

CHAPTER SIX

ACTIVITY 32
A Weekend Toward the Enablement
of Adults and Young People to
Become Youth Advocates
(Mary Byrider)

Purpose: To help adults and young people to be aware of the need for youth support, for understanding of youth needs and gifts, and for representation of the position and insights of young people in the parish.

Background: "An advocate for youth shows dedication by interpreting and speaking for youth before the Church and secular community." (*A Vision of Youth Ministry*)

A quality needed by a ministerial advocate to youth is *listening*. Before one can speak out for another individual or group, she/he must be in touch with the needs, desires, potentials, and gifts of the people she/he will speak for. In many situations an adult can best serve as the link between young and old but often a young person can more accurately represent the youth's position. Therefore, the purpose of this project is to help adults and young people be aware of the need for youth advocacy in the parish.

Two additional requirements for a youth advocate are (1) he/she must be living the Christian faith and openly sharing it with others. It is essential that as the person represents and understands the young people, he/she must also be representing a personal Christian life-style to the ones he/she serves. The primary goal of a youth minister should be to offer opportunities and activities in which young people can hear and respond to the Spirit of God and the gospel message as they experience it in their lives and in the lives of others. The greatest opportunity one has to offer is the Spirit of God present and alive in one's own life, and (2) he/she must be a person with *vision* for young people. A youth advocate must understand a bit of where young people are and encourage them in their potentials and gifts beyond their present fulfillments. When an adult or young person can help teen-agers to realize their self-identity and value and offer them an opportunity to grow, then she/he is being a *real* advocate for that teen-ager.

Audience: Adults interested in young people who want to learn to serve their needs, and young people seeking leadership roles among the youth and who can share "where they're at" and teach others by their experience.

Time: A weekend retreat experience at the beginning of a formation process of a youth ministry program or committee of the youth ministry group.

Procedures: For a retreat to be effective and meet the needs of the people it is intended for, it should be planned and organized by a group directly involved. Therefore, the retreat model I present here is an outline to be filled in, altered, and worked from rather than a "prepackaged" retreat weekend.

Three questions to help focus a group and clarify objectives (prior to discussing the model) are: (1) What are we doing? (2) Why are we doing it? and (3) What's the best way that *we* can reach our objective? With the answers to these questions in mind, a planning group can work from the following model.

Friday night should include: Games or activities to facilitate getting to know everyone else on the retreat. In small groups, a discussion by individuals why they came on the retreat and what they hope to gain from it. Then the small groups should report briefly what the commonalities and differences were in the small groups. An explanation of the objectives and goals of the weekend by the planners. A large group discussion to come to group consensus of what the objectives and goals will be for the retreat in view of the small groups' input and the ideas of the planners. Prayer and music.

(Note: this plan must be flexible in relation to Friday night.)

Saturday should include: Formation of small groups to facilitate discussion. Talks by young people and adults concerning the needs of young people; the needs of the parish; the areas for youth involvement in the parish; and, how young people's presence in the parish can be best nurtured, respected, and when necessary—represented.

Open discussion with insights, ideas, and questions will best facilitate reaching objectives and goals. The talks can be by a parish council member, clergyperson, or other staff person to express the position of the coordinating (controlling?) body. One or two young persons telling how they view their role in parish and what they would like to see happen would help keep the group focused on the needs of teen-agers in the present situation. Free time for people *to be* together. An important function of a retreat is to provide an opportunity for the creation of community. This can happen through praying together, talking with one another, and *being* together. Worship is a coming together to recognize the presence and power of the Lord present. The liturgy can be either Saturday night or Sunday morning and include prayer and music.

Sunday should include: A pulling together of ideas expressed Saturday that may not yet be focused toward an objective or goal. Small group discussion and then sharing in the larger group of, "Where do we go from here?" "Can we realistically remain a workable group?" "Who should be included in our group who was not here this weekend?" An evaluation of the goals and objectives set Friday night. Were they realistic? Which ones did we meet? Which ones were not met? A discussion of "As a youth advocate I see myself . . ." A real sensitivity to where people are, where they may be leaning, and where they have come from. Prayer and music.

RESOURCES:

Edwards, Maria, R.S.M. *Total Youth Ministry: An Approach for Parish Workers.* Winona, Minn.: St. Mary's College Press, 1976.

Flynn, Elizabeth W. and John F. La Faso. *Group Discussion As Learning Process: A Guidebook.* New York: Paulist Press, 1972.

Moran, Martin. *Some Ideas, Suggestions and Models for Organizing and Conducting Youth Retreats.* Diocese of Richmond, 1977.

A Vision of Youth Ministry, U. S. Catholic Conference, Dept. of Education, 1312 Massachusetts Ave., NW, Washington, DC 20005, 1976.

Youth Magazine, Herman C. Ahrens, Jr., ed., 1505 Race Street, Room 1203, Philadelphia, Pennsylvania 19102. "We Did It Ourselves!" Special Issue on Youth Action, July–August, 1976, vol. 27, nos. 7 and 8.

Chapter Seven
DIAKONIA: THE MINISTRY OF TROUBLEMAKING

We are afraid of religion because it interprets rather than just observes. Religion does not confirm that there are hungry people in the world; it interprets the hungry to be our brothers and sisters whom we allow to starve.

—Dorothee Soelle

In both the Hebrew Bible and the Christian New Testament, a passion for peace and justice characterizes the truly religious ideal. In text after text, from Psalms to Amos to Jeremias, Yahweh is a God of justice whose challenge culminates in Isaias:

> Is this not the fast I choose
> To loose the bonds of wickedness,
> To undo the thongs of the yoke
> To let the oppressed go free and to
> break every yoke?
> Is it not to share your bread with the hungry
> and bring the homeless poor into your house;
> when you see the naked to cover them,
> and not to hide yourself from your own flesh?
> (Isaias 58:6–7).

Similarly, in the New Testament, Jesus' first words describing his mission are about the poor and oppressed (Luke 4:17–19), and the dramatic scene of the final judgment in Matthew still stands as the test for those who would enter the Kingdom:

I was hungry and you gave me food, I was thirsty and you gave me drink. I was a stranger and you welcomed me. I was naked and you

*clothed me. I was sick and you visited me. I was in prison and you
came to me. (Matt. 25—35-36).*[1]

From the time of the first gathered Christian community, these
challenges have been a motivating ideal. In Acts we read of the impulse, put into immediate practice, of ministry directed to sharing
with all, giving to each as necessary, even selling what was one's
own to help another (2:45). The ministry of *diakonia,* of outreach,
service or mission is being described. This prophetic impulse is the
focus of this chapter.

Outreach has three meanings: to reach out, to extend outward,
to go beyond or surpass. My intention in this chapter is to do the
religious task of interpreting that kind of activity for our own time
and in our own circumstances. Because the religious world of the
Hebrew Bible and early Christianity is not our world, we need to
search our own circumstances to find the most appropriate exercise
of *diakonia,* rather than to translate and repeat. We must find
ways for this prophetic element in ministry to be taken up by the
young. In Chapter 1, I suggested the ministry of *diakonia* as *troublemaking,* directed to institutions rather than individuals. My ecclesial warrant begins in the scriptures and grows out of Christian
social doctrine that teaches there can be no genuine renewal of
mind and heart without concern for social reform. It is inspired by
innumerable women and men among the saints. Bernard Häring,
for example, in *A Theology of Protest,* speaks of the true Christian
as an all-out revolutionary, seeking to overthrow out of a stance of
hope and nonviolence. "I am on the side of Teilhard de Chardin,"
he writes, "whose fundamental position is that the world belongs to
those who can offer it greater hope. We can generally say that
youth and youthful men and women involved in protests are those
who still have that greater hope."[2] I am inspired too by Daniel Berrigan, he of the long haul, who has always known the intimate relationship of resistance and contemplation.[3] And I am inspired by
the presence in our midst of young people in each new generation
whose deepest religious cry is that of outraged, social protest.

---

1. See John R. Donahue, "Biblical Perspectives on Justice," in John Haughey
(ed.) *The Faith that Does Justice* (New York: Paulist, 1977), pp. 68–112 for extended
commentary on this theme.

2. (New York: Farrar, Straus and Giroux, 1970), pp. 6–7; 152.

3. See for example his *The Dark Night of Resistance* (Garden City: Doubleday,
1971).

When Merton Strommen's 1974 study was published, one group of young people stood out as deeply concerned over injustice.[4] At that time, Strommen distinguished them by means of five major characteristics. They were humanitarian, oriented to change, socially involved, concerned over national issues, critical of the institutional church, while at the same time remaining in and considering themselves a part of it.[5] To the sisters and brothers of these young people of the late sixties and early seventies, what does the Youth Minister call for as the contribution to today's world? I suggest it is *diakonia* under the guise of troublemaking, that is, vexing, stirring up, making uncomfortable, inconveniencing, bothering. More specifically, it is these activities directed to institutions. It is the church working to feed the hungry, secure justice for the poor, freedom for the oppressed and sight to the blind by directing attention not to individual persons, but to the social systems in which they live. "If it is true that the church's mission is to offer humanity the hope that God will remain faithful to the divine promise of justice and love, then the church's prophetic role is to keep history open to the fulfillment of this promise and to resist the institutional stabilizing of things."[6] Because acts of troublemaking are directed to institutions, they require social and political skills; because they are done on religious grounds, they arise from nonviolence and humility rather than self-aggrandizement; and because they almost always upset the status quo, they are destined to end in failure, disillusionment and loneliness. At best they will be tolerated, and like Berrigan, those who do them will have to say, "Even if we are tolerated, the tolerance has little of virtue about it; in a time of public irrational upheaval, we are simply another instance of those who fly the coop, kick over traces, or anticwise, hang around to make trouble."[7] Nevertheless, in every group of young people, there are those whose vocation is *diakonia* in the sense of such makers of trouble. And in every age, the church's ministry is incomplete without them. In this chapter I will describe some forms this ministry might take when offered to four institutions: the church itself, schools, work, and government.

---

4. *Op. cit.* See pp. 52–71, "The Cry of Social Protest."

5. *Ibid.*, pp. 53 and 60.

6. David Hollenbach, "A Prophetic Church and the Catholic Sacramental Imagination," in Haughey, *op. cit.,* p. 242.

7. *Op. cit.,* pp. 180–181.

BOTHERING THE CHURCH

Michael Warren and Richard Costello tell of an experience they had a decade ago among eight parishes in Flushing, New York. Having spent four months listening to teen-agers' views and complaints about the church, they and others went to the pastors of the eight parishes and asked them if they would be willing to let the young people try to establish a ninth parish, separate and autonomous, composed of and run by the young people themselves. The pastors agreed, and although the parish was eventually discontinued, it is the example I wish to cite here as opportunity for *diakonia*.[8] Separate, satellite churches are a bother; they are also part of the tradition.

Smaller units born from large churches are a continuous occurrence in Christianity. From Jerusalem, Antioch, Ephesus and Rome, the missionary, diaconal impulse has always been a going-out to establish and set up new communities. In our own times, this move is reoccurring with great strength. One example is the base-satellite church.

There are numerous varieties within this basic style, but the essential principle is the same. There is the large mother congregation housed within a large facility. It becomes a base of outreach ... it is only through a satellite that a church is able to penetrate certain communities. There may be a language or cultural barrier. In some cases the satellite groups may come in regularly to the mother church. In some situations the smaller groups come in once a month for the Lord's supper. In some cases, the satellite congregation never shares.[9]

Even better known examples are the *communidades de bases* or base-communities of Latin America, endorsed by the Catholic bishops at Medellin, Colombia in 1968. These are composed of people reflecting upon their faith and the existential and social consequences of that faith. The purpose of these latter communities is to develop the kind of personal conviction characterized by a greater responsibility for others. Theirs is what Segundo calls "a histori-

---

8. Warren and Costello, *op. cit.*, pp. 117–118.

9. Francis M. Dubose, *How Churches Grow in an Urban World* (Nashville: Broadman, 1978), p. 88.

cal consciousness which, in accord with the gospel, is intent on the social signs of the times, (and) in search of concrete symbols of liberation."[10]

It seems to me that separate youth churches could be established on similar grounds and for similar purposes: (1) a church is needed where the particular emphasis of the members is on social action; (2) the cultural and language barriers may be so great between mother church and young people that the separate church is called for. Both may occur in the same church or youth churches may be set up to take one or the other as their main concern.

(1) Some youth churches will be formed by satellite communities specifically directed to care for the needy by heeding the cry of social protest coming from the young. Decisions about membership, organization, services, finances, minister and place will all be made with the youth themselves. But the qualifying concern will be for social justice. The major ministry of such a church will be to serve people within and beyond the community, to train its members in helping the lonely and rejected, to exercise political skills, and perhaps to remind the church establishment just what it was established for. Certain issues seem to provide natural ministries for such groups. The first issue is hunger. On the domestic level, a youth church can become directly involved in day-care meals, school breakfasts, and malnutrition in its own community by working with church agencies or with groups such as the Food Research and Action Center.[11] On a global level, it can become associated with its own denominational agency or *Bread for the World,* the Christian citizens' movement whose work the socially moved young people will want to know.[12] Another ministry is one such as *Amigos de las Americas,* a group made up of teen-age U.S. volunteers who bring medical assistance and information to families in rural Latin America. Founded by Guy Bevil, a youth director in the Baptist church of Houston, Texas, *Amigos* is a nonprofit organization that encourages any community which wishes to form a local chapter.[13] Over six months are spent in training for a three-week term of duty

---

10. Alfred T. Henelly quotes this in *Theologies in Conflict, The Challenge of Juan Luis Segundo* (Maryknoll: Orbis, 1979), pp. 90–91, 103.

11. 25 West 43 Street, New York, New York 10036. The Food Research and Action Center has a primarily legal thrust, but also serves as a major source of information on food assistance. It is important for local groups.

12. See Arthur Simon, *Bread for the World, op. cit.*

13. Amigos de las Americas, 5618 Star Lane, Houston, Texas, 77027.

in the summer. In learning to bring medical information and services to communities beyond them, the church members learn to address such needs within their own neighborhood borders as well.

A third ministry is with the handicapped, especially with handicapped teen-agers. In 1978, the National Conference of Catholic Bishops approved a pastoral statement which affirmed that "very few people would admit to being prejudiced against handicapped people, yet handicapped people are visibly, sometimes bluntly different from the 'norm' and we react to this difference."[14] Such reactions are difficult for any handicapped person to take, but especially so for handicapped teen-agers. The pastoral statement emphasizes that what handicapped persons need first is acceptance, but it then goes on to suggest that local churches do the following, which could easily provide a ministry for the youth church: (1) Conduct a census aimed at identifying parishioners either with or without church affiliations who have significant disabilities, and invite them into the church. (2) Place emphasis on education of church members on the rights and needs of local handicapped people. (3) Correct the physical design where it hampers the presence of the handicapped; and if new construction is impossible, devise alternate ways to reach the handicapped. (4) Make realistic provisions for handicapped persons to take part in worship services, e.g., signing for the deaf. (5) Design worship services not only toward attendance, but toward full participation and role-taking by the handicapped. Such a program, in a small youth church, can be an invaluable ministry for all concerned; the major caveat would be that the young do not "use" the handicapped as a cause, but engage in a ministry *with,* rather than *to.*

(2) A second kind of youth church is one established as a mission church for young people whose culture is so different that they would not think of participating in the mother church. The Rev. Eugene Langevin of Quincy, Massachusetts, has been pastor of such a church since 1966. At that time, working for the Boston Baptist City Mission Society, he found the recreational programs he ran attracting plenty of "street-corner kids" but was struck by the fact that "all my attempts to speak a word about Christ fell upon deaf ears." Eventually, however, a small group of delinquent boys, whom he called the "unrighteous remnant" and who had been put

---

14. See Lawrence Cronin, "It's Not an Option/Break Through," in *Newsletter* (Religious Education Office, Archdiocese of Boston, 1979), p.4.

out of one church's recreational rooms, began to meet for Bible study several afternnoons a week at a local school.

As we rapped our way through the traditional Bible stories on those autumn and then winter afternoons, the idea gradually emerged that what these kids really needed was a church of their own, a church that could cater to the specific needs they had. For instance, we got the idea that maybe even rock 'n' roll music could be used to praise the Lord. The kids liked the idea of a teen-age church and decided to call it "The Way" after that other little band of folk, the early Christians, who had also been put out of the religious establishment of their day. (Acts 9:2; 19:9, 23; 22:4; 24:14, 22.)[15]

The Way was started. At the same time, to support its work, Langevin took a job as a juvenile probation officer. Some of his probationers began drifting into the program. For the last fourteen years, it has been in operation (Langevin currently doubles as pastor of a small "regular" church; his salary helps pay for the storefront out of which *The Way* operates; the rest is funded entirely by contributions.) As it presently exists, it is a missionary center; its target population is young people between twelve and nineteen presently outside of any Christian church, but its basic goal is "to transmit the spark of God's Holy Spirit to other persons and to nourish the relationship with the living God which that spark will inflame. The purpose of the youth church ... is to provide a setting in which a young person can encounter Jesus Christ for him or herself and then grow in the relationship which that encounter has produced."[16] Langevin describes the church's operation thus:

The youth church takes its origin initially from the faith of one or more Christian individuals who are concerned enough about a particular group of young people to undertake a mission to that group. Eventually, the youth church becomes a spiritual fellowship rooted in the covenant that its young members make to each other. It has officers and committees like other churches. It receives new persons into membership after a suitable period of discipleship training, fol-

---

15. Eugene A. Langevin, "The Youth Church as a Viable Means for Dealing with Juvenile Delinquency" (Newton: unpublished manuscript, 1977), p. 7.

16. *Ibid.,* p. 8

lowed by a believer's baptism. Membership in any case lasts only six months and lapses if not renewed. Membership can be renewed for six months by reading the covenant publicly with the other members at the time each month when the covenant is read during the regular Sunday services.[17]

The objections to such youth churches are predictable. Perhaps the most obvious one is that such settings promote divisiveness and exclusivity. Certainly, this is a possibility. However, the youth church forms described here are established for particular purposes and the second has a terminal point of membership. In both cases, the members are present by choice. (For a church wishing to establish a youth church social-justice mission, the church might want to do so prior to confirmation with that ceremony being a terminus point. However, since a central characteristic of this type of church is the choice element, that could be undermined if all candidates for confirmation were required to belong.) In the case of *The Way*, the teen-age congregants do not belong to any other church; in addition, they can belong only until they are nineteen. At that time, their mode of participation is changed to "adult fellowship," which is an adjunct to the youth church, a reversal of the situation in most Protestant churches that have "youth fellowships." Most important, however, is that each church takes seriously the disaffection the young may have for a more traditional setting, and sees itself providing an opportunity for the young to worship and to hear the gospel in a setting that is "home" to them.[18]

The second objection is that what is being described is not really a church but a social agency. The two responses I would make are (a) churches *are* social agencies, that is, they are *social* in being groups of people who unite in communal, societal and social forms; and they are *agencies* in being initiators of activities. However, they are *not only* social agencies; (b) ministry is both priestly and pro-

---

17. *Ibid.*, p. 13. Those wishing further information can write to the Rev. Eugene Langevin at *The Way Up*, 329A Newport Avenue, Quincy, MA 02170.

18. I hope the reader will not read these Youth Church suggestions as contradicting advocacy for full participation in the church as suggested in Chapter 6. They are intended, instead, as an example or a complement of such participation. Experience suggests no one way as the best or only way. For some, it may be more politically expedient to speak not of Youth *Churches,* but of a Youth *House* Church; a Youth Ecclesiola; or of Youth Communidades de Bases.

phetic, and at one time or another, persons will emphasize different aspects of that ministry. Most times, the priestly elements of teaching, prayer and community are to the forefront. Such churches as I am describing, while including these, are geared to the more prophetic aspects of ministry: *kerygma* and *diakonia*. The church as a larger corporate body, in its national and international forms, can certainly tolerate and most certainly needs smaller congregations within it that emphasize these ministries.

A third objection is that when a church is established for social justice, it may be more for the benefit of the members than those toward whom help is directed. This is the most serious objection, to my mind, but a superb way of learning the political skills and realities of troublemaking. Just as the North Atlantic nations have had to learn that their social and economic policies contribute to the exploitation and dependency of Latin American nations, so too a Youth Minister must learn that the ministry of *diakonia* is a standing in solidarity with, and never a doing to. If the first is their intention and attitude, those among whom they minister will recognize it and do them the graceful favor of eventually explaining that they are no longer needed.

In the long run, the advantages of such moves outweigh the possible and sometimes quite real disadvantages. The poor, the needy, the oppressed are kept from being marginalized. Young people have the opportunity to grow in their religious identity, and in the first case to do work to which they feel called. In many cases, such participation proves to be an apprenticeship for a life's vocation in ministry. And for most, participation in a youth church can be a powerful learning about the nature of the church as a body engaged in many ministries, acting from many different perspectives. "This pluralistic approach is liberating in itself since it presents the Gospel not as a finished system imposed on us by the church but as an open-ended tradition," writes Gregory Baum.[19] Speaking precisely to the appeal of an ethic of social justice, he comments that the appeal of such an ethic may, ironically, become important for the young "especially if this approach is *not* made normative for them. Only after living with the new ideas for a while in a non-threatening situation do many of us become moved to action and capable of assimilating these ideas as our own."[20]

---

19. "Spirituality and Society," in *The Social Imperative, op. cit.,* p. 145.
20. *Ibid.,* p. 146.

UPSETTING THE SCHOOL

Throughout this book, I have spoken many times about the institutional form of schooling, primarily because it is the place where most young people spend most of their time. In this section, I want to address the school as a place of *diakonia*, of social and political troublemaking. The ministry may take place best among those schools operated by church bodies, although ideally this ministry should be directed to all schools.

In Chapter 3, "*Didache*, the Ministry of Teaching," I named several curricular emphases, one of which is social reconstruction.[21] In that emphasis, teaching is directed to social issues, to understanding the gospel in the light of bringing a new social order into existence, and to protesting oppression. Among teachers and students, some—not all—will see this as their main educational purpose. In my judgment, if we accept educational principles of pluralism, they should be encouraged to try. "Protesting students are engaged in a struggle against many forms of oppression, but they are willing to put a good deal of their considerable energy and talent to work in the struggle against the oppression most immediate to their own experience, and that is the oppression of schooling."[22] If this exists, ministry could begin with a talking stage where students discuss the oppression they experience and possible ways to address it.

One set of activities that might accomplish this is: (1) engage in analysis of current school practices, and if necessary, formulate alternatives to these practices. (In one high school intent on this ministry, the principal encouraged students to examine the price of junk foods sold within the school, to discover if this was a source of exploitation); (2) become involved not only in learning one's own political and legal powers and rights, but also the distribution of and legal constraints upon power in and around the school system. This extends to the powers others such as groups of teachers have, especially within their unions; (3) begin to engage in political action over specific issues, some of which may have to do with curriculum, others with more broadly political overtones (school-board appointments; busing).[23]

---

21. See p. 63, above,
22. John S. Mann, "Political Power and the High School Curriculum," in Eisner and Vallance, *op. cit.*, pp. 148-149.
23. *Ibid.*, p. 151.

The next step would be gaining acceptance of these activities within the school itself. If the above are admitted as valid procedures, social action might be the focus of one or another "extracurricular" club, but is more valued if included as part of the curriculum for a semester or two, perhaps in the junior or senior year. As with the church within a church, the best form might be a school within a school. In such a design, students could then concentrate on (a) the examination of materials for sexism, racism and classism, which can be aided by innumerable agencies, from the federal government to the *Council on Interracial Books for Children;*[24] (b) learning the techniques and procedures by which education becomes oppressive, whether intended or not (using such resources as Brian Wren's *Education for Justice*[25] and Paulo Freire's *Education for Critical Consciousness;*[26] and (c) forming alliances with like-minded teachers, while cultivating support in related professional and paraprofessional groupings. Mann writes that such an approach will "strike a responsive chord in a large number of teachers who entered the profession with ideals they have long since learned out of necessity to keep buried away."[27]

Let me stress here that such troublemaking is not envisioned as a copout or escape from the need for the tools and skills of literacy that are necessary in the society. Instead it is directed to a schooling that is equitable and just for all. The second volume of the Carnegie Council on Children's Report (*All Our Children* was the first) was published while this book was being written, and serves to underscore these concerns. A sobering and troubling report, entitled *Small Futures: Children, Inequality and the Limits of Liberal Reform,*[28] it has both good and bad news about schooling. The good news is that while gaps in unemployment and income between blacks and whites have not closed since the sixties, the educational gap has closed somewhat. This testifies to the positive force schools can be. The bad news is that schooling continues to hurt many. Low-income students are more subject to suspension or expulsion than others and are disproportionately classified as mentally re-

---

24. *Council on Interracial Books for Children* publishes a bulletin eight times a year directed to these issues, and includes suggested and precise activities for students and teachers. 1841 Broadway, New York, New York 10023.
25. (Maryknoll: Orbis, 1977).
26. (New York: Seabury, 1973).
27. Mann, *op. cit.*, p. 152.
28. Edited by Richard Delone (New York: Harcourt, Brace, Jovanovich 1979).

tarded or learning disabled. As a result they are assigned to classes where they receive minimal teaching. Indeed, intensive observation finds that teachers of low-income children minimize discussion and interaction while emphasizing pure rote learning.[29]

Obviously, the fault is not the individual teacher's or even an individual school's. It is the fault and responsibility of an entire society that persists in denying justice. The argument I am making here for troublemaking is that to change this society, our young people must learn the forms that social injustice takes, and the political and social processes that can remedy them. These learnings are an essential subject for study and teaching, but ideally such schooling in justice will go beyond rhetoric.

In a world of grave injustice, where all yet have a fundamental equality, education for justice will ... seek to increase people's knowledge of injustice and inequality, to widen their range of comparison and to create a critical consciousness which turns grievance or guilt into hopeful and constructive action ...

Yet, because it is concerned with justice, it must itself be just. It cannot be a propaganda exercise that gives facts-with-slogans and tells or persuades people what to do. It has to be a dialogue holding together conviction and commitment with openness and trust.[30]

INCONVENIENCING THE WORK-WORLD

The report of the Panel on Youth of the President's Advisory Committee begins:

As the labor of children has become unnecessary to society, school has been extended for them. With every decade, the length of schooling has increased, until a thoughtful person must ask whether society can conceive of no other way for youth to come into adulthood.[31]

The report documents the reality that school is not, nor can it be, an environment giving all the necessary opportunities for becoming

---

29. "Educational Equity? Not in U.S.," in *Boston Sunday Globe* (August 26, 1979), p. 81.

30. Wren, *op. cit.*, p. 56.

31. Coleman, *op. cit.*, p. 1.

adult, and concludes by making a number of alternative proposals, which allow youth to be more than "students." In the two previous sections, I have discussed youth communities as one alternative and a change in the school structure as another. In this section I encourage action toward a third, this one associated with the world of work. I want to emphasize it as an alternative, presently not appropriate for all young people, any more than is the youth church, or the social-justice-schooling project. However, considering it is an activity Youth Ministers can engage in as they seek to minister among the young.

One way young people might acquire opportunities for wider experience, especially in assuming responsibility and mixing with a variety of ages, is the encouragement of alternation of school and work. Work-school alternation has three basic forms: (1) the alternative of schooling; (2) schooling and a job together; (3) a job alone as an alternative to schooling. Presently the first and the second are available; I am suggesting all three as options. Present practice already includes the second alternative under the title "work-study." However, the current design and purposes are in rather specific instances: planned for lower-class and poorer students seeking jobs because they need money, geared to those wishing training in manual skills who are not considered "academic material," offered for young people terminating high school who do not plan any further schooling. Scharf and Wilson criticize the ideology behind many such programs, pointing out that where they operate, "certain students end up being 'sorted' into a social caste of undereducated 'laborers,' " and the learning techniques often employed "fail to provide the kinds of experiences likely to facilitate necessary development growth."[32] Two undesirable results then occur: the first, capable poorer youth tend to overlook careers that might require college training; the second, middle or upper-income young people ignore skilled labor careers that might be more economically viable. "In addition to stratifying the interests of youth prematurely and often inappropriately, the overall social consequence of such programs is to create a fixed undereducated working class with anachronistic skills and a white-collar, socially advantaged elite with overpopulation and insecurity."[33]

Equally disadvantageous, however, and my concern for ministry is the situation created by keeping *all* young people isolated

---

32. Scharf and Wilson, *op. cit.,* p. 434.
33. *Ibid.*

from others of different ages and from the social possibilities the work-world offers but schooling does not. Even for those who continue to choose the alternative of schooling, full time, a difference occurs with a both/and option rather than an either/or, as is the case for most students after high school in college or graduate programs. I am also concerned to challenge the meaning of *work* as the *equivalent* of a job. As I have suggested, at least three possibilities exist. For some, school is their full-time work; for others, school plus job provides two ways of working; for still others, a job may be the main work experience.

To secure the benefits of such alternation, Youth Ministers would need to engage in several troublemaking activities. One is to find job openings and/or businesses willing to take on the young as full-time workers. The range of work opportunities would have to be extensive, since they would be designed for all young people, including the college bound. This would mean securing the help of such institutions as hospitals, clinics, law firms and government agencies as viable environments, in far greater numbers than now allowable. The second activity is to end time-limit restrictions, as we presently do post-high-school, for completion of high school, and for jobs during the year. This would make jobs available for a year, or two, or three, or a semester, or however long appears feasible. Presently, the anachronistic summer vacation is the only acceptable time allowing for all-day work outside school. This means the Youth Minister will have to lobby for extension of the school year to a year-round situation, perhaps on a trimester basis, where alternation would be possible throughout the entire year. Side benefits would be more efficient use of physical plants, year-round employment of teachers and the end of a pejorative meaning to the term "high-school drop-out." No longer would it be any more unusual to leave high school for a year or two than it presently is to do the same in college.

A third activity is the sticky one of pointing out the need for salaries to be paid to the young. We are not talking about playing at a job or volunteering, although the latter may provide a foot in the door. Coleman proposes in this event "broad experimentation with a dual minimum wage, lower for youth than for adult workers."[34]

Once the value of alternation is agreed upon as important for all young people because it provides far more complexity, respon-

---

34. *Op. cit.,* p. 168.

sibility, experience and justice than presently offered, the partnerships needed for the venture must be taken into account. For young people and Youth Ministers who see the importance of this ministry, the central activity will be making alliances. Often, nothing is attempted because people work on far too individualistic a basis. To accomplish work-school alternation, three major alliances could be formed: (1) Among Youth Ministers themselves, across denominational and church lines. Presently Youth Ministers do meet, but often it is toward exchange of intra-church programs only, and in narrow parochial groupings. (2) With both school and business or professional agencies, especially persons in authority willing to encourage the participation of the young in the work-world. (3) With juvenile advocates in denominational, community, and governmental agencies. To believe that Youth Ministers are the only ones who care for or are working for the interests of young people is naïve. The search for like-minded persons in school, business, government and the professions should yield a corps of dedicated people eager to help this generation of youth move toward adulthood with enriched and extended opportunities beyond the structures of the present.

STIRRING UP THE GOVERNMENT

City, state and federal governments already have much to say about young people. In concluding this chapter, I want to address three governmental policy areas related to a Youth Ministry of *diakonia*. Each could be an extraordinary means of promoting justice for all young people; presently, each is in an area that needs some stirring up, since it disproportionately affects the poorer and less fortunate youth in our society.

(1) *Military Service.* During the suspension of the draft, the United States government has had to rely on other procedures to encourage the young to enlist in military service. Several programs now exist that are directed toward recruitment of high-school people: the Junior Reserve Office Training Corps, the Delayed Entry Program, the Armed Services Vocational Aptitude Battery, and the Program for Increased Education. Although the general public may not know of these, high-school administrators and personnel are well aware of them since the target population for each is the fourteen to seventeen year-old age range.

In addition to the enormous questions of pacifism and war that are distinct but related issues, these programs need to be studied carefully. In a recent well-documented and trenchant criticism, Eileen Lindner pointed out the inequities of such programs:

> ... *relatively few middle- or upper-class Americans have direct contact with the military recruitment program and little experience of the pressures which make the program work. It is no accident that most schools with JROTC units are populated by the children of the working poor, children for whom college and graduate school are out of the question, whose older siblings are already unemployed or underemployed, and who will themselves emerge into the job market with few "contacts," little in the way of commercially useful skills, and very likely, little sense of direction.*[35]

She details the errors, false claims, and disproportionate federal backing of such programs. Youth Ministers who encourage young people to enter the military out of altruistic motives for their future would do well to study government investment in these plans. We need continuing examination of the kind of leadership-training materials provided, the existence of false or inaccurate information in the recruitment literature, and the need for federal monitoring so that no young person is unwittingly "conned" into believing a promise that does not get fulfilled. Such study means careful homework and is an important, although troublemaking and trouble-generating ministry.

(2) Military programs should be studied in tandem with alternative service programs. Where the United States government now spends, via the Department of Defense, more than $1000 per recruit to encourage young people to enter military service,[36] it should be challenged to expend at least as much for presently existing programs such as the Peace Corps, VISTA, Teachers Corps, Neighborhood Youth Corps, Youth Conservation Corps, and the University Year in Action. Recruitment for these could be widened considerably, providing young people far more valuable and diverse options than military service.

For this to happen, several elements of alternative service programs would need to be changed. Besides an increased budget, they would have to be made available prior to age eighteen, be shortened

---

35. "Our Classist Army/ How the Pentagon Cons Kids," in *Christianity and Crisis* (May 16, 1977), p. 109.

36. *Ibid.*, p. 106.

to a one-year commitment if desired (presently they require two), and extended to and publicized among all young people. On their part, as I have pointed out in a previous section, states and cities would have to change compulsory school-attendance laws to allow for a one or two or several year absence from high school with the option of returning if the young person wished that. Once more I should note that presently such possibilities are perfectly permissible in college and graduate school.

The particular benefits of alternative service programs are many. In *Youth, Transition to Adulthood,* the authors suggest several motives for a young person to engage in them. Among these are a dissatisfaction with school and with the isolation it often fosters, always being asked to prepare and never to do, the gaining of opportunity for responsible activity affecting others, interdependent work with persons of all ages toward commonly held goals, and the management of one's own affairs.[37] As with contemporary work-study programs, however, such programs often are biased toward only one segment of society, and even seen as ways of relieving hard-core unemployment. As long as this view exists, all young people will be losers, as will be the society itself.

(3) The discomforting issue of vouchers still needs attention. Until this time, with the exception of the state of California,[38] funding for parochial school is the main public association people have with the voucher question, and Youth Ministers have not always seen this issue as theirs. They need to realize that the present governmental policy of giving money to any young person who wishes to stay in school after age sixteen, and even more prevalent, the issuance of grants to college and graduate-school students is discriminatory as it exists. That is, by virtue of financial grants, the government gives a disproportionate value to schooling as an option for young people, which (a) discriminates against those who do not wish this option; (b) at times is chosen solely because this is the only way the young can get funds. A young person wishing training in fields less compatible with school courses (for example, newspaper reporting, horse racing, and portrait painting) or a young person whose style of learning is different from a cognitively oriented college or university education is not given equal opportunity under the particular laws offering federal grants.

---

37. Coleman, *op. cit.,* pp. 171–172.

38. See especially John Coons and Stephen Sugarman, *Education by Choice, The Case for Family Control* (Berkeley: University of California Press, 1978).

In contrast, a voucher system that would make funds available to all young people, for training or education at some other public or private institution besides a school, ought to be instituted. Engaged in small, experimental situations, this possibility is an ideal one for churches and/or local communities to take on and could be administered by a team of Youth Ministers initially with small groups of teen-agers. If the federal government is averse to the proposal, state and/or city governments could be bothered enough to try. The President's Advisory Committee suggests that as brief a time as a three-year-span is enough to determine the benefits of such programs.[39]

The ministry of troublemaking described in this chapter is by no means complete. Major issues such as juvenile justice and institutional racism have been alluded to only in passing. My intention has not been to ignore them, but to suggest some possible options for activity that are good in themselves and that may be catalysts for other issues more pertinent to particular situations. No matter what is chosen, however, Youth Ministers must realize their actions will make them unpopular. In political matters, we tend to separate justice from peace at least in part because the latter *appears* to be less trouble. The school, the church, the work world, and the government are comfortable as they are and do not like to be upset; they are, they believe, at peace, and wish everyone saw them so. In this event, it is good to read these lines on troublemaking from *The Social Imperative:*

The governing bodies of society are perceived as the guardians of harmony, they are the representatives of God's will, and hence it is sinful to make trouble, to rock the boat, or to organize dissent. A certain Christian spirituality suggests that in a situation of conflict it is the powerless who are to blame. But Jesus was a troublemaker from the beginning. He was willing to disrupt peace and unity for the sake of justice and truth. The revolution brought by him demands conversion and change of life.[40]

---

39. *Op. cit.,* pp. 170–171.
40. *Op. cit.,* p. 83.

Chapter Seven
STUDY AND PRACTICE

ACTIVITY 33
Troublemaking and the School
(Lyle Jenks)

The following situations are designed to provoke and encourage discussion/action with reference to possible occurrences in schools. The procedure used might be simple discussion, or you may use the following more structured format.

1. If the group is large enough, ask each person to choose one of the situations.
2. Participants should group with others who have made the same choice.
3. Decide together the *issues* raised by the situation.
4. Explore what *options* exist to address the situation.
5. Evaluate the reasons *pro* and *con* for choosing a particular option.
6. After forty to forty-five minutes, be ready to report back to the group using this form: "Given the situation considered, we recommend ... , for the following reasons. ..."

A. You are an eighth-grade student who has been recognized for your special interests and abilities in science; you've been placed in an advanced-standing class that meets in the senior high wing, at the far opposite corner of the floor plan from where you have your previous class. That previous class is gym, and you find it a near physical impossibility to shower, dress, and move to the other end of the building in the few minutes allowed.

Under the new discipline code, which makes no exceptions and listens to no excuses, you've been given demerit points twice in the last week for being late to the advanced-standing science class.

B. You are an administrator, given responsibility by your superior for enforcing the discipline code in your building. Responsibility, but not the authority. You're personally convinced that any code is valuable only as a guide against which you compare the merits and circumstances of each discipline "problem," and should not be used as absolute law. You recognize, however, that certain students have already learned how to manipulate the system, and are buying their way out. Too, you see that most teachers on your staff will sell cheaply—demerits are not assigned for "punishable offenses" in a hope that the kids will save their real acting out for someone else's classroom.

And, as the administrator, you listen to your superior's ravings about how your conversations with students who have ended up in the "BOX," an oversized closet used as a solitary confinement for detention, defeat the whole philosophy and purpose of this discipline style.

C. You are a senior high teacher. One of your nonacademic responsibilities is to monitor the twelfth-grade study hall. Seniors are free to adjourn to the outside courtyard for smoking and conversation, but they are forbidden to cross the street to a newly opened sub and soda shop.

The principal instructs you to enforce this new regulation.

D. You are a parent who is very much concerned, among other things, with the lack of career counseling offered through the guidance department of the regional school. Your letters to the editor of the local paper have been rather sharp, critical, and specific; you recently listed percentages of the graduating class who would be going on to college or joining the armed forces. Gleaning these statistics from the administration's newsletter to the townspeople, your purpose was to question whether other options are held up for the students to examine, or whether seniors are basically left hanging if they fit neither of these molds.

Through the grapevine, you hear that the guidance department staff has been called on the carpet, and asked whether they know you, under what circumstances they have talked with you, whether they have ever released information to you, or have ever caught you in acts of unauthorized snooping in the school's confidential files of individual students' performances and potential.

E. You are an older adult whose only direct connection to the local school system is in your role as taxpayer. A decade ago, you were sold on the need for a new regional high school; you're still paying for it. Now, ground is being broken for two decentralized middle schools; the architects indicate that they will be show places.

The new property-tax rate came out earlier this month. It's up 45 percent, and the increased school allocation is in large part the reason. While the town is growing rapidly, the tax base is being outrun by the school-age population.

By law, the town select board cannot curry and scrutinize the school budget as it must all other public expenditures. Rather than a "base zero" funding, the school budget is by and large a lump-sum deal.

Town meeting is tonight.

ACTIVITY 34
"Can You See? Then Help!":
An Activity for a Youth Church
Engaged in Social Action
(Barbara Sinclair)

PURPOSE:

The long-range goal: to encourage young people to participate in outreach activities all of their lives.

The short-range goal: to encourage the young people to participate in an outreach program for the blind.

The objective: to become aware of the needs of the blind, and to realize that a youth group is able to help the blind in an outreach program.

BACKGROUND:

The topic of outreach is viewed here from this perspective: a youth minister can help her or his youth group to reach out to others instead of being exclusively, or almost exclusively, self-centered.

In order to reach out, they must be aware of the needs of others, and what those specific needs are. Youth can reach out to many (elderly, shut-ins, the deaf, blind, retarded, emotionally disturbed, orphans, juvenile offenders), but in our small group, we began talking about possible avenues of outreach to the handicapped, and focused on blind youth. It was these discussions that sparked our interest in this design.

193

CHAPTER SEVEN

INTENDED AUDIENCE:

This activity is designed for senior high-school students. However, the design is universal enough for seventh graders through adults.

TIME:

approximately two hours.

MATERIALS NEEDED:

Blackboard, chalk and eraser, *or* newsprint, tape for hanging it, and markers
Double-coated tape and glue
Paper and pencils for each participant
Blindfolds for each participant
Different textured materials such as felt, yarn or construction paper shapes, spools, tinfoil, crayons

PROCEDURE:

1. The leader explains that everyone is going to simulate a situation that will aid him or her in understanding blindness.
2. The members divide into small groups, preferably of five or six.
3. Each group chooses a recorder and a leader. The recorder writes down observations he or she makes about what he or she sees or hears; the leader oversees the project.
4. Each member of the group is blindfolded, except the recorder and the leader.
5. A. Distribute materials evenly between groups.
   B. Ask members to decide upon a theme in each group, to be the subject of a collage or picture.
   C. While the members make the collage or picture (allow twenty minutes), the recorder writes down observations, and the leader facilitates the making of the group collage.
6. Remove the blindfolds.
7. Each leader asks the following of the group members, while the recorder notes the answers:
   A. What did you feel like when you tried to communicate with each other?
   B. What would have helped you communicate better? What skills did you need?

194

    C. What type of thing would you like to do, but cannot, when you are unable to see?

    D. What could a seeing person, or a group of sighted persons, do to help those who cannot see?

8. The recorder then shares her or his observations with the group, describing what he or she noticed during the process.

9. The leader of each group then asks how that group, as unhandicapped, can help the blind in the wider society; the recorder notes the answers.

10. All come together from the groups. Time should be given to each group's responses; the Youth Minister highlighting these on board or newsprint.

11. The leader offers other concrete ideas for helping the handicapped, which have been prepared in advance: people who are resources in the area; community agencies; bibliography—and discusses these with the group.

12. The group discusses the possibility of following up one of the suggestions made by doing some concrete activity.

EVALUATION:

This can take place afterward among the leaders, with leaders and a representative group of the young people, or with the entire group at the end of the meeting. The following questions can be used as guidelines: 1. What was the young people's response to the design? 2. Did they decide on further concrete action? 3. If yes, why? If no, why not? 4. What should the group do next?

ACTIVITY 35
Establishing a Youth Church:
A Blueprint

The following activity is designed to outline essential elements for a group wishing to set up a youth church. The elements may take as long as a year to accomplish or may be initiated and begun in a few weeks. Each church will eventually take on its own character. The blueprint is for the church, not the church for the blueprint! After gathering the group together you might proceed as follows:

1. Opening Prayer: Recite together the *Veni, Sancte Spiritus,* the Sequence for Pentecost, or another appropriate prayer to the Holy Spirit.

2. Opening Reading: Read from Acts 2 or choose another reading close to the history and characteristics of the persons involved.

3. Overall Goal: Have the group write a statement that attempts to describe the group's ultimate purpose in coming together.

4. Overall Objectives: Have the group write the more specific activities which it hopes to accomplish together. (These might be few and modest as a beginning.)

5. Tasks and Processes: Have the group list some of the tasks and processes that they agree to engage in together.

6. Resources: Have the group list resources that can be called upon. Include the following: people, places, things, hardware, software, materials, music, color, dreams, food.

7. Commitments: Have the group list the commitments they agree to make with one another.

8. Closing: Close with worship/liturgy.

ACTIVITY 36
Studying the Services:
A Letter-Writing Project

The purpose of this exercise is to gain information, approaches and understanding of military service by contacting as many informed and diverse sources as possible. If personal interviews are possible, these can be follow-up actions to the letters.

1. Have the groups decide whom they will contact.

2. Have the groups decide what kinds of questions they wish to ask. Some suggested background reading would include: the section on Youth and the Military in Chapter 7 of this book; the article, "Our Classist Army/How the Pentagon Cons Kids," by Eileen Lindner (*Christianity and Crisis,* May 16, 1977, p. 109); promotional material from local recruitment centers and so on.

3. Suggested contacts:
   Local recruitment personnel for the services
   Local and state government officers from all major parties
   Representatives of the American Civil Liberties Union
   Military Chaplains
   Representatives of Pacifist Groups
   Representatives of the Society of Friends (Quakers)
   Division of Church and Society, National Council of Churches

4. Have the group members report back regarding responses they have received.

5. Have groups formulate some specific conclusions and recommendations based upon their experience.

ACTIVITY 37
Capital Punishment and Prisons
(Timothy Morrison)

Capital punishment—the death penalty—has received and continues to receive a lot of consideration these days. Is it right, is it proper to condemn individuals to death? Is incarceration the answer to the breaking of the law? Do our prisons need reforming? Most of us simply talk about these issues without actually getting too involved with the emotions and the reality of arrest, search, booking, incarceration. This program offers a suggested format for the experiencing of these situations.

PURPOSE:

To enable the youth to have a greater sensitivity for the plight of the imprisoned individual; to develop modes of ministry to the imprisoned.

CHAPTER SEVEN

PROCEDURE:

The following is an outline for a four-session program on these concerns. It is the feeling of the writer that a minimum of four sessions is necessary to explore fully the aspects of these issues.

SESSION I. CAPITAL PUNISHMENT

Suggested Resource: *Criminal Justice Issues,* Volume 1, Number 6, January 1975, a news service of the Criminal Justice Priority Team of the Commission for Racial Justice of the United Church of Christ. This particular issue considers capital punishment both pro and con. A written debate is offered within the issue. An annotated bibliography of films, pamphlets, and books on the topic of captial punishment is also found within this newsletter. Copies can be obtained by writing to: United Church of Christ, Commission for Racial Justice, 132 West 31st Street, New York, New York 10001.

Perhaps one's own denomination would have some publication on this issue, in which case that probably should be the one to utilize. Procure some copies of some material that lift up both the pros and cons of capital punishment; distribute them a week in advance of the program, then meet to discuss and to debate the issues. The U.C.C. C.R.J. publication listed above gives material that highlights religious considerations, biblical writings, Christ and the new covenant. These should most assuredly be a part of any consideration of capital punishment.

Important in this consideration is that both sides be raised fairly. An advisor should seek to maintain that sense of fairness and should prevent any youth from being excoriated for his/her beliefs and position on the issue. This particular session should end with a spirit of reconciliation and acceptance so that the group does not leave feeling divided. This can be realized by summarizing the positions and then going into a short reflection on the importance of acceptance of each other, the sense of community that we seek and share. Close with prayer.

SESSION II. PRISONS, PAROLE, PROBATION WITHIN THE STATE (COUNTY)

In this second session invite someone from the State corrections department. (If your State is too large to permit that, then seek out someone on a county level.) Have the guest describe what the prison-probation-parole system is like in the State. What are the usual sentences for various crimes; do judges have leeway in sentencing or do the law codes prescribe a specific sentence? Consider how this particular department is structured in the State and what this suggests about the priority of criminal rehabilitation and the persons serviced (e.g., in the State of Maine prisons, probation and parole fall under the jurisdiction of the Department of Mental Health and Corrections). What does the guest see as the primary problem in the penal system in the State? What corrections or advancements need to be made? Of what should citizens be aware? What might citizens do to help in/with the correctional institutions and with those on probation or parole? This type of presentation should lead to a free and open questioning by the youth.

SESSION III. THE REAL THING?

Quite simply, this program carries a hidden agenda. There is the program that is announced and that the group believes is going to take place. Then there is the program that happens in the midst of the first.

Schedule an activity that is pertinent to the theme at hand. This could be a further consideration of some issues raised in the previous week(s). One might wish to play a tape or film on prison situations. Check through the resources that are available. All that is needed is about a fifteen-minute lead-in . . . and now for the other program . . . :

Arrange with the local police department to crash the group's meeting with a "warrant" for the arrest of two of the group members. Pre-arrange *with these two persons* and *with their parents.* Explain that this is to be a mock arrest but that it will seem very real. The youth will be frisked and taken to the police station for "booking." Parental permission is needed in writing both for the church and the police station. Ask for complete confidentiality. In discussion with the two youth and the police determine some offense that is believable, i.e., when the police come to make the mock arrest, it will seem very real and very possible; otherwise, the play will be seen through. (When my youth group had this experience, I was fortunate to have an attorney as a youth adviser. He accompanied the youth to the police station as legal counsel; I remained with the group. You might plan on sending an adviser with the arrested members as an added measure.) Arrange with the police to arrive about fifteen minutes into your program so that all of your youth will be present and all will seem natural. After the officers and youth and adviser leave, be sensitive to feelings. Draw out reactions but do not force; otherwise, some may not believe it to be real. Attempt to go back into the scheduled program and continue with it if the group seems amenable; however, emotionally, they most likely will simply want to sit and wait for the youth to return or to get a telephone call to find out what is happening.

Have the adviser who accompanied the arrested youth telephone the meeting place to report that the parents have been notified and that the youth will be released and will return shortly to the meeting. Share this with the group. When the youth are brought back, invite the arresting officer to join the group (inform officer in advance). Bring the officer into the group with an introduction similar to this: "I sensed some rather angry feelings when Officer ... came with this job to do and had to take ... away. I thought perhaps it might be good if we could sit and talk about what happened and why and what our feelings were. It might help us feel better." Allow questions and conversations to flow freely a while. Officer and advisers should be prepared for some bitter feelings or anger to surface. When the feelings seem dissipated or the moment opportune, then share with the group that the experience was a set-up.

Now discuss the reasons for doing such a program. This type of situation is common, virtually an everyday experience to various segments of our society. Sometimes it is justified and at other times one would question the necessity of it. Most of those gathered in the group for the program will never know the trauma of having a family member taken off to jail or even experience in any manner an arrest. This program has given them that experience. How did they feel and why? Can they understand how police are sometimes held in disdain by certain segments of society? What might be done to minister to families and individuals who experience arrest?

SESSION IV. LOCKED UP

This is perhaps the hardest aspect of the program to arrange. One must find a county sheriff or local police chief who is willing to take the risk and to cooperate. Arrange for the members of your group to be locked up overnight in a jail. This particular youth group met at the church early in the evening on a Friday. Here they sat with a district judge, also a member of the parish, who spoke to the youth about the court room proceedings and sentencing procedure at which point the judge "sentenced" us all to an overnight in the jail. The group proceeded to the county jail house where each person was booked on a possible but phoney offense, frisked, photographed, fingerprinted and jailed. All was done by the book except that the group was not strip-searched as is the common practice. After breakfast, the following morning, the group was set free.

In planning this experience, meet with the law official to discuss the full aspect of the program and to explain why being locked up would be such an invaluable experience. Consider the possible legal problems. This group procured trip insurance along with receiving parental permission for the experience. Parents and youth were assured that the cells in which the youth would be incarcerated would be separate from the regular inmates.

A caution is to request that no publicity take place before the event. Local media oftentimes hear rumor of the pending stay and want to do a story on it. This is to be avoided if at all possible. Follow-up stories are fine, though.

Process this jail experience at the next regularly scheduled gathering of the group. To do the processing, give the following discussion guide to the youth as they are released from prison:

Our program this Sunday evening is to be a relaxed sharing time. It is my hope that those of you who have gone through the jail experience will be able to convey some of the feelings of that to those who have not. I would hope that this entire month's experiences as you encountered them personally might be explored and shared.

I would ask you to read the following material and questions and give them serious thought; perhaps you might even jot down a few notes. This will enable you to better remember your night in jail.

Some things to think about:

"The dilemma of how to maintain domestic peace without killing, maiming, or banishing those who were identified as 'offenders' was solved in the late 1700's by the invention of 'doing time' in a prison. The realization of the total failure of that invention has touched off here in the middle and late 1900's a trial and error search for 'alternatives.' "

(*World Update* #3)

In Maine we have a Bureau of Mental Health and Corrections. In many states the department which oversees the prison-probation system is entitled "the Bureau or Department of Corrections." How does this title reflect the reality of the major aspect of such a bureau, i.e., prisons and persons?

"Prisons, as they exist in this country, are set up for one reason—to punish... Bars, fences and walls are the actual restraints that separate the incarcerated from the rest of society. Within this mini-society, the movements and activities of those inside are very tightly controlled and monitored."

(Criminal Justice Issues Oct. 1976)

"Parole ... is ultimately a paradox. Parole is deemed a reward for good behavior in prison. The 'good risks' are released early, under supervision, for a fixed number of months or years. That leaves the 'bad risks' in prison to serve out their sentences and return to the streets with no supervision at all. And even those who are granted parole are often denied a real chance to re-integrate by the inadequacy of community services and programs for vocational training and job placement, family counseling, mental and physical health care, housing and financial assistance."

(Criminal Justice Issues Nov.-Dec. 1975)

What were your feelings as you were booked, i.e., fingerprinted and photographed? How did you feel as you were issued your bedding and took the walk to the cell? What were your reactions when you saw the toilet–wash bowl facilities? How did you feel and what did you think as the cell door went shut? How do you think serving time in jail rehabilitates an inmate? After this month of experiences how do you now view the corrections system?
Please read the following passages: Matthew 25:31–46; Colossians 4:2–4; Hebrews 13:1–3.

These are a few of the references within the Bible to prison. In light of your experience, how do you feel about Jesus' teachings in verses 36, 39, 40, in the twenty-fifth chapter of Matthew?
Paul was one of the major apostles of the church. His ministry and teaching were most crucial in the lives of the early church. Much of what we have of Paul's writings indicates that he was im-

prisoned when he wrote the letters to the people in the churches. What do you think he must have felt being a man of God, imprisoned for his faith? Do you think that you would have heeded his advice on faith matters knowing that he was in jail?

What is the role of the Christian pertaining to prisons and the whole system of corrections?

What can we do as a Pilgrim Fellowship as an expression of what we have learned and experienced through this month's programs?

RESOURCES:

National Council on Crime and Delinquency, Continental Plaza, 411 Hackensack Avenue, Hackensack, New Jersey 07601.

"New Media News No. 8", October, 1974, Office for Audio Visuals, United Church of Christ, 1505 Race Street, Philadelphia, Pennsylvania, 19102.

"Criminal Justice Issues," Commission for Racial Justice, 132 West 31st Street, New York, New York 10001.

"Prison" filmstrip and cassette, $15, Urbex Affiliates, Inc. 474 Thurston Road, Rochester, New York 14619.

"An Eye for an Eye," by M. Jack Griswold, Holt, Rinehart and Winston, New York, N.Y.

"The Problems of Prisons," by David Greenbert, 25¢, American Friends Service Committee, 160 North 15th Street, Philadelphia, Pennsylvania 19102.

"Trends", July–August, 1972, 75¢, Geneva Press, Room 200, Witherspoon Building, Philadelphia, Pennsylvania 19107.

"Case for Reform," 24-minute 16mm color film, free, WCAU-TV, City Line and Monument Avenues, Philadelphia, Pennsylvania 19131.

"Prisons and the Christian Conscience: A Kit for Study and Action," $4.25, Friendship Press, Room 772, 475 Riverside Drive, New York, New York 10027.

SECTION THREE

Chapter Eight
THE YOUTH MINISTER

Youth are big business. Millions of people's economic and personal well-being is invested in them. A partial list would include record-company executives, recording artists, clothing manufacturers, magazine editors, operators of fast-food chains, school teachers, counselors, guidance personnel, coaches, legal-aid volunteers, social workers, and scout leaders. Each has a somewhat unique focus; some are exploitative, even manipulative. Others are genuinely altruistic and dedicated in their efforts to serve young people. In this diverse cast, where does the Youth Minister fit? What are the qualities most needed in those who would be Youth Ministers? What institutional relationship is needed for them in the churches, both locally and nationally? And what is their future?

In this concluding chapter, I will address these questions, sharing some of the insights we now have about this particular work. I will begin with comment on qualities and expectations, move to concerns for the church as a whole, and end with recommendations for the future.

EXPECTATIONS

Expectations are always twofold: adults of youth and youth of adults. Recently at the University of Minnesota, a conference concerned with youth focused on these mutual expectations from the perspectives of five different persons, each of whom represented a different discipline or profession working with youth.[1] Included

---

1. Miriam Seltzer (ed.) "Expectations-Youth of Adults, Adults of Youth," in *Center for Youth Development and Research Quarterly Focus* (St. Paul: CYDR, Spring, 1978).

were a psychologist, an educator, a physician, a sociologist, and a social worker. The psychologist focused on parent-child relationships. He found that if both groups are questioned about their perceptions of the expectations each holds for the other, one finds a discrepancy between what parents say they expect of adolescents, and what adolescents seem to think parents expect of them; and between what adolescents think of themselves and what they think parents say of them. Both groups believe the other group thinks less of them than the group actually seems to think. The educator focused on discipline: his research indicates that in general, working-class people bring an authoritarian approach to discipline that is rigid and demanding of their children, whereas to middle- and upper-class parents, it appears to be more important that their children achieve. The physician in the group, asked to speak from that point of view, pointed out that nothing in physicians' training qualifies them to deal with the problems of adolescence. Apparently, there are only 300 physicians who have been identified as knowing or expressing an interest in adolescent health care and there are only 12 in the United States who practice adolescent medicine on a full-time basis. The sociologist in the group noted that in that discipline, one-to-one expectations were not of interest; sociology is concerned with patterns of relationships and with such questions as: How clear are the expectations? How complex? How changeable? What happens when you don't fulfill them? Where are these expectations institutionally lodged? Who decides which are the most important? The social worker broke down the issue by commenting that youth workers had three areas of self-expectation: modeling or coaching, recharging their own batteries, making things better. They saw these three as the reasons they themselves were in the work and as criteria for judgment. On the other hand, for her, adolescents' expectations were more complex and difficult to detect, but did tend to cluster around (a) what the young people wanted from the adults most significant to them (which appears to be the sense of a genuine, trusting relationship that will not be violated); and (b) in many cases, a fantasized, idealized role model—often hard to live up to on the part of the youth worker.

What strikes me in the above, despite their diversity, is how close many of these perspectives come to those of Youth Ministers whose ministry is so broad, and covers so many areas that they find themselves placed in every one of the above roles: psychologist, educator, physician, sociologist, social worker. Nevertheless, if it is possible, I am concerned to isolate more specific expectations among the young and those who minister among them, and to do so, I recommend a two-pronged approach. The first is a probe and analysis of the individual situations in which we find ourselves; the second is a search for informed and authoritative sources.

Individual Situations. In the past four years, I have approached the question of expectations informally with many Youth Ministers. As a starting point, I have asked: "If your youth group were writing a job description for a Youth Minister, what would be their top three priorities?" "What qualities are most important in a Youth Minister?" "How do you do youth ministry?" Many of them, in turn, have put similar questions to the youth with whom they work and to veteran Youth Ministers. Each time we have done this, we have received detailed, complex and often divergent responses, some predictable, some genuinely novel. Certain qualities are invariably mentioned more than others, such as "someone who is caring, who listens, who is understanding, who is really concerned about you." Less often, but enough to be remarkable, both Youth Ministers and young people will mention someone who is young, the qualification apparently being the hope that the closer the Youth Minister is in chronological age, the more understanding she or he will be. Athletics or sports often rank high, as does "personality." Groups do not seem to care about the gender of the Youth Minister, and religion as a topic is mentioned in every possible way and no way—from groups who wish to study the Bible to those who want no contact at all with religion. Because the answers have been so diverse, the young people so different (for example, from twelve to twenty), and the Youth Ministers differing so widely in experience; and because the procedure is so unscientific, I draw no conclusions. Instead, I share some of the responses, with the suggestion that the reader carry out a similar exercise in her or his own situation.

Specific Qualities:

Qualities for a Youth Minister:
A person who listens.
A person who will help us to do what we would like to do.
A person who is honest with us.
A person who will go on retreats and overnights.
A person who cares about what we do.
A person who is fun to be with and doesn't have too many rules and
     doesn't yell too much.

A person who has *some new ideas for us to try.*
A person who will let us run our own group.
A person who can care about us.
A person who can talk about religion/God in a way we can understand.

—collected from senior-highs.

I found six adjectives predominated: young, honest, understanding, open-minded, experienced, and a good listener. When stated by the young people these words seemed to point to deeply felt needs they were experiencing. I found this perception verified when the Youth Minister spoke to me of the skills (e.g., listening), qualities, and background that have been invaluable to her. The youths' notion of a young person being preferred seemed to speak to their desire to have someone who wasn't a parent-figure, but rather who could relate more personally to what they were going through.

—from eighth-graders and high-schoolers.

Most of the youth in one group said "friendliness and patience" were the key qualities needed in an adult leader. This was noted by most; the overlap of the remaining qualities was not as pronounced. The rest of the qualities had one or two under each. These included: sense of humor, nice personality, authority (or leadership, which may not be the same thing in the eyes of youth), liberal and unprejudiced. Two youths, one male (sixteen) and one female (fifteen) listed "be married" as a quality. One thirteen-year-old girl wrote that a leader should like to work with kids; and a fifteen-year-old girl wrote that the leader should "understand the attitudes of youth."

—thirteen-to-eighteen-year olds.

Many of the qualities listed were: genuine interest and care for members of the group, willingness to listen, compassion or simply ability to relate to youth.

—thirteen-to-eighteen-year olds.

From the point of view of the youth worker the most important qualities were believed to be sincerity, a love for youth, a sense of humor, lots of energy, patience, kindness, unselfishness, firmness but with restraint and the ability to receive a lot of criticism, not all of it constructive. This was interesting to me because it describes the qualities of a good leader in anything. The only exception would be the love of youth. This makes sense and anyone who has all or most of the above qualities should make an effective youth leader.

I expected to find sincerity and a genuine concern high on the list when I asked the young people about the kind of person they would like to have ministering to them. What I found was slightly different. The qualities they emphasized the most were the ability to plan and organize effectively and a good sense of humor.

This was a very difficult question to ask the youth group which I have been working with the last two years. The difficulty came in the fact that no one had ever asked the kids what they thought a Youth Minister should be.

General attitudes:
The reasons the youth leaders felt ministry to youth was important (and they all did) varied widely. Some felt it was important as youth was the future of the church and the world; while others felt that youth minstry gave youth an opportunity for growth experiences outside the home and school. Only one said that it was an opportunity to present Christ.

Youth are everywhere, and unfortunately, can also be nowhere. At times they experience isolation, loneliness, fear, rejection, and having someone in particular to turn to who really cares can make quite a difference. Likewise, there are times of great joy for a teen (a joy that too often "older" folks forget having experienced) and here, too, having someone to share this with can make it even nicer.
—Youth Minister, female, twenty-six.

I have found through my work that they want someone who cares and wants to be with them. They see through phoniness very quickly and therefore honesty is very important. Patience and tolerance is needed as well as assertiveness and openness. I'm truly amazed at how even though I was once "one of them" I still have much more to learn in understanding youth and what that entails.
—Youth Minister, female, twenty-five.

Having to summarize, I think youth are asking for a leader whom they can respect and trust. Someone who sincerely dares to care; someone who will help enable them to discover and be themselves.
—Youth Minister, female, twenty-five.

211

Most of the youth seem to be at odds with their parents, and seek acceptance elsewhere. They treat the Youth Minister not as a parent, but as an adult in whom they can trust and confide. The youth have a great amount of energy, that is usually wasted because of inadequate programming. Under proper leadership this energy has been released creatively and with group consent.

—Youth Minister, sex, age unknown.

On Religion:

The majority that I spoke with saw the Church as something that was important, but something which they hadn't come to terms with yet. They saw one's involvement to be a personal decision ("they should not be forced") and in general acknowledged their own uncertainties and the questioning that often predominated (Why go to Mass? etc.).

—thirteen-to-eighteen-year olds.

Significant in both youth and adult responses was the lack of a sense of God or faith. There are so many "social" needs at these ages that the faith needs take second place, if they are present at all. Mostly youth groups seem either to be an alternative to loneliness/boredom, or they take the place of largely defunct social/secular groups such as Scouting. Is youth ministry really going to become merely an anodyne for the growing pains of youth, or is it to engage in the growing process to focus, clarify, and educate?

They wanted someone who could make the Bible interesting. It seems that the age-old problem of boredom has once again reared its ugly head. This is important, but I think this involves teaching techniques, not just the qualities which would make a good youth worker.

—Youth Minister, male, twenty-six.

The overriding flavor of these youths is strong will and a "suspiciousness of being programmed ideologically." They want nothing to do with the organized church teaching but do want a place to become themselves and discuss issues of importance to them. Although individual counseling is available to them by lay leaders or the minister they rarely take advantage of it except interestingly, when in need of abortion information.

—Youth Minister, male, thirty-one.

It would be good for a youth minister to be able to teach religion in ways that are interesting to young people. Also, the minister should be able to assist us in working out problems and disagreements that arise in the study of religion and in our own lives.
—twelve-to-fifteen-year olds.

Too many programs for youth came into an area, ran for a while, and then pulled out or were closed down. Young Life had a commitment to staying, and that was important; it implied a stability about the Christian faith. This is related to a feeling that the kids in a church setting are always the group being experimented with, and led by people on their way to other ministries.
—from an interview with a Young Life Director.

On Programs:

It is important that Youth sense an involvement in the Church's life. Youth in our church serve on committees, help with Church School, conduct worship, usher, greet, and help with church workdays, suppers, etc. I think it is most important for Youth to feel a sense of personal ownership of their group, to understand that Christianity can be challenging, alive and relevant to their needs and concerns. Especially significant is the role-modeling and sense of acceptance and Christian community that is provided. A recent retreat on "Creativity" allowed Youth to try new creativeness in a context of acceptance and trust. Interest groups in drama, photography, baking, snow-sculpturing, cake-decorating and performance of skits and role-plays freed up many up-tight Youth. I know that this rundown of issues and concerns does not seem to focus on advocacy but it is what we consider important in Youth Ministry.
—Youth Minister, male, n.a.

In dealing with youth within the context of the church I try to follow a few simple rules of thumb.
1. Youth need to see themselves and be seen as an integral part of the church, yet be regarded as persons with special interests and needs at this time in their lives.
2. A program for youth in a church should be viewed as a vital part of the church's ministry and *not* as a subsidiary organization.
3. It is necessary for youth ministry to be performed by adults and youth alike in mutual responsibility and involvement.
4. My youth ministry is open to all faiths and goes beyond the doors of the church. Example: Swimming and soccer-coaching.

5. The church's ministry to youth is both a ministry of the entire church to them and a ministry of theirs to the community, their peers and to the whole church.
6. My ministry is an integrated rather than a fragmented program.
7. Youth Ministry is viewed by my advisors and myself as a servant of purpose and program rather than an end in and of itself.
8. A ministry to youth should be well structured and yet give the appearance and feeling of being informal and relaxed.

—Pastor, male.[2]

Research. I believe that most Youth Ministers, engaging in similar probing, would arrive at similar responses. A second exercise, however, is necessary. This is making oneself familiar with the work of those who have undertaken such questioning in a more systematic and detailed way. The benefits are confirmation, in many cases of what are apparently only one's individual experience; awareness of divergence that might put us on guard; and the support and security that come from working out of an informed perspective.

The best-known research in this area is the last chapter of Merton Strommen's *Five Cries of Youth,*[3] given additional prestige and circulation when it was reprinted in Michael Warren's 1977 collection *Youth Ministry: A Book of Readings.*[4] Strommen asked the questions, "What ways of approaching youth have you found helpful?" and "How do you get next to them?" and discovered the responses falling into six groupings of skills: building relationships, being genuine, being available, showing interest, communicating, and leading. Each of these is then described in detail with a subset of additional but related skills.[5] To the question "What are you doing to accomplish your purposes with youth?" three new groups of skills were named, each of which is closely allied to ministry: teaching, creating a community, and encouraging involvement.[6] Less well known, but in my judgment equally valuable, are the findings of Gisela Konopka's study listing the qualities most admired in

---

2. For the interview data shared here, I am grafetul to the compilers, especially Walter Pitman, Judy Westerhoff, Susan Wilson, Anne Squire-Buresh, Bob Bixler, James P. Dowse, Sue Olmstead, Nancy Adams, Bruce Sandy, Thomas Cabezas, William Donoghue, Kenneth Murray, Stephen Corso and Bruce Burnham.
3. *Op. cit.,* pp. 112–126.
4. *Op. cit.,* pp. 162–171.
5. *Op. cit.,* pp. 119, 120.
6. *Ibid.,* pp. 120–121.

adults. The first three were the most frequently mentioned: generally friendly and fun to be with; understanding (they listen and care about us, they respect us, they are helpful to us); older, more experienced and knowledgeable, and can tell us the rights and wrongs; these were followed by easy to get along with, good people, they trust us, they respect us for what we are, patient with us, fair and just, independent—they speak their own minds.[7]

INSTITUTIONAL ALLIANCES

Any Youth Minister who has been in the role more than a week will be able to confirm that although essential, the qualities just noted are not sufficient. Ministry is not only private and individual, it is ineluctably social. To be successful, but more important, to be ministry, the church as a social unit and religious body must own it. Thus, the Youth Minister will need to engage in one crucial alliance above all—the alliance with the church. For a very few, such as those engaged in Youth Ministry on a school campus, or prison, or hospital setting, this may be in relation to the church at a wider state or national level. For most, however, the alliance will be within the local church.

Underlying the alliance is the basic assumption that in answer to the question, "Who owns Youth Ministry?" the only appropriate response is "The entire church." The one called Youth Minister is a delegate, a deputy, a spokesperson, a liaison, but Youth Ministry does not belong to the Youth Minister. Despite assurances to the contrary, this appears to be very much a problem in most churches, Protestant and Catholic. On the church's part, a subtle pressure exists to give over this aspect of its life to the Youth Minister, for whatever reason. On their part, Youth Ministers are tempted to say to the rest of the church, "Hands off, this is my territory." Neither position is desirable. On its part, the church must exercise ownership of this ministry by invitatory, financial, attitudinal and validating support. The Youth Minister must respond by relatedness, flexibility and open communication.

A. THE CHURCH

The church's invitatory support. By invitatory support, I refer to the initial moves a church makes toward the Youth Minister in

7. *Op. cit.,* p. 61.

inviting her or him to be the chief person in its ministry to the young. The church as a whole, or acting through a carefully chosen, fully representative committee, must place priority on the kind of adult it chooses to work with the young. This would include concern for the qualities enumerated at the beginning of this chapter, but would also include looking for persons who accept the young as equals in society, understand the great variety among them, have the capacity to show deep respect regardless of race, ethnicity, social and economic status, and gender, and know the impact and lure of drugs and alcohol.[8] When a church is satisfied, by careful conversation, interview and prayer, then an invitation should be extended by the church. It should be one that promises support, ongoing assistance, warmth and continual welcome.

The church's financial support. Primary among the forms of support a church offers will be its financial support. Most Youth Ministers will be looking for a decent, although not exorbitant salary (they are not in this ministry for money!) and ought to be granted the same as the going rate (a) for other full-time ministers; or (b) for high-school teachers in the area, with adjustments made for different vacation, schooling, and day-night time schedules. Judicatory and diocesan bodies can be especially helpful here in providing suggested base salaries, with cost-of-living differences duly noted and acted upon. Financial support must extend to two additional areas. The actual conduct of programs is one. Here, the church must set aside enough money to provide adequate resources for the program, in consultation with the Youth Minister and the young people, so that it is clear *beforehand* what is and is not available. Ongoing education is the second. A church would do well to choose its Youth Minister from its own ranks on occasion, sending her or him for study, and underwriting the training needed for this ministry. If an invitation is extended to a Youth Minister from outside the parish, however, this financial support should continue with a yearly allowance set apart for continuing education.

The church's attitudinal support. I refer here to that kind of support which is often absent or damaged in far too many churches. Sometimes, a climate of suspicion or distrust, if not outright resentment, is directed toward youth ministry in an individual local church. Missing here is an attitudinal support, which in turn depends on the youth and Youth Minister keeping the lines of com-

---

8. Konopka, *op. cit.*, pp. 166–167.

munication open and on some integrated planning so that youth, even if apart at some times, are still visible and included in the total church life. It seems to me that what must be clear for a positive and encouraging attitudinal support is a recognition by all in the church that the young will often need to go apart. However, the situation is analogous to a young person shutting the door to his or her room, but still remaining *within* the house. That is quite different from being put out, segregated, and treated as not belonging to the wider community. Both church and Youth Minister will need to keep alive an attitude that accepts and even celebrates the inevitable tension which exists when a group finds it necessary, as a youth group often does, to be by itself. Paradoxically, this may be one of the surest roads to a full participative life in the church later on.

The church's validational support. I have known Youth Ministers who have been in a church as long as six months and still not been introduced to the congregation as a whole, a situation that in my judgment demonstrates a lack of validational support. What I would urge here is not only initial introduction of the Youth Minister to the church, but the validation of the person's ministry through some kind of ritual, ceremony or celebration. Ideally (perhaps Confirmation is an appropriate time), such ritual could be designed so that the ministry of the youth of the church is affirmed and validated at the same time and in the same ceremony. The opportunities for doing this are many: the setting up of a youth church, the beginning of the school year, an annual retreat. To be truly effective and a genuine symbol of validation, such a ritual should be repeated on a regular, possibly yearly basis.

B. THE YOUTH MINISTER

Alliances are made among partners; therefore, all of the obligations are not on the side of the church. Youth Ministers must demonstrate, from their position, a complementary set of attitudes. The first is relatedness.

Perhaps no attitude is more critical for the Youth Minister than a sense of *relatedness* to the church. The primary place this finds expression (exclusive of with the young) is with the other members of the ministerial team. For those in very small churches, who embody in one person—themselves—the roles of pastor, DRE, Youth Minister and parish president, this is not a problem. But for almost everyone else, the manner and procedures whereby the

Youth Minister engages with the others is most important. To avoid the very real danger of territorial propriety (this is mine—you stay away), a team is well advised to meet *at least* weekly to pray and to share with the other team members their plans for that week as well as to comment on previous or completed ministerial activity. In addition, it is a time to solicit comments and suggestions from the other team members. Such meetings may appear to be time wasters or may appear unproductive. Nevertheless, if there is one activity that should never be cancelled, this is it. Praying together and sharing concerns together will not solve every issue; but if they are not engaged in, the isolation and antagonism endemic to far too many ministries is almost certain to develop. I would even go so far as to say that refusal to engage in such meeting is ground for termination.

Youth Ministers should also demonstrate *flexibility.* Throughout this book, I have tried to describe a variety of ways for engaging in youth ministry with the assumption that because situations, needs, circumstances and people differ, flexibility is essential. The most obvious example of this is my recommending advocacy toward integrating youth into the church's life at the same time I can advocate a youth church, positions that ought not be considered antithetical. Similarly, a Youth Minister must not be tied to only one way of acting with youth. The young people of this decade are not the same as those of the last decade; nor is this year's group the same as last year's. Twelve-year-olds are not nineteen-year-olds. What helps some can hurt others. For this reason, a Youth Minister must take time to know the church and the young people with their individual characteristics this year, encouraging others, such as advisors, to do the same so that no one is locked into an inappropriate or impossible form of ministry. In addition, Youth Ministers cannot bring the qualities of their former positions to a new situation. Rather the present place and people in all their distinctness must be engaged, studied, understood and cherished.

For these attitudes to become realities, the Youth Minister must stress *open communication* in her or his approach. On the one hand, this means the Youth Minister's taking time to learn what else is going on in the parish as a whole and in the wider neighborhood community, besides the program of youth ministry. Companioned rather than competitive activity is the key. Arriving at a basketball game or a school play or a block party, at a rotary club, PTA or Al-ateen meeting may itself prove a symbolic ministry; it is a way of saying the other's plans and programs are as important as mine. Even short of physical presence, however, a note of support, or good luck or congratulations to another parish team member is a small but powerful gesture. At the same time, the Youth Minister must do all in her or his power to notify the rest of the team, the church membership, the community, and all young people, even those not in the program of what is occurring. This may be one of the surest signs that the ministry of *koinonia*, or communion, is a reality in the Youth Minister's life. If it is done and, along with the information, a request is made to join in for those who wish to, the Youth Minister may be surprised when what seems a small, unpretentious ministry begins to burgeon, to grow and to flower.

C. ACROSS BOUNDARIES

Support for youth ministry can be given a strong boost with the presence of alliances on a broader level. Judicatory and diocesan offices can supply resources, credentialing, criteria, ideas and personnel services and set up occasions for Youth Ministers to come together. Two other alliances should be stressed. First are the seminaries in the area. Often, seminarians in training are given, as their field-education assignment, the job of "youth work," seen as a stepping stone or base for other ministry. A place to work toward changing this is seminary education itself, which might encourage youth ministry as part of the total church's work. Pastoral ministry must be taught as including youth ministry, and the role of the pastor as Youth Minister should be explored. Special attention might also be directed to examining the practice of assigning youth ministry to the youngest ordained staff person, a practice in many churches. One way of accomplishing such examination is to design small, seminar-type meetings with seminary faculty and Youth Ministers so that exchange of views, of purposes and of information can occur.

Perhaps the most fruitful alliance, at least for the present, however, will be among Youth Ministers themselves. We need to continue the regional, national and denominational meeting that exist in this area, but attention at such meetings must be directed to setting up ongoing support systems in between such times. Exchange of programs and procedures must continue to be undergirded by exchange of philosophy and ideals, so that no one need feel or in actuality be alone in carrying on youth ministry.

CHAPTER EIGHT

WHERE DO WE GO FROM HERE?

The establishment of local and regional networks is a first step in exploring the question of directions for the future. No one is fully equipped to say where youth ministry will be a year, five years, or ten years from now, but together let us try. Certain constants can be named that have been with us for some time; these provide an agenda for the foreseeable future. Those items that prove inconsequential can be discarded; those deserving further attention can be explored more deeply. Many of the areas for further study have been named in this book. In conclusion, let me name those that to my mind are most important.

(1) Youth Ministers must continue to study. We need to know the history of adolescence, its sociology, its special problems, and the rights and laws surrounding it. We need to question how much of a fictional social construct it might actually turn out to be. We need to keep our ears to the ground for the results of each new Gallup poll on youth, and to take seriously the work of special committees and commissions (the Carnegie Report and the National Council of Churches Family Justice project are two examples) where years of painstaking action-research have uncovered deep and profound issues. I am not convinced this is accepted as serious business; many of our meetings appear to deal with "entry-level problems" that suggest a beginning level of involvement as the norm for Youth Ministers, who tend to be unaware of or uninterested in research data or carefully thought-through reflection and theory about their work.

(2) More adult role models must be available to the young. The story is told that almost every young black boy in the middle 1950's, when asked what he wanted to do when he grew up, said "Play center field for the New York Giants." Willie Mays was one of the few black adult males the young saw doing something they too wished to do when they grew older. Not only for young black people, but for all young people, it still is the rule rather than the exception to be cut off from adults in adult activities who can provide role models for the next generation. Most of the adults with whom the young come in contact are met in relation to themselves; they are their parents or their school teachers. For the rest, young people do not have occasion to spend any significant time with those who might widen their horizons.

Thus, a vital concern in youth ministry is more adult involvement, with a focus on sharing the variety of worlds adults know: the legal profession, medicine, politics, tending animals, theater and museum work, business, newspaper production. The most obvious benefit is role-modeling; a second is a greater integration of the world of work into daily life. A third, however, is attention to ministry beyond the church and a sense of how the Christian religious life might be lived in those settings that are primary for most grown people.

(3) This brings us to the need for continued exploration of the young person's own involvement in ministry. Michael Warren is known for insistence on youth ministry being done *with*, not *to* young people, and it is this insistence that is the starting point for a person coming to understand her or his ministry as a member of the church. If it is true that ministry is the priestly and prophetic work of the church; and if it is true that we, all of us, are the church, then it is also true that when I am expressing my Christian commitment, I am also taking on that commitment in and toward the world. I have tried, in this book, to describe the basic forms of this ministry as rooted in a tradition of Word and Sacrament, learned in study and prayer (*didache* and *leiturgia*), directed outward toward communion with all that is *(koinonia)*, and expressed both toward individuals (*kerygma*) and toward institutions (*diakonia*). Grounded in tradition, this ministry is there for the young person in her or his individual life and circumstances, and given a strong base, personal ministry *will* be discovered. This is, I believe, what is meant by vocation, and to discover one's vocation in life is to discover the harmony that appears when inner call and outward expression become one. Often, the fullness of vocation does not appear for fifty or sixty years, but if it has a starting point, it is most often in the green wood of youth.

The deepest questions are frequently the simplest to state: "Who are you?" "How are you?" "Where are you from?" "Where are you going?" At the level of ordinariness, my hope is that the answer to where we go from here is not dependence, but interdependence with the young; not toward the tragic but toward the lightness of the comic; not toward an individualistic, privatized religious life, but toward one of communion. Beyond the ordinary, however, there is both more conviction and more paradox concerning the eventual goal of youth ministry. For all of us, God willing—church, its Youth Ministers, and the growing persons who are receiving their first calls to full participation and ministry—are journeying in the same direction. We are going toward light and darkness, toward wisdom and unknowing, and toward the ultimate home of death and resurrection. We dare not make this journey alone.

Chapter Eight
STUDY AND PRACTICE

ACTIVITY 38
Clarifying Expectations

The following are *some* of the questions to be asked prior to the invitation to a Youth Minister to join in a community. The questions should be asked of the young people, of the church community, and of prospective Youth Ministers. Each community will, of course, have questions more specific to its own situation.

1. What is your understanding of youth ministry?

2. If the youth group were writing a job description for a Youth Minister, what would be the top three priorities?

3. What qualities are most important in a Youth Minister?

4. What ways of approaching youth have you found helpful? How do you get next to them?

5. What are you doing (or do you plan to do) to accomplish your purposes with young people?

ACTIVITY 39
Inventory for the Local Church

This inventory-item is designed to suggest key areas a local church or search committee might consider before inviting a prospective Youth Minister to become part of the ministerial team. What does the church plan to provide:

1. *in its invitation to the person selected:* by way of support, ongoing assistance, concern, expression of welcome?

CHAPTER EIGHT

2. *in terms of finance:* on what grounds, and comparable to what work is the salary offered? in terms of program resources? in terms of continuing education?

3. *in terms of attitudes:* what expectations need to be made clear, especially with reference to the young going apart, and with reference to the young taking roles in church activities?

4. *in terms of ritual:* what rite, ceremony, or celebration will mark the Youth Minister's entrance into the church community? Will this rite be a once only or repeated event?

ACTIVITY 40
Inventory for the Prospective Youth Minister

1. How will you establish relationships with the other members of the church's ministerial team?

2. What are some alternative programs you envision for youth ministry?
—In Teaching
—In Prayer
—In Community and Communion
—In Advocacy
—In Prophetic Troublemaking

3. What persons and/or groups in the church and community do you think it important to establish communication with?

4. Where do you expect to find professional support in your work as a Youth Minister? What groups or individuals can assist you?

5. What do you expect from your diocesan and/or judicatory staff?

STUDY AND PRACTICE

ACTIVITY 41
Inventory for All in the Church,
Including Youth Ministers

1. What gifts and talents do you bring, personally, to ministry with youth?

2. What gifts and talents do you bring, communally—in this church—to ministry with youth?

3. What gifts and talents do you hope to encourage and develop personally among the youth of your church?

4. What gifts and talents do you hope to encourage and develop communally and corporately among the youth of your church?

5. If you can/could choose one priority for youth ministry in the next three years, what would it be? Be decisive—choose it!